Ethical
Profess
Compu

D1378980

FASTTRACK

Ethical, Legal and Professional Issues in Computing

Penny Duquenoy, Simon Jones and Barry G Blundell

THOMSON ™

Australia · Canada · Mexico · Singapore · Spain · United Kingdom · United States

THOMSON

Ethical, Legal and Professional Issues in Computing

Penny Duquenoy, Simon Jones and Barry Blundell

Series Editor
Walaa Bakry, Middlesex University

&
Middlesex
University
PRESS

Publishing Partner
Middlesex University Press

Publishing Director
John Yates

Commissioning Editor
Gaynor Redvers-Mutton

Managing Editor
Celia Cozens

Content Project Editor
Leonora Dawson-Bowling

Manufacturing Manager
Helen Mason

Marketing Manager
Jason Bennett

Production Controller
Maeve Healy

Text Design
Design Deluxe, Bath

Cover Design
Matthew Ollive

Typesetter
Keyline Consultancy, Newark

Printer
C&C Offset Printing Co., Ltd, China

Disclaimer

The publisher reserves the right to revise this publication and make changes from time to time in its content without notice. While the publisher has taken all reasonable care in the preparation of this book, the publisher makes no representation, express or implied, with regard to the accuracy of the information and cannot accept any legal responsibility or liability for any errors or omissions from the book or the consequences thereof. Products and services that are referred to in this book may be either trademarks and/or registered trademarks of their respective owners. The publisher and author/s make no claim to these trademarks.

British Library Cataloguing-in-Publication Data

A catalogue record for this book is available from the British Library

Contents

The FastTrack Series

Thomson Learning and Middlesex University Press have collaborated to produce a unique collection of textbooks which cover core, mainstream topics in an undergraduate computing curriculum. FastTrack titles are instructional, syllabus-driven books of high quality and utility. They are:

- **For students**: concise and relevant and written so that you should be able to get 100% value out of 100% of the book at an affordable price
- **For instructors**: classroom-tested, written to a tried and trusted pedagogy and market-assessed for mainstream and global syllabus offerings so as to provide you with confidence in the applicability of these books. The resources associated with each title are designed to make delivery of courses straightforward and linked to the text.

FastTrack books can be used for self-study or as directed reading by a tutor. They contain the essential reading necessary to complete a full understanding of the topic. They are augmented by resources and activities, some of which will be delivered online as indicated in the text.

How the series evolved

Rapid growth in communications technology means that learning can become a global activity. In collaboration, Global Campus, Middlesex University and Thomson Learning have produced materials to suit a diverse and innovating discipline and student cohort.

Global Campus at the School of Computing Science, Middlesex University, combines local support and tutors with CD-ROM-based materials and the Internet to enable students and lecturers to work together across the world.

Middlesex University Press is a publishing house committed to providing high-quality, innovative, learning solutions to organisations and individuals. The Press aims to provide leading-edge 'blended learning' solutions to meet the needs of its clients and customers. Partnership working is a major feature of the Press's activities.

Together with Middlesex University Press and Middlesex University's Centre for Learning Development, Global Campus developed FastTrack books using a sound and consistent pedagogic approach. The SCATE pedagogy is a learning framework that builds up as follows:

- **Scope:** Context and the learning outcomes
- **Content:** The bulk of the course: text, illustrations and examples
- **Activity:** Elements which will help students further understand the facts and concepts presented to them in the previous section. Promotes their active participation in their learning and in creating their understanding of the unit content
- **Thinking:** These elements give students the opportunity to reflect and share with their peers their experience of studying each unit. There are *review questions* so that the students can assess their own understanding and progress
- **Extra:** Further online study material and hyperlinks which may be supplemental, remedial or advanced.

Ethical, Legal and Professional Issues in Computing

In both a local and global sense, computer-based technologies underpin almost everything we do; they directly affect us all. It is therefore vital that those working within the computing industry are aware of their professional responsibilities in guiding the development, deployment and interconnection of computer-based technologies in order to ensure that they bring positive benefits to society and to the environment. The British Computer Society (BCS) and other professional computer organisations, such as the Association for Computing Machinery (ACM), recognise the need for today's graduates to be aware of the issues surrounding the use of computers in all aspects of society. The BCS is committed to raising the awareness of future computing professionals, and requires that the social, legal and professional issues of computing be included in degree programmes in order for them to receive accreditation.

We have said that computerisation can bring both benefits and losses. But how do we know what is beneficial or not? At the heart of this chapter is the subject of ethics: the discussion of 'good' and 'bad', 'right' and 'wrong'. It can sometimes be difficult to know what we 'should' do in a specific situation, particularly where there are conflicting priorities. We shall be looking at different ethical positions and discussing them in a computing context.

The purpose of this book is to introduce students to some of today's most contentious issues in the field, to inform them of the arguments surrounding the issues, to encourage critical thinking, discussion and debate. Many issues are not clear-cut, and often there are no obvious 'right' or 'wrong' answers. Finding solutions to some of these issues can be difficult, but through the process of thinking and discussion you will have a clearer picture of the situations presented.

Using this book

There are several devices which will help you in your studies and use of this book. **Activities** usually require you to try out aspects of the material which have just been explained, or invite you to consider something which is about to be discussed. In some cases, a response is provided as part of the text that follows – so it is important to work on the activity before you proceed! Usually, however, a formal answer will be provided at the end of each chapter.

The **time bar** indicates *approximately* how long each activity will take:

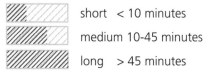

short < 10 minutes

medium 10-45 minutes

long > 45 minutes

 Review questions are (usually) short questions for each chapter to check you have remembered the main points of a chapter. They are found at the end of each chapter; feedback is provided at the back of the book. They are a useful practical summary of the content and can be used as a form of revision aid to ensure that you remain competent in each of the areas covered.

About the authors

Penny Duquenoy

Penny Duquenoy is Chair of Working Group 9.2 (Social Accountability) of the International Federation for Information Processing (IFIP) and is a senior lecturer at Middlesex University, with a PhD in Internet Ethics and a background in philosophy. Penny is a leading researcher in the field of Ethics and ICT, with more than 30 publications on aspects of ethics in relation to applied information technologies; she advises on issues of ethics at EU level for ethical reviews of, and within, EU research projects. Her research interests are in the areas of the ethical impact of computer technologies, particularly of intelligent systems and ambient environments. In addition to long-term membership of the IFIP Special Interest Group on Ethics (SIG9.2.2) Penny is Manager of the British Computer Society's Ethics Forum.

Simon Jones

Simon Jones is a lecturer in Computing Science at Middlesex University and has taught courses on the social, legal and professional aspects of computing. His academic background is in communication and cultural studies and he is currently researching the impact of Internet technologies on popular music.

Barry Blundell

Barry Blundell is a physicist with many years of experience in teaching computer and IT-related courses and in developing digital systems. His research interests are multidisciplinary, and he is a leading researcher in the area of emerging 3D display and interaction systems for the advancement of human/computer communication. He is actively involved in forums promoting the ethical usage of computer technologies. Barry is the author of three research textbooks, several technical and undergraduate teaching books, and he is currently working on an introductory undergraduate computer graphics book.

Visit the accompanying website at **www.thomsonlearning.co.uk/fasttrack** and click through to the appropriate booksite to find further teaching and learning material including:

For Students

- Activities
- Multiple choice questions for each chapter.

For Lecturers

- Downloadable PowerPoint slides.

CHAPTER 1

A general introduction

OVERVIEW

In this chapter, we present some general background discussion and so lay the foundations for subsequent chapters. We will show how discussion of ethics and the major ethical theories are relevant to debates surrounding the use of computer technology, and to the increasingly complex decisions that face today's computing professionals. We will also address the question of why making a 'good' decision does not always necessarily mean following the law blindly. Not all law is good law, and laws should be looked at critically for their impact on citizens.

Ethics is rather an abstract concept and is often considered to be a 'fuzzy' area of discussion. Most people have some idea of what is 'ethical' and what is 'unethical', but are not generally confident about articulating why this should be so. An important part of this chapter concerns the ability to recognise what is actually an ethical issue, rather than just a decision between taking one action or another. We shall therefore spend some time on recognising an ethical issue, identifying stakeholders (those affected), and the winners and losers in a given situation.

Even if we understand the issue, it can be difficult to know what the right course of action might be. We will present two of the major ethical theories that are useful in decision making, and discuss the role of professional codes of conduct in the decision-making process.

Finally, we bring together ethical theory, social norms (approved conduct that is laid down by society), the law, and professional codes of conduct as guiding principles for forming an opinion, and making an informed and rational judgement that can be understood by others. When faced with a difficult ethical dilemma, professionals should know why they have pursued a particular course of action, and they should be able to justify their actions and decisions to others.

Learning outcomes	By the end of this chapter you should be able to:

- Understand the relationship between the law, ethics and computer technology

- Identify an ethical issue

- Understand at least two basic ethical theories

- Understand the application of law and professional codes of conduct to the IT and computing industries.

1.1 Computer ethics: an overview

Computer systems perform tasks and the way they perform tasks has moral consequences, consequences that affect human interests.

Johnson & Powers, (2004)

As a field of academic research, computer ethics had its beginnings in the early 1980s, and was defined by James Moor in a paper published in 1985: *What is Computer Ethics?*

Computer ethics represents:

The analysis of the nature and the social impact of computer technology and the corresponding formulation and justification of policies for the ethical use of such technology.

Moor argues that computer ethics is unique because computers have certain properties that raise unique issues and, according to Moor, there are three properties that make computers a special case:

- **Logical malleability**
- **Impact on society**
- **Invisibility factor.**

These are summarised in Figure 1.1 and are briefly outlined on the following pages.

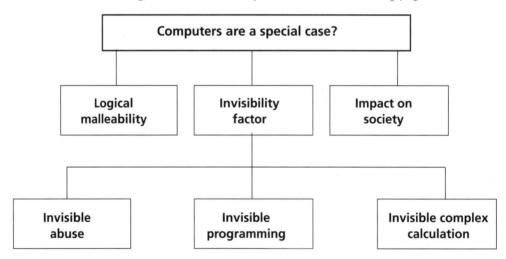

Figure 1.1: Moor makes the case that characteristics of computer-based technologies are such that they raise ethical issues that are somewhat unique. Others have suggested that computer ethics is no different from any other branch of professional ethics.

Logical malleability

What Moor means by 'logical malleability' is that computers can be shaped and moulded to perform any activity that can be characterised in terms of inputs, outputs and connecting logical operations. This is in contrast to the majority of manufactured products. For example, a car, television or refrigerator has well-defined, and quite specific, functions.

The logic of computers, however, can be shaped in infinite ways through changes in hardware and software and in terms of their usage. This enables computer-based technologies to exhibit tremendous flexibility. Moor writes:

> Just as the power of a steam engine was the raw resource of the Industrial Revolution so the logic of a computer is a raw resource of the Information Revolution. Because the logic applies everywhere, the potential applications of computer technology appear limitless. The computer is the nearest thing we have to a universal tool. Indeed, the limits of computers are largely the limits of our own creativity.

Impact on society

The extensive impact of computerisation on society is clear. Naturally, in 1985, when Moor wrote his paper, relatively few could foresee the extent of that impact, nor did anyone envisage the Internet and the World Wide Web. Moor did, however, foresee the changing workplace, and the nature of work:

> Computers have been used for years by businesses to expedite routine work, such as calculating payrolls. However, as personal computers become widespread and allow executives to work at home, as robots do more and more factory work, the emerging question will not be merely *How well do computers help us work?* but *What is the nature of this work?*

Invisibility factor

An important fact about computers is that most of the time, and under most conditions, computer operations are invisible. Moor identifies three kinds of invisibility that can have ethical significance:

- Invisible **abuse**
- Invisible **programming**
- Invisible **complex calculation.**

We shall now discuss these in further detail.

Invisible abuse

Moor describes this as: 'the intentional use of the invisible operations of a computer to engage in unethical conduct'. He cites the example of the programmer who realised he could steal excess interest from a bank:

> When interest on a bank account is calculated, there is often a fraction of a cent left over after rounding off. This programmer instructed a computer to deposit these fractions of a cent to his own account.

Another example of invisible abuse is the invasion of the property and privacy of others – for example, computers can be programmed to surreptitiously remove or alter confidential information.

Invisible programming values

These are values which, according to Moor, are embedded into a computer program:

> A programmer makes some value judgements about what is important and what is not. These values become embedded in the final product and may be invisible to someone who runs the program.

Invisible complex calculation

In this context, Moor writes:

> Computers today are capable of enormous calculations beyond human comprehension. Even if a program is understood, it does not follow that the respective calculations are understood. Computers today perform … calculations which are too complex for human inspection and understanding.

He argues that the issue is how much we should trust a computer's invisible calculation. This becomes a significant issue as the consequences grow in importance. For example:

> Computers are used by the military in making decisions about launching nuclear weapons. On the one hand, computers are fallible and there may not be time to confirm their assessment of the situation. On the other hand, making decisions about launching nuclear weapons without using computers may be even more fallible and more dangerous. What should be our policy about trusting invisible calculations?

There are those who disagree with James Moor and say that computer ethics is no different from any other branch of professional ethics such as legal ethics and medical ethics (for example, Gotterbarn, writing in Johnson & Nissenbaum (1995). Spinello (1995) warns against thinking in terms of uniqueness, and advises that the digital environment simply requires a different approach to resolving problems such as, for example, privacy.

Whether we favour the arguments put by Moor, or Gotterbarn and Spinello, there is no disagreement that information communication technology (ICT) has an impact on our lives in good and bad ways, and certain rights, such as privacy, are increasingly threatened by digital technologies. As new developments in technology emerge it is clear that the issues within the field of computer ethics require constant review and consideration.

Activity 1.1

Background to computer ethics

By means of examples, explain the terms 'logical malleability'; 'impact of society'; and the 'invisibility factor'. If possible, obtain a copy of Moor's article and read it in full.

1.2 Identifying an ethical issue

Most people have a clear ability to distinguish between what is 'ethical' and what is 'not ethical'. However, when asked to explain our reasons for deeming an action to be ethical or unethical, we often experience difficulty. This is often because we base our judgement on a complex set of criteria that may include those remarkable human traits – common sense, instinct and wisdom (based on experience). In addition, we tend to use the terms 'ethical' and 'moral' interchangeably – although it is interesting to note that we normally use their opposites 'unethical' and 'immoral' more specifically.

In fact, 'ethics' is derived from the Greek 'ethos,' whereas 'morality' is derived from the Latin word 'moralis'. The ancient Greeks were greatly interested in issues of philosophy and thus we may consider ethics to relate to the philosophical study of the way in which we act.

The *Oxford English Dictionary* defines 'ethics' as:

> ...the science of morals in human conduct.

We can, however, consider 'morality' to be a more practical term – representing 'ethics' in action.

Morals are concerned with good and bad, right and wrong, justice and injustice. In certain cases the distinction between right and wrong is clear – helping someone in trouble is acting ethically; stealing from someone is acting unethically. However, there are many cases where the degree of 'wrongness' is not clear, or where choosing the right action conflicts with another action that causes harm.

For example, consider the case of a person who steals food to feed a starving family. Although we generally perceive stealing to be wrong, we can see that under certain circumstances, it may be the only course of action and may alleviate suffering. Furthermore, it is important to note that different people may perceive moral standards quite differently. For example, in the second world war, members of the French Resistance were perceived by the German occupiers as being criminals and murderers. If the outcome of the war had been different, this view would most likely have continued and would have been established within the history books. However, given the allied victory, the history books record the courage and bravery of Resistance workers whose actions are both applauded and perceived as being morally justified.

In this book we will generally not distinguish between ethics and morality – for simplicity, we will use these concepts interchangeably. However, when referring to their opposites, we will normally avoid the term 'immoral' as modern society has tended to associate this word with issues that are of a sexual nature and, to some extent, its generality has therefore been eroded.

Let us turn now to issues that relate directly to computer ethics (morals). Key issues include:

- **Stealing** (to be discussed under the topic of hacking in Chapter 2)
- **Intellectual property** (Chapter 4)
- **The right of privacy** (Chapter 6)
- **The right of equality** (Chapter 7)
- **Keeping promises** (such as professionals meeting a deadline)
- **Not lying.**

A useful guideline in recognising an issue that has some ethical (moral) component is to watch out for the word 'should'. If the question 'what should I (he/she/they) do?' is asked, then very often the issue is an ethical one. This is because, when used in this context, the word 'should' implicitly implies a desire to 'do the right thing' – to take the most appropriate/professional/ moral course of action.

Activity 1.2

Identifying an ethical issue

Read the following, and identify the issues that you consider to involve ethical issues.

Spend a little time thinking about your concerns as to the ramifications of the general deployment of such computer-based technologies; if you have the opportunity of discussing this with fellow students, friend or colleagues, then this would be very useful.

In February 2003 an article appeared in the *Philadelphia Inquirer* describing a United States project aimed at safeguarding US troops in foreign urban areas (Sniffen, M J, *'Pentagon project could keep a close eye on cities'*).

'Using a combination of computer technologies and cameras, information about a vehicle could be recorded. The software program underlying the project can also recognise drivers and passengers by face. The software is capable of issuing an alert if the monitored vehicle appears on any 'watch' list, and is capable of searching records to locate and compare vehicles seen around the sites of terrorist incidents. According to scientists, law enforcement officers and privacy advocates this technology could also be used within the United States to monitor US citizens, although the article also reports that a representative of the Defense Advanced Research Projects Agency (DARPA) 'insists that CTS technology was not designed with local law enforcement or homeland security in mind', and that sweeping alterations would be needed to implement it in such a way. However, a member of the Federation of American Scientists was quoted as saying that he 'can easily foresee pressure to adopt a similar approach to crime-ridden areas of American cities … or any site where crowds gather'. This view is supported by a comment from the New York deputy police commissioner that the police would encourage the adoption of this type of technology. The immediate 12 million-dollar plan is to deploy CTS technology over the next four years in two stages. First, to install 30 cameras in a fixed site to improve troop protection, and second to set up around 100 cameras in support of military operations incorporating software that can analyze the video recordings with a view to noting abnormal activity.'

1.3 Ethics and the law

We could ask why we need ethical principles to guide our decisions when we have the law to turn to. Laws, should (at least in principle) tell us when it is right or wrong to do something.

However, laws are not always ethical – they are created by governments and may be introduced to further ethical or not-so-ethical aims. For example, laws can promote equal rights (such as the Disability Discrimination Act in the UK), or reduce rights (such as the US Patriot Act).

As far as law and ethics are concerned, we can have laws that are ethical, and laws that are unethical. When we pursue a course of action it can be:

- Legal and ethical
- Not legal but ethical
- Not ethical but legal
- Not ethical and not legal.

In Figure 1.2 these possibilities are illustrated within a simple 2-by-2 array; although four combinations exist we cannot assume these are fixed in scope; there is not always a simple boundary between ethical and non-ethical decisions. By way of example, in our everyday conversations we may describe something as being 'not quite ethical' or 'totally illegal' – thereby indicating that we perceive a sliding scale of legality and ethicality.

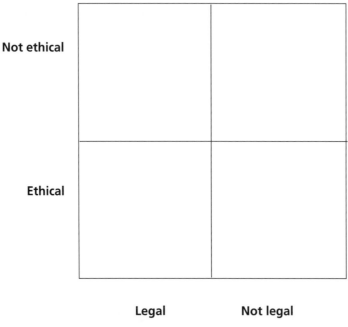

Figure 1.2: Legality and ethicality

When faced with a difficult decision, reference to the law is often a good starting point. It should not be assumed, however, that simply following the guidance of the law will result in 'good' (ethical) decision making. Later in this chapter we will propose a framework for making an informed ethical decision.

Activity 1.3

Ethics and the law

Select actions to be placed in the array presented in Figure 1.2 to illustrate each of the four combinations (choose one action for each of the four sections). Explain your reasons for choosing each action.

1.4 Ethical theories

Theories are commonly used to explain natural phenomena and so provide us with an understanding of the world in which we live. Theories are put forward, assessed and discussed – and either generally accepted, revised, or discarded. There is also usually more than one theory put forward on a specific topic, and some people will be convinced by one theory and not by another.

In all of these respects, ethical theory follows the same pattern. Ethical theories attempt to explain human morality, and why we think some actions are good, while other actions are bad. Ethics falls within the domain of philosophy and, as with other theories, different philosophers have come up with different ethical theories. Coverage of a broad range of types of theory is beyond the scope of this book.

Here, we briefly refer to two influential western ethical theories. These theories can be useful in ethical decision making, and they are also helpful in providing a basis for critical thinking. Taking different perspectives on an issue provokes thinking, and helps to form opinion.

Aspects of two theories are outlined below. These are:

- **Kantianism** (a theory provided by Immanuel Kant)
- **Consequentialism** (sometimes called utilitarianism).

Kantianism

The German philosopher Immanuel Kant (1724-1804) believed that how we behave ethically comes from within us, and the things that we decide are 'good' or 'bad' are based on whether we could imagine everyone doing them.

He embodies this idea within a 'categorical imperative' (that is to say, a moral rule that is absolute and which therefore has no conditions attached to it):

> Act only according to that maxim by which you can at the same time will that it should become a universal law.

Thus, we could simply say that we must not lie – and according to Kant, there are no circumstances in which a lie could be justified. The point to note is that if we believe that it is *acceptable* to lie, then in accordance with the above categorical imperative, we must then accept that telling lies should become the norm – everybody can lie. As a result, truth and honesty would become things of the past – in an extreme case, they would no longer exist.

By way of a further example, consider the breaking of promises. It would be logically inconsistent to say that breaking a promise is good – because if everyone broke their promises there would be a loss of trust in promises, and the whole nature of a promise would be lost. Therefore, he says, certain things cannot be 'universalised' (that is, they would not work if everyone did them), and these things are wrong. Examples include: killing, lying, stealing, breaking promises. Moreover, in Kant's view, things that we view as wrong are 'essentially wrong' – that is, they are always wrong and there is never any circumstance where they would be right. This conflicts directly with the theory of consequentialism (see below).

It is interesting to note that Kant's categorical imperative, as outlined above, is in essence equivalent to the Christian teaching 'do unto others as you would have done unto yourself'. In short, the concept of right or wrong and the entire ethical ethos comes from within ourselves; furthermore, Kant believed that it is the underlying motives that lie behind our actions that determine how good or bad they in fact are. However, Kant's model is inflexible as we illustrate in the simple cartoon presented in Figure 1.3.

Here, two friends – Alice and Bob are talking. Bob wishes to share a confidence with Alice but first seeks a promise that the conversation will be treated as being strictly confidential. Alice promises confidentiality and has every intention of keeping the promise. The great secret is revealed – Bob is having an affair! Some time later Bob's astute (suspicious) wife approaches Alice and asks her whether or not she has any idea as to whether or not Bob is having an affair. On the basis of Kant's model, Alice is now in a very difficult (impossible) situation.

If she tells Bob's wife the truth, then she will be breaking her promise to Bob. On the other hand, if she lies to Bob's wife then she is accepting that lies can be the norm. Unfortunately the inflexible nature of Kant's theory does not accommodate such a situation!

Figure 1.3: Kant's model is inflexible – Alice must either break her promise to Bob (by telling the truth to Bob's wife), or keep her promise to Bob and lie to Bob's wife. Neither of these possibilities fit with the objectives of Kant's 'categorical imperative'.

Consequentialism

Consequentialism, as its name suggests, deals with consequences of actions rather than the actions themselves (in contrast to Kant's theory). So, for example, it could be argued that stealing could sometimes be the right action to take, provided the outcome is for the 'good'. What 'good' is has always been a matter for extensive discussion among philosophers, but for our purposes we use the definition provided by utilitarianism (which is a type of consequentialism). Utilitarian theory says that a good outcome is that which brings 'the greatest benefit to the greatest number of people'. Therefore stealing, for example, is a morally permissible act if it brings greater benefit to the greatest number. Consider, for instance, that a dictator has a warehouse full of food while most of the people in the country are starving. In this instance, stealing the food to distribute it to the starving people would be considered the 'right' thing to do.

Discussion of the theories

Both of the above theories have strengths and weaknesses.

- In favour of Kant's theory is that it assumes *equality*. It is based on logic and rationality (on the premise that human beings are rational agents). Therefore, if something is good enough for one person, logically it must be good enough for another person. Arguments against this theory are that it does not take into account conflicting priorities, or special circumstances, such as those given in the example regarding the stealing of food. To claim that stealing food from someone who has more than enough is wrong, seems to go against human intuition.

- Consequentialism, on the other hand, takes into account different circumstances and can (as the example of stealing shows) accommodate conflicting priorities. A major argument made against this type of theory is that it does not take into account the individual, or accommodate minority groups. This theory, as we have said, looks for the greatest benefit for the greatest number of people.

The approach would therefore ignore minority groups such as the disabled. The theory would, therefore, make it morally acceptable to produce computers that some people with disabilities cannot use, thus denying them access to information technology and the ensuing benefits (see Chapter 7). It is also important to remember that, although this theory supposes that a certain action is good if the *consequences* are good, it is often impossible to predict the consequences at the time of an action being taken. By way of an example consider the simple scenario depicted in the cartoon presented in Figure 1.4. Here, a president wishes to rid a country of a corrupt and homicidal dictator. He decides the best approach is by military invasion. If we accept his motives at face value, then it follows that, at the time of making the decision, he is acting for the good of the majority (the population of the country). However, it is impossible for him to predict with certainty the ultimate consequences of his actions. In short he opens up a Pandora's box – and others use the chaos of invasion for their own ends. Here, we note that although the basic objective (regime change) may, under the circumstances, have been ethical, the way in which this objective was implemented (invasion) is likely to have influenced an undesirable outcome. Thus we must view conseqentialism not in terms of a single decision but rather as it applies to a series or set of decisions.

In summary, both of these theories have something to offer but are far from ideal. However, they do provide an interesting framework for debate.

Figure 1.4: Unforeseen consequences

Consider a president, who wishes to remove a dictator from power and chooses to do so by military force. It is possible that his objective is ethical – he may be trying to rid the country of a despot and have the good of the countries citizens in mind. However, he cannot predict with certainty the ultimate consequences of his actions. Others may use the chaos brought about by invasion for their own purposes – it is possible that the president has inadvisably poked a stick at a hornets' nest! Generally, conseqentialism should be viewed not in terms of its application to a single isolated decision, but rather as it applies to a series or set of related decisions. These trigger a train of events and make it extremely difficult to accurately predict consequences.

Applying ethical theories

A programmer, after returning from a holiday to an underdeveloped country, was deeply affected by the level of poverty. When he returned to his job in a large international corporation, it occurred to him that he could write a program that filtered off small amounts of money from the advertising account and pay it in to a private account. His idea was to collect enough money to provide IT equipment and training to the people in the town he had visited on holiday. However, he is not sure about his decision. What should he do?

a) What solution does a Kantian approach offer?

b) What solution does a consequentialist approach offer?

c) Are their conclusions the same?

d) What do *you* think he should do?

1.5 Professional codes of conduct

Most professional bodies have codes of conduct, or codes of ethics (for our purposes the precise title is unimportant). Their purpose is to offer guidance to members, and set standards for the professional body. The British Computer Society Code of Conduct, 2001 (**www.bcs.org/server.php?show=nav.6030**) sets standards for computing professionals in the UK and lays out a number of principles.

Under the heading 'The Public Interest', the Code states:

> In your professional role you shall have regard for the public health, safety and environment.

Therefore, in any situation where public health, safety or the environment is affected, members of the British Computer Society must always make sure these aspects are not threatened. Not only do codes of conduct offer guidance; they are also useful as a defence. If, for instance, an employee were asked by their organisation to carry out some action that they considered unethical, the employee could point out that their own code of conduct did not allow such action to be taken.

1.6 An ethical dilemma

In some of the chapters of this book we present ethical dilemmas. Some of these describe actual, real-world situations; others are of a hypothetical nature. In the final chapter, we discuss aspects of these dilemmas.

By and large, we do not place ourselves in situations in which we seek out ethical dilemmas – these are simply situations that we encounter (often by chance) and must deal with. As mentioned previously in this chapter, in the case of the BCS Code of Conduct, the first statement made under the heading of 'Public Interest' is that members of the BCS shall have regard to the protection of the environment.

This first (actual) ethical dilemma relates to this statement.

Several years ago, a colleague of the editor of this book was faced with an ethical dilemma specifically relating to the impact of computer equipment on the environment. One morning, on the way to her computer science department, she noticed two enormous industrial refuse containers loaded with a sizeable mountain of computer workstations. Upon enquiry she found that these computers were destined for the local rubbish dump. The university was disposing of its large network of SUN™ workstations. During the course of the morning, two additional rubbish containers arrived and over a hundred workstations were soon ready for disposal.

She was well aware that, although the metallic and plastic components that form the workstations would gradually decompose, the lead glass from which the displays were constructed and the toxic materials (heavy metals) contained therein represented an environmental hazard; certainly in the case of the glass this hazard would not lessen with time.

Given the large number of computers being disposed of, this person decided to act in an ethical manner – within the scope of the BCS Code of Conduct. She began by visiting the university's Health and Safety department, only to be told that at that time there was no legislation in place concerning the disposal of computer systems: in short, the university was acting within the law. She attempted to explain the ethical nature of the problem and the negative impact of this bulk disposal on the environment. The only response was a further reassurance that the university was acting within the law. Subsequently she discussed the matter with the head of computer science and several colleagues. Nobody seemed to be particularly interested.

Is this an ethical issue of importance? Do you feel that she should have taken this matter further and, if so, what should she have done? What would you have done? Was the university acting in an unethical way by disposing of computer equipment in this manner simply because at the time there was no law precluding the dumping of computer systems?

In the final chapter of this book we draw some conclusions from some of the 'ethical dilemmas' described in the chapters.

1.7 A framework for ethical decision making

Many ethical issues are complex; deciding on the best course of action can be difficult. We have briefly outlined aspects of the relationship between ethics and the law, the role of codes of conduct, and have introduced two ethical theories. These ideas, coupled with social norms and that remarkable human attribute 'common sense', can help us to develop a rational approach to making an ethical choice.

Ethical choices are not made with absolute certainty; they are not deductive, in the same way as mathematical problems and solutions. Ethical decisions are made through judgement and by validation through a rational appeal to a number of principles (see, for example, Table 1.1). There is often no unique correct solution to a moral dilemma. However, in assessing moral positions, a person can rationally examine alternative options and choose the correct one for themselves. This does not mean others will necessarily agree with them but, by rationalising their point of view, individuals can be confident that they have thought thoroughly about the issue, and are not simply 'following the crowd'.

Guiding principles	Questions to consider
Law	Is there a law applicable to this issue? What does it say? Is it a good law?
Codes of conduct	Do professional codes of conduct have anything to offer on this issue?
Ethical theories	What solution does a Kantian approach offer?
	What solution does a consequentialist approach offer?
	Are their conclusions the same? If not, which provides the most convincing argument?
Social norms and other arguments	What do social norms say about this? Are the arguments valid? Are there other arguments that might help – for example, economics?

Table 1.1 A framework for understanding ethical issues, and making informed decisions

In subsequent chapters we refer to laws, to professional codes of conduct and to ethical theories. By and large, though, we do not focus on social norms – these are formed by the society in which we live and work, and may be heavily influenced by culture or religion. It is important to bear in mind that what is normal and acceptable to one society may be very different in another.

1.8 Summary

This chapter has set the context for the module as a whole by introducing some general concepts relating to computer ethics. We have shown how discussions of ethics, and the major ethical theories, are relevant to debates surrounding the use of computer technology, and the decisions that face today's computing professionals.

An important part of this chapter is the ability to recognise what is an ethical issue, rather than just a decision between taking one action and another. Recognising an ethical issue, identifying stakeholders (those affected), and the winners and losers in a given situation is not always easy; even if we understand the issue, it can be difficult to know what the right course of action might be. We have outlined aspects of two of the major ethical theories and have discussed the role played by professional codes of conduct in the decision-making process.

Finally, we brought together ethical theory, social norms (the approved conduct of a society that is laid down by that society), the law, and professional codes of conduct as guiding principles for forming an opinion, and making an informed and rational judgement that can be understood by others.

1.9 Review questions

? **Review question 1.1**

Briefly describe the three kinds of invisibility mentioned by James Moor with regard to computer operations.

? **Review question 1.2**

What are the arguments for and against a Kantian position?

? **Review question 1.3**

Explain utilitarianism in your own words, giving your own example.

? **Review question 1.4**

What are the four guiding principles for understanding ethical issues, and making informed decisions?

1.10 Feedback on activities

Feedback on activity 1.1

i When James Moor talks about logical malleability, he means that computers can interpret any logical command. Therefore, computers could be programmed to do anything that we could logically instruct them to do – which in principle amounts to almost anything. He says the limits of computers are only the limits of our imagination. We could, for example, program a computer to make ethical decisions on our behalf.

ii Moor claims that computers have a big impact on society, and computers will transform institutions and the way we work. For example, computers and the Internet have provided an environment for distance learning – the teaching material is delivered in a totally different way than if tutors only had personal interaction with students. The way tutors work has been totally transformed.

iii The invisibility factor includes a number of different aspects. One of them is that because the operations of a computer are invisible, they can be intentionally abused. An example of this is a computer programmer who intentionally programs the computer to transfer small amounts of interest to their own bank account.

Feedback on activity 1.2

We note from the article reported that a surveillance technology has been developed to 'watch' US troops and vehicles in foreign urban areas. However, the concern expressed in the article is that this technology could also be used for surveillance in non-combat situations in the United States – in other words, to watch United States citizens. There are serious privacy issues in that the monitors can read licence plates and identify facial characteristics, and match details to a database of records. Law enforcement agencies (or other government agencies) could use this technology in specific areas of the United States – saying that they are combating crime. Civil liberties groups are afraid of this 'misuse'. So, the original idea put forward would seem to be 'good', in offering some protection to US troops in life-threatening situations. However, it could also be used to monitor innocent citizens, which raises ethical questions such as 'what citizens', 'why are they being watched', 'do they know they are being watched', 'do they have any choice over being watched'? We could ask, is the ordinary citizen's life likely to be better or worse if this technology is introduced in the United States? We could also be concerned with the ultimate ramifications of such technologies – as technologies advance, how could this type of activity develop?

Feedback on activity 1.3

For the purpose of the activity the following acts have been selected from the topics covered in this module:

Not ethical	Sending junk email (spam). *It is not illegal to send junk email from the US as it has an opt-out policy*	Sending a malicious virus. *This is in violation of the Computer Misuse Act*
Ehical	Providing good security measures to protect personal data. *The Data Protection Act requires that where personal data is stored on a computer it must be secure*	Gaining unauthorised access to a computer to reveal information that is in the public interest. *The law against unauthorised access is the Computer Misuse Act*
	Legal	**Not legal**

Feedback on activity 1.4

a What solution does a Kantian approach offer? Taking the Kantian approach, we have to ask 'what would happen if everyone did it?' – that is, can it be 'universalised'? We have to decide whether this is stealing. If it is (which it certainly looks like: he is, after all, taking something which belongs to someone else), then he would be morally wrong in taking this action. There is no provision in Kantian terms for taking something from someone else that they are not going to miss. In other words, it does not matter that the third party has plenty. It could be, though, that these small amounts of money are the fractions of percentages that are left over after calculating interest (as in Moor's example cited earlier in the chapter). In this case the programmer is not 'stealing' anything, because the small amounts would be lost in any event, and would not be used. In this case, the programmer would be making good use of the money, and he would be in the right.

b   What solution does a consequentialist approach offer? The consequentialist position would look for the greatest benefit to the great number of people. We could say that the population of the country would benefit and therefore, whether the programmer is stealing or not, it would be a morally right thing to do. However, we have also to take into consideration the large number of organisations and the beneficiaries of advertising. Who are in the greater number?

c   Are their conclusions the same? This depends on certain factors – whether he is stealing (Kantian), and how we calculate the benefits to the largest number (population of the underdeveloped country versus advertisers and beneficiaries). If this is not stealing, then the outcome is good. If it is stealing, then Kant would say no. If the population is the greater good, then consequentialism/utilitarianism would say yes.

d   What should he do? If the percentages of money would be lost anyway, the programmer could put the proposition to the company that they could usefully use the money in a good cause. This would benefit them from a public relations perspective. If he would be stealing, our answer would be that he should not do this, regardless of the numbers of the population versus the beneficiaries of the company. It seems then, that we hold a Kantian position!

References

Johnson, DG & Nissenbaum, H (eds) (1995), *Computers, ethics & social values*, Prentice Hall

Johnson, DG & Powers, T M (2004), 'Computers as surrogate agents', in *Challenges for the Citizen of the Information Society*, Proceedings Ethicomp 2004, University of the Aegean.

Kant, I (2002), *Groundwork for the Metaphysics of Morals*, translated by Zweig, A and edited by Hill, TE Jr. and Zweig, A, Oxford University Press.

Moor, J (1985), 'What is computer ethics?', *Metaphilosophy*, 16 (4).

Further recommended reading

Ayres, R (1999), *The Essence of Professional issues in Computing*, (Chapter 1), Prentice Hall

Baase, S (2003), *A Gift of Fire: Social, Legal and Ethical Issues for Computers and the Internet*, (Chapter 1), Pearson.

Black, E (2001), *IBM and the Holocaust*, Little, Brown and Company.

Spinello RA (1995), *Ethical Aspects of Information Technology*, Prentice Hall

CHAPTER 2

Computer hacking

Overview

In this chapter we outline ethical, legal and professional issues relating to computer hacking. In recent years, 'hacking' has become something of an emotive term; from stories in the media, we might think that all hackers are irresponsible, destructive criminals, intentionally releasing computer viruses, stealing personal data and disrupting businesses. However, there are other people – who call themselves hackers – who do none of these things. This chapter will look at some of these conflicting definitions of hacking, and explain how the connotations of the term 'hacker' have changed over time. We will be looking at some of the motives behind hacking, as well as the technical tools involved in the more malicious aspects of this activity, particularly viruses, worms and Trojan horses.

We shall also be considering what the law has to say about hacking, focusing particularly on the Computer Misuse Act 1990, as amended by the Police and Justice Act 2006, as well as the professional constraints that exist in codes of conduct of bodies such as the British Computer Society. Do these provide useful or appropriate ethical guidelines on hacking? Most importantly, this chapter will consider the main arguments for and against hacking. Can it be justified, and if so, under what circumstances? And what principles can be called upon to defend such actions?

Learning outcomes	At the end of this chapter you should be able to:

- Understand and define some conflicting definitions of hacking

- Understand the application of relevant national and international legislation to hacking

- Have a basic knowledge of malicious and invasive programs

- Understand the application of professional codes of conduct to hacking

- Construct defensible arguments from an ethical point of view concerning the issue of computer hacking.

2.1 Introduction

This chapter begins by considering different definitions and connotations of the term 'hacking'. Subsequently, we examine some of the motives behind hacking, as well as various technical tools used in support of malicious aspects of this activity. The main piece of UK legislation relevant to hacking, the Computer Misuse Act, is discussed, along with the relevance of professional codes of conduct. These will be applied to particular cases of hacking.

We will look at the principles of the 'Hacker Ethic' and other viewpoints that defend hacking. In particular we will be exploring the argument that computer hackers are like public 'watchdogs', disclosing information that the public has a right to know. Finally, we will consider how these conflicting ethical principles fit into wider debates about democracy and power in society.

2.2 Definitions of hacking

The computer ethicist, Duncan Langford (1995), states that in the 1960s and 1970s the term 'hacker' was used to describe an individual working with computers who was technically gifted. From a traditional perspective, therefore, a hacker was considered to be an expert, skilled programmer, rewriting code to customise and improve it. In the early days of computing there was no implication that someone known as a computer hacker would act illegally.

Nonetheless, the social and computing environment has changed greatly since the 1960s, and the use of the term 'hacker' has expanded and its definition broadened. Forester and Morrison (1990) outline several different definitions of the term 'hacker', which include:

- A person who enjoys learning the details of computer systems and how to stretch their capabilities, as opposed to most computer users who prefer to learn only the minimum amount necessary
- Someone who programs enthusiastically, or who enjoys programming, rather than just theorising about it
- A person who is able to create programs quickly
- An expert on a particular program, or one who frequently does work using it, or on it
- A malicious inquisitive meddler who tries to discover information by poking around. For example, a password hacker is one who tries, possibly by deception or illegal means, to discover other people's computer passwords.

Today, hacking is often defined in terms of individuals who seek to gain 'unauthorised access' to computer systems, and the currently broadly accepted view of a hacker is someone who uses specialised knowledge of computer systems to obtain illegal access to them. Langford defines hacking as:

> obtaining and exploiting unofficial access to a computer system.

The connotations of the term 'hacker' have clearly shifted away from the earlier benign meaning, towards a legal definition which is used by the authorities. Although the term suggests something malicious or subversive, this is not always the case. Typical malicious actions now covered by hacking include: breaking into public and private databases to steal, corrupt or modify data, defrauding banks, stealing credit card details, finding out private information, and spreading viruses.

The technical means of hacking have become ever more sophisticated. Information on how to accomplish hacking is often posted on specialist bulletin boards. Hackers may use a succession of computers as staging posts, to route a continuing series of attacks on different systems. In his book *The Cuckoo's Egg*, Clifford Stoll describes how, in the 1980s, US military computers were attacked by a hacker located in Germany . This was accomplished through a whole series of staging posts as the German hacker broke into dozens of US computers, including military systems, looking for information to sell to the Soviet Union.

One of the more notorious and widely publicised security breaches happened to the *New York Times* on 13 September, 1998. Their website server was invaded by a group of belligerent hackers who posted pornographic material and printed this threatening message for all to see:

> 'FIRST OFF, WE HAVE TO SAY ... WE OWN YOUR DUMB ASS. S3COND, TH3R3 AR3 SO MANY LOS3RS H3R3. ITZ HARD TO PICK WHICH TO INSULT MOST.'

The site was closed for nine hours while IT personnel cleaned up the offensive messages and plugged the security breach.

In 2001, Raphael Gray, a teenage hacker from Wales, broke into several online stores and stole thousands of credit card numbers. He then published the numbers on the web and, using one of the stolen card numbers, despatched a shipment of Viagra tablets to Microsoft boss Bill Gates. His actions sparked an international investigation that brought the FBI to the door of his parents' home in Pembrokeshire.

Why do hackers hack? The motives behind hacking are varied (see Figure 2.1) and complex. One suggestion is the satisfaction gained from the intellectual challenge involved, breaking into systems simply to see if it is possible – the challenge has been said to be similar to solving an elaborate crossword. The guessing of passwords and bypassing of file protections pose intriguing problems that some individuals will go to enormous lengths to solve, according to Forester and Morrison, (1990).

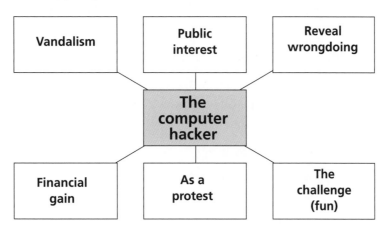

Figure 2.1: Computer 'hacking' may be undertaken for many reasons. Some motives are summarised here – see text for discussion.

A motive commonly stated by hackers themselves is the exposure of loopholes and vulnerabilities in computer systems. Hackers also expose bugs in software and alert software developers so that fixes (or 'patches') can be made. Hackers in this sense are like unpaid security consultants. In fact, some may be employed by security companies or intelligence agencies as consultants; others may go on to start their own computer security firms.

There is an international community of these 'professional' hackers, some of whom attend conferences, where competitions are staged in which contestants are invited to break into rigged computer systems.

There is the playful side of hacking, where it is no more than a practical joke, albeit a disruptive or offensive one, but no harm is intended. The malicious side of hacking – as we will discuss shortly – involves the creation and distribution of viruses, or the defacing and disruption of websites. In many instances, it has involved acts of vengeance, particularly by disgruntled employees against former employers, or by individuals with grudges.

Hacking can also be conducted as a form of political activism, to make a protest, to get a particular message across, or to correct a perceived injustice. Then there is the national security aspect, where hackers are employed by government agencies or by the military to engage in espionage, sabotage or cyber war with other countries. Hacking can also be conducted on behalf of law enforcement agencies for the purposes of crime prevention and detection, or increasingly, counter-terrorism.

Finally, there is the straightforwardly criminal aspect, where hacking is a tool to commit crimes of theft, fraud, extortion or forgery. These will be covered in greater detail in the next chapter.

Activity 2.1

Researching hacking cases

Research one of the following hacking cases by either typing one of the keywords into a search engine, or consulting one of the recommended textbooks:

- Kevin Mitnick
- Mafiaboy
- Raphael Gray
- Legion of Doom
- Master of Deception
- Robert Morris' Internet Worm

From your research, answer the following questions:

- What was this case about?
- Who were the protagonists and parties involved?
- Did any prosecutions result?
- If so, what were their outcomes?
- What ethical issues are raised by this case?

2.3 Destructive programs

Traditionally, hacking involved knowledge of programming and a certain degree of skill. Nowadays, hacking software can easily be obtained from the Internet, and hacking accomplished with rudimentary knowledge. Software can be downloaded to crack passwords or serial numbers for software installation, or to bypass other protections and security measures. Individuals, often describing themselves as hackers, anonymously release destructive software known collectively as computer viruses (because of the manner and ease with which they spread).

Let us first consider the nature of a computer virus. Quite simply, a virus is a self-replicating piece of programming code inserted into other programs to cause some sort of unexpected, and usually undesirable, event. Viruses can be transmitted by downloading a program from another computer, or can be present on a disk. The virus lies dormant until circumstances (typically a particular time or date, or the user activating another program) cause its code to be executed by the computer. Some viruses are playful in intent and effect, while others can be harmful, erasing data or causing a computer's hard disk to require reformatting. Viruses can attach themselves to the computer's operating systems, and other key programs, using up memory, and corrupting or erasing files. Measures for preventing and removing viruses in the form of anti-virus software will be discussed, along with other security technologies, in the next chapter.

Examples of viruses include:

- **Trojan horses**
- **Worms**
- **Time or logic bombs**
- **Denial-of-service.**

Some of these generic, destructive or malicious programs will now be discussed.

Trojan horses

The term 'Trojan horse' comes from Homer's *Illiad*. In the Trojan War, the Greeks presented the citizens of Troy with a large wooden horse, in which they had secretly hidden their warriors. During the night, the warriors emerged from the wooden horse and overran the city.

In the computing field, a Trojan horse is a program in which malicious or harmful code is disguised inside some apparently harmless programming or data (perhaps an image or sound file, or e-mail attachment). The victim is tricked into executing the program code by opening the file or attachment, initiating a malicious sequence of events. This may include damage to files, programs or the hard disk, or modification of data. It may enable unauthorised access to a computer, through a 'back door', in such a way as to gain control of that computer. Trojan horses can involve the insertion of false information into a program in order to profit from the outcome – for example, a false instruction to make payments to a bogus company.

Worms

A worm, like a virus, is self-replicating code, that situates itself in a computer system where it can do harm. Like most computer viruses, worms usually come in Trojan horses. Worms, however, tend to take the form of stand-alone code. In other words, they do not require a specific host computer, but run independently, travelling across networks. Worms tend to exist in memory and are non-permanent, whereas viruses tend to reside on disk where they are permanent until eradicated. In addition, worms are network-orientated, with segments of the worm inhabiting different machines. Worm programs entail the deletion of portions of a computer's memory, thus creating a 'hole' of missing information. Crucially, they use up system resources, slowing down a network, or shutting it down completely.

One of the first widely distributed worms, with global consequences, was Robert Morris' Internet Worm – a program written by Morris and released onto the Internet in 1988. The worm did not destroy files, and there was some disagreement about whether Morris intended or expected it to cause the amount of disruption that it did.

However, the worm spread quickly to computers running particular versions of the UNIX operating system, effectively jamming them and preventing normal processing. It was estimated that a few thousand computers on the Internet were affected (note that this represented a large proportion of the Internet at the time).

Time bombs and logic bombs

Time or logic bombs are programs triggered to act when they detect a certain sequence of events, or after a particular period of time has elapsed. They involve the insertion of routines that can be triggered later by the computer's clock or a combination of events. When the bomb goes off, the entire system will crash.

- Time bombs can be activated on a particular date; for example the 'Friday the 13th virus' wakes up whenever a Friday is the 13th of the month, copying itself, and attaching itself to other programs. It increases the size of the programs or files it attacks, using up computer memory, and eventually shutting the computer down

- A logic bomb is activated by a particular event or set of logical conditions. For example, a popular form of logic bomb monitors employment files and initiates systems damage (such as erasure of hard disks) once the programmer's employment has been terminated. A simple variation on this theme is a logic bomb virus. This is a virus that begins to replicate and destroy a system after it has been triggered, either by a time lapse, a set of pre-programmed conditions coming into existence, or by remote control, using the appropriate password.

Denial-of-service

Another hacking tool is a denial-of-service attack in which a server, hosting a particular website, will be targetted with a massive volume of fake traffic in the form of e-mails or requests for pages or other information. These overwhelm the server and block legitimate traffic, effectively shutting down the site. The execution of such an attack usually involves the coordination of many linked machines which are often 'hijacked' for this purpose.

Activity 2.2

Researching notorious viruses

Research one of the following viruses, by either typing the keyword into a search engine or consulting one of the recommended texts:

NIMDA virus	*Code Red* virus
I Love You virus	*Anna Kournikova* virus
Melissa virus	*MyDoom* worm

- How and where did the virus originate?
- Who was responsible for creating and distributing it?
- How did the virus work, and what effects did it have?
- What prosecutions were brought, if any?

2.4 Hacker ethics

Early hackers took their position seriously enough to establish their own ethical code, known as The Hacker Ethic (Langford, 1995).

The Hacker Ethic was comprised of five principal values:

- Access to computers, and anything which might teach you something about the way the world works, should be unlimited and total. Always yield to the hands-on imperative
- All information should be free
- Mistrust authority – promote decentralisation
- Hackers should be judged by their hacking, not bogus criteria such as academic excellence, age, race or position
- You can create art and beauty on a computer.

Hackers as public watchdogs

One way in which hackers have been represented is as public watchdogs, revealing information the public has a right to know, and exposing the truth. Given that more and more personal information is now being stored on computers – often without our knowledge or consent – it might be reassuring (the argument goes) to know that some citizens are able to penetrate these databases to find out what is going on. It is not always in the public interest – it is argued – to have information about us withheld.

In this sense, hacking continues a long tradition of investigative journalism (involving information leaks to the press and whistle-blowing by insiders). This is the same kind of journalism that uncovered the Watergate and Iran-Contra affairs in the US. Such journalism has the power to break a government's control of information flow to the public, and can ultimately even destroy corporations or governments that have been shown to be guilty of unethical or criminal activities.

An example of hackers acting in this manner can be seen in the events that surrounded the Chernobyl disaster in the former Soviet Union in 1986. A major explosion at the Chernobyl nuclear power plant in the Ukraine caused a serious radiation leak that threatened large areas of Europe. The Soviet government of the time tried to keep the disaster quiet, as did the then West German government. Hackers from the 'Chaos Computer Club' in West Germany released more information to the public about the Chernobyl disaster than did the West German government itself. All the information was gained by illegal break-ins carried out into government computer installations.

Hackers can indeed be an intelligent and critical check against governments who withhold information from the public or abuse their power. In this sense it could be argued that hackers represent one means by which we can attempt to avoid the creation of a more centralised, even totalitarian, government. This relates to the third principle of the Hacker Ethic which advocates decentralisation of power and information.

Hackers as security consultants

Another key argument, from a hacker's perspective, is that the breaching of systems can provide more effective security in future, so that other, presumably less well-intentioned, hackers are prevented from causing real harm. Given the possibility of terrorist acts becoming more and more technologically sophisticated, perhaps we can also look to hackers as a resource to be used to foil such acts and to improve our existing security arrangements.

Forester and Morrison (1990) write:

> To some extent this is already happening: in the US, convicted hackers are regularly approached by security and intelligence agencies with offers to join them in return for amelioration or suspension of sentences. Other hackers have used their notoriety to establish computer security firms and to turn their covertly gained knowledge to the benefit of commercial and public institutions.

2.5 Legal constraints: the Computer Misuse Act, 1990

In the UK, in 1989 a working paper on computer misuse by the Law Commission made several specific recommendations for changes in the law regarding computer hacking. However, despite government promises to legislate, no official measures were taken until 1990. In that year, Michael Colvin MP introduced a Private Member's Bill on computer misuse that incorporated many of the recommendations from the Law Commission paper, but included greatly increased penalties. In August 1990, the Bill eventually became the Computer Misuse Act.

As summarised in Figure 2.2, the Act introduced three new criminal offences:

- **Unauthorised access to computer material:** this is described as 'simple hacking', that is, using a computer without permission. It carries a penalty of up to six months in prison or a £2,000 fine, and is tried in a magistrates' court.

- **Unauthorised access to computer material with the intent to commit or facilitate commission of further offences:** this section of the Act covers actions such as attempting to use the contents of an e-mail message for blackmail, or stealing credit card numbers. This is viewed as a more serious offence; the penalty is up to five years' imprisonment and an unlimited fine. This offence is tried before a jury.

- **Unauthorised modification of computer material:** this section of the Act covers distributing a computer virus, or malicious deletion of files, as well as direct actions such as altering an account to obtain fraudulent credit. This offence is also tried before a jury.

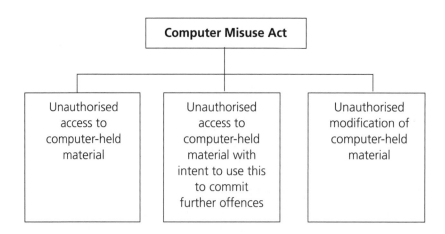

Figure 2.2: Three criminal offences detailed in the Computer Misuse Act

The Act also includes the offences of *conspiracy to commit*, and *incitement to commit*, the three main offences. This aspect of the Act makes even discussion of specific actions which are in breach of these three main sections a questionable practice. Merely to be associated with an offender in planning an illegal action, or to suggest carrying out the action, are sufficient to be committing an offence under the Act!

If a hacker, or anyone else, gains access to a system containing personal data, and then copies all or some of that data to their own system, they are liable to prosecution under not only the 1990 Computer Misuse Act, as amended by The Police and Justice Act 2006, but also the 1998 Data Protection Act. (Privacy will be discussed later in Chapter 6.)

Jurisdiction of the Act

The Computer Misuse Act (as amended) also attempts to cover international computer crime. Under the Act, an individual can be prosecuted in the UK as long as there is at least one 'significant link' with the UK. For example, hacking into a computer in Belgium from a computer terminal in London is illegal, as is hacking into London from Belgium. Using the UK as a staging post is also illegal under the Act (such as breaking into the Pentagon from Belgium via a UK university or company) and could result in UK prosecution, even if the hacker had never been in England.

Activity 2.3

The Computer Fraud and Abuse Act

Find out about the US *Computer Fraud and Abuse Act* (CFAA).

How does this Act compare with the UK *Computer Misuse Act?*

The following URL is recommended as a starting point for your research, though you may also want to consult some of the recommended texts and other articles:

www.eff.org/Legislation/CFAA

2.6 Professional constraints: BCS Code of Conduct

As we saw in Chapter 1, professional codes of conduct, such as those of the British Computer Society (BCS) and other professional bodies, provide a set of ethical and professional guidelines for computing professionals. The BCS Code of Conduct has a number of clauses that may be applied to hacking. Two of these, in the section on Public Interest, are as follows:

> Members shall have regard to the legitimate rights of third parties.': The term "third party" includes professional colleagues, or possibly competitors, or members of "the public" who might be affected by an IS project without their being directly aware of its existence.

> Members shall ensure that within their professional field/s they have knowledge and understanding of relevant legislation, regulations and standards, and that they comply with such requirements': As examples, relevant legislation could, in the UK, include the UK Public Disclosure Act, Data Protection or Privacy legislation, Computer Misuse law, legislation concerned with the export or import of technology, possibly for national security reasons, or law relating to intellectual property. This list is not exhaustive, and you should ensure that you are aware of any legislation relevant to your professional responsibilities.

In the international context, you should be aware of, and understand, the requirements of law specific to the jurisdiction within which you are working, and, where relevant, to supranational legislation such as EU law and regulation. You should seek specialist advice when necessary.

Activity 2.4

BCS Code of Conduct

Visit the *British Computer Society* (BCS) website and read through the BCS Code of Conduct at the following address: **www.bcs.org/BCS/Join/WhyJoin/Conduct.htm**

Consider which clauses in the BCS code of conduct are most relevant to hacking, and explain how and why.

Can hacking be consistent with any of these professional codes of conduct, or is it contrary to all of them?

2.7 To hack or not to hack? Ethical positions on hacking

Information ownership

As we will discuss in Chapter 6, many organisations and businesses collect personal information about us from a huge range of sources. But who gave these organisations the right to gather such information, and to provide or sell it to other organisations? And what if this information is inaccurate? Should we own information about ourselves, and have a right to correct it if it is wrong? Or, as a database operator, should I own any information that I have paid for to be gathered and stored?

If we imagine a hacker penetrating a system so that they can correct the records of those who have been denied the right to correct inaccurate data, which of these two – the database owner or the hacker – has committed the greatest ethical error? Are they both equally guilty?

If hackers are finding out who holds what information, on whom, and for what purposes – if they are checking whether corporations are adhering to the data protection laws, and exposing abuses that the government cannot or will not terminate – then in what ways are their actions unethical?

Hacking as trespassing

If computers are viewed as material possessions, then electronic entry to a computer system can be looked on as similar to physical entry into an office or home. Unless there is a specific invitation, or previous permission to enter, this could be considered trespassing, if not unlawful entry. The typical defence that hackers offer to this charge is that they are entering to test for loopholes in the software. But is this realistic or convincing? This is comparable to having a burglar break into your home in the hope that the burglar may reveal security weaknesses. Indeed, what would most people think of someone who broke into your home and went through your desk, reading any letters and personal material they happened to find?

In such a case, there seems to be a clear legal and ethical case against hacking into someone else's computer system. One counter-argument to this is to suggest that computers cannot be viewed as material possessions owned by one business or another. Langford (1995) argues that, in an undefined global community of computing (such as that represented by the Internet) physical ownership of machines is secondary to the benefit of its users. Exploring this electronic world is somehow above such considerations as 'yours' or 'mine' – electrons belong to no one.

Activity 2.5

Arguments against hacking

Write a summary of the main arguments against hacking – from a legal, professional and ethical perspective.

Activity 2.6

Ethical justifications for hacking

Can hacking be justified ethically, even when it involves breaking the law? How and under what circumstances?

Describe a situation where hacking might be excused on ethical grounds. You must support your argument with cases drawn from the Press, Internet articles or textbooks.

Activity 2.7

The medical centre scenario

Consider the following scenario:

'A Dutch hacker who copied patient files from a University of Washington medical center (and was not caught) said in an online interview that he did it to publicise the system's vulnerability, not to use the information. He disclosed portions of the files to a journalist after the medical center said that no patient files had been copied.' (Baase, 2003)

Prepare a five-minute presentation analysing the ethics of the hacker's actions. In your presentation, you should try to answer the following questions:

1. Was this honourable whistle-blowing or irresponsible hacking?

2. What arguments and good reasons would you give for your answer?

3. What ethical theories and principles (from Chapter 1) could you draw upon to analyse this case?

2.8 An ethical dilemma

A government employee believes that there is a secret agenda in connection with microchips currently being inserted into passports; he believes that there is a plan in place by which the microchips are in fact to store a broad range of personal information, and thinks this to be a somewhat sinister exercise that will impact negatively on the liberty of the individual. To obtain evidence concerning the use ultimately to be made of the microchips, the employee gains access to confidential memos and takes a copy of this material. Let us assume that the memos confirm the employee's suspicions. He sends the memos to the press and this brings the matter out into the open. As a direct result of ensuing public opinion, the use of microchips in passports is terminated. In parallel, the employee is identified as the hacker.

Despite having broken the law, has the employee acted ethically? Can he have a clear conscience? How do you think the employee's actions will impact on his future career? Were the actions ill-advised?   Under such circumstances, what would you have done?

2.9 Summary

This chapter has presented some of the ethical, legal and professional issues invoked by computer hacking. We have looked at some of the conflicting definitions of hacking, and have explained how the connotations of the term 'hacker' have changed over time. We also looked at some of the motives behind hacking, as well as the technical tools involved in the more malicious aspects of hacking, particularly viruses, worms and Trojan horses. In this chapter we have considered what the law has to say about hacking, focusing particularly on the UK's Computer Misuse Act, as well as the professional constraints that exist in codes of conduct of bodies like the British Computer Society. We also considered the main arguments for and against hacking, looking at instances where hacking might be justified, and the kind of principles that might be called upon to defend such actions. We looked at the principles of the Hacker Ethic and other viewpoints that defend hacking. In particular, we explored the argument that some computer hackers are like public watchdogs, disclosing information that the public has a right to know.

2.10 Review questions

Review question 2.1

How have the connotations of the term 'hacker' changed?   Describe the two main definitions of a computer hacker, focusing on the difference between a computer programmer's idea of 'hacking' and the type of activity described as 'hacking' by the media.

Review question 2.2

Identify and describe three different potential motives for hacking.

Review question 2.3

List and describe two forms of destructive programs a computer hacker can release.

Review question 2.4

Describe the five values that comprise the Hacker Ethic. Write a sentence on each, stating whether you think it is valid and why. What does the Hacker Ethic leave out? What principles could be added?

Review question 2.5

What legal constraints exist for cases of computer hacking in the UK and the US?

Review question 2.6

What are the three main categories of offences under the Computer Misuse Act? Give examples of each.

2.11 Feedback on activities

Feedback on activity 2.1

To demonstrate how you might approach this activity, we have focused on the case of *Mafiaboy*.

Within one week in 2000, almost a dozen major websites were shut down, some for several hours, by *denial-of-service* attacks. The sites included *Yahoo, eBay, Amazon, Buy.com, CNN* and others. The FBI traced the denial-of-service attacks to a 15-year-old Canadian who used the name *Mafiaboy*. Within a week, the FBI had Mafiaboy's real name.

Mafiaboy was identified as a suspect, because like many young hackers, he had bragged about his exploits on newsgroups. Law enforcement agents searched the archives of these message boards looking for other posts by the same person that yielded clues to his real identity. Mafiaboy had posted a message including his first name and e-mail address two years before the incident.

Mafiaboy pleaded guilty to a long list of charges, including that of 'computer mischief'. The US government estimated the cost of this incident at $1.7 billion. A key aspect of the case was that Mafiaboy did not write the destructive programmes himself; he had found them on the Internet.

The motives of Mafiaboy were unclear, but common motives among teenage hackers are the challenge, excitement and, above all, recognition and status, that come from executing such attacks.

Mafiaboy was sentenced to eight months in a juvenile detention facility.

The case raised a number of issues. Was shutting down major commercial websites a political statement against the commercialisation of the web – or was it, at best, a serious act of mischief, and, at worst, disruptive vandalism? If teenagers who are not especially technically skilled can easily obtain and use hacking programmes, what implications does this case have for the term 'hacking'?

Before the attacks were traced to the 15-year-old, some people speculated that they were the work of terrorists. This raises the problem of how to distinguish between non-malicious hacking and much more serious acts of theft, terrorism or espionage.

Feedback on activity 2.2

To demonstrate how you might approach this activity we have focused on the *Melissa* virus.

The *Melissa* virus of 1999, spread by mailing copies of itself to the first 50 people in the computer's e-mail address book, on systems using popular Microsoft software. Each new copy sent 50 more copies and the virus quickly infected approximately 1 million computers worldwide, including those of government and military agencies (including the US Marines) and hundreds of businesses. Many of the clogged systems shut down.

Law enforcement agencies arrested David Smith, who admitted to writing the Melissa virus (believed to have been named after a Florida stripper Smith knew).

Smith had illegally accessed America Online for the purpose of posting the virus onto the Internet. Although Smith had used someone else's AOL account, AOL's logs contained enough information to enable law enforcement authorities to trace the session to Smith's telephone line. Because the virus was originally located in a word-processing file (as a macro virus), security experts were also able to use this information to trace the Melissa virus to Smith.

David Smith pleaded guilty to releasing the Melissa virus which resulted in more than $80 million worth of damage. The $80 million total was partly related to the time spent by systems administrators to clear the virus off affected computers.

Smith was charged with three offences – interruption of public communication, conspiracy to commit the offence and attempting to commit the offence. He was also charged with two lesser offences – theft of computer services and damage or wrongful access to computer systems. Smith was eventually sentenced to 20 months in a federal prison in May 2002, and fined $5,000. He could have faced up to five years in prison, but prosecutors suggested a lesser term because he had assisted the authorities in thwarting other viruses. In 2003 Smith was still assisting computer crime authorities in the investigation and prosecution of other virus writers.

The case also raises a number of issues about the appropriate penalties for offences involving hackers who are young, who do not intend to do damage, or who, through accident, ignorance or immaturity, do more damage than they can pay for.

Feedback on activity 2.3

The *Computer Fraud and Abuse Act* (US) was passed by the US Congress in 1986 and is similar in many respects to the *Computer Misuse Act* (UK). The provisions of the act make it a crime to 'knowingly access a computer without, or in excess of authority, to obtain classified information'. The statute also makes it a crime to access any 'protected computer' without authorisation, and as a result of such access to defraud victims of property or to recklessly cause damage. Protected computers include those used by the government, financial institutions or any business engaged in interstate or international commerce.

In addition to the *Computer Fraud and Abuse Act* (CFAA) each state in the US has its own anti-hacking laws and penalties. The CFAA covers areas over which the federal government has jurisdiction: government computers or those used by government agencies, financial systems and medical systems. It also covers activities that involve computers in more than one state. Denial-of-service attacks and the launching of computer viruses are covered by the law in sections addressing the altering, damaging or destroying of information and the prevention of authorised use of a computer.

Feedback on activity 2.4

The BCS Code of Conduct sets out the professional standards required by the Society as a condition of membership. It applies to members of all grades, including students, and affiliates, and also non-members who offer their expertise as part of the Society's Professional Advice Register. The most relevant clauses to the issue of hacking include the following:

2. *You shall have regard to the legitimate rights of third parties.*

Comments: Third parties could be defined as businesses, government bodies or the general public. By engaging in any kind of unauthorised access that involves modification of data, distribution of viruses or other malicious actions, you could be denying the rights of these parties.

> 3. *You shall ensure that within your professional field/s you have knowledge and understanding of relevant legislation, regulations and standards, and that you comply with such requirements.*

Comments: Unauthorised access which falls under any of the 3 main offences of the *Computer Misuse Act,* or constitutes an offence under any other legislation, would obviously contravene this clause. This would also include hacking in an international context, where computing professionals have a responsibility to be aware of, and understand, the jurisdiction of the law in the country in which they are working.

> 10. *You shall uphold the reputation and good standing of the BCS in particular, and the profession in general, and shall seek to improve professional standards through participation in their development, use and enforcement.*

Comments: It would be difficult to reconcile hacking with this clause, especially if the consequences brought the computing profession as a whole into disrepute. Disaffected computer programmers turning hackers does not create a good public image of the IT profession. However, this depends on the circumstances of the hacking. If an act of hacking can be justified ethically (alerting the authorities of an impending terrorist act and saving lives?) this might exonerate the hacker and *improve* the good standing of the profession.

Feedback on activity 2.5

Some of the main arguments against hacking are as follows:

- Hacking is illegal, and if one accepts that the law is still one of the best guides as to what constitutes ethical/unethical behaviour, then if an action is criminal it is also indefensible, ethically

- Hacking can be enormously disruptive of business and communication, using up valuable system resources that may be needed by emergency services, security or law enforcement agencies

- Hacking constitutes trespassing of personal/private property and/or invasion of privacy

- It can be argued that public disclosure of information is not always in the public good. Some information should remain classified (for example, military and national security information, information that might threaten public order). We will discuss these free speech restrictions in greater detail in Chapter 5

- Hacking is unprofessional and cannot be reconciled with the codes of conduct of any professional body in the computing field.

Feedback on activity 2.6

Some of the main ethical defences of hacking are as follows:

- Hackers can act as public watchdogs, disclosing information which the public has a right to know, or where the public might be in danger, for example in the case of Chernobyl

- Hackers can expose abuses of power, corruption and wrong-doing by governments or big business

- Hackers can provide a check against the centralisation of power and information in societies

- Hackers can improve security, by breaching systems in order to expose vulnerabilities and loopholes

- Hacking can be conducted for the purposes of counter-terrorism, law enforcement and crime detection.

Feedback on activity 2.7

We need to know much more about this hacker's motives and intentions in this case but from the information provided we can identify a number of key issues and questions:

- Was this hacker breaking the law? Do his actions constitute 'unauthorised access'? What about the jurisdiction of the law, given that the hacking was conducted across international boundaries?

- Exactly what kind of confidential medical records did he disclose? We are told he disclosed portions of these records – did he disclose any really confidential information, such as names and identities of patients?

- Should the medical centre shoulder some of the blame in the case, by failing to take adequate security measures to protect the data of its patients? Should it have admitted publicly that it had been hacked, rather than trying to cover up the incident?

- Relevant ethical theories and principles in this particular case are utilitarianism (hacking for the greater good, or the public interest) and consequentialism (the consequences of an action justify the action itself). Do the consequences justify illegal or unethical actions – particularly if they bring about some benefit to the wider public? Was the end result – exposing security vulnerabilities at the medical centre – a good-enough reason to disclose the patients' files?

References

Baase, S (2003), *A Gift of Fire: Social, Legal and Ethical Issues for Computers and the Internet*, (Chapter 1), Pearson.

Forester, T & Morrison, P (1990), *Computer Ethics: Cautionary Tales and Ethical Dilemmas in Computing*, MIT Press.

Langford, D (1995), *Practical Computer Ethics*, McGraw-Hill.

Spinello, R (1995), *Cyber Ethics : morality and law in cyberspace*, Jones and Bartlett.

Stoll, C (1998), *The Cuckoo's Egg: Tracking a Spy through the Maze of Computer Espionage*, Pocket Books.

Further reading

Ayres, R (1999), *The Essence of Professional Issues in Computing*, (Chapter 4), Prentice Hall.

Baase, S (2003), *A Gift of Fire: Social, Legal and Ethical Issues for Computers and the Internet*, (Chapter 7), Pearson.

Erickson, J, (2003) *Hacking: The Art of Exploitation,* No Starch Press

Jones K J, Bejtlich R & Rose CW, (2005), *Real Digital Forensics: Computer Security and Incident Response*, Addison Wesley

Levy, S (1984), *Hackers: Heroes of the Computer Revolution*, Delta.

Mitnick KD & Simon WL, (2005),*The Art of Intrusion: The Real Stories Behind the Exploits of Hackers, Intruders & Deceivers*, John Wiley & Sons

Mitnick KD, Simon WL & Wozniak S, (2003), *The Art of Deception: Controlling the Human Element of Security*, John Wiley & Sons

Schneier B, (2004), *Secrets and Lies: Digital Security in a Networked World*, John Wiley & Sons

CHAPTER 3

Aspects of computer crime

Overview

This chapter explores the topic of computer crime, a serious and growing problem which raises a number of important legal, technical and professional issues. One such issue is how to define 'computer crime', and whether we are dealing with new categories of crime. If so, what are these crimes, who commits them, and how should they be tackled, legally and technically? What legislation exists to address computer crime, and is it adequate? We will be looking at the role of computer security in preventing computer crime, especially technical measures that can be implemented to protect computer systems. We will also address some of the professional issues raised by computer crime: for example, whether it is important for computer professionals to be aware of the kinds of crimes that exist, and whether organisations have a duty to provide adequate security measures and protections against computer crime.

Learning outcomes At the end of this chapter you should be able to:

- Appreciate the scope and nature of computer crime

- Understand the problems of combating computer crime

- Describe the work of national/international government initiatives to combat computer crime

- Appreciate the role of computer security in preventing computer crime

- Have an overview knowledge of protective measures.

3.1 Introduction

This chapter examines some of the key issues raised by computer crime. We begin by defining computer crime, and thinking about the extent to which computer crimes are 'new' kinds of crimes. We then outline some of the forms that computer crime takes, and examine some of the perpetrators of these crimes and their motives. In Section 3.4, we outline government initiatives to detect and tackle computer crime, and explain some of the difficulties of this work. In particular, we shall be considering why there is more computer crime than is realised or publicly known. This chapter provides an overview of the security measures that can be implemented to prevent the threat of computer crime, including passwords, encryption, biometrics, firewalls and access control software. Finally, we address some of the professional and ethical issues raised by computer crime, both for organisations and for computing professionals as individuals.

3.2 What is computer crime?

Computer crime can be broadly defined as a criminal act that has been committed using a computer (or computer-based hardware) as the principal tool. When most people talk about computer crime, they are usually referring to the fact that a computer has either been the object, subject, or instrument of a crime. As summarised in Figure 3.1, a further distinction can be made between crimes where the role of the computer is purely incidental, and those where the computer is an essential part of the crime. In the first category are computer-assisted crimes, many of which were committed long before the advent of computers. These include electronic versions of 'traditional' crimes, such as fraud, forgery, extortion and theft. In the latter category are crimes that could not have been committed without a computer and which require some degree of computer knowledge and expertise. This definition of computer crime is a narrower one, and includes 'new' cyber crimes which are specific to computers, such as hacking, virus attacks, and identity theft.

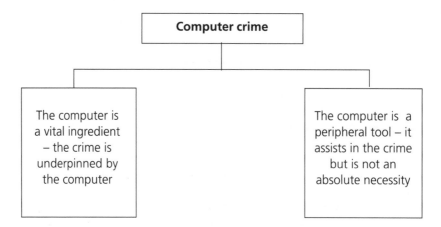

Figure 3.1: In terms of computer crime, a computer (or computer-based hardware) may facilitate the crime or may play a fundamental role.

Activity 3.1

Computer-assisted crime

Give examples of two crimes in which a computer plays an incidental role. In each case, explain how computers have made a difference to the particular crimes that you describe.

Types of computer crime

The field of a computer crime is highly fluid – many new crimes, and new versions of more traditional crimes, are continually emerging. This section looks at some of the different types of computer crime. The areas we discuss are indicated in Figure 3.2.

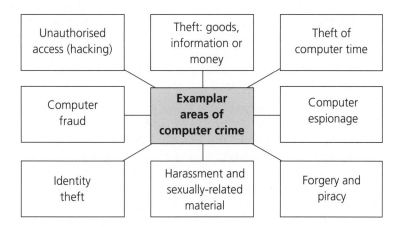

Figure 3.2: Examples of computer crime that are briefly described in the text

Unauthorised access

As outlined in Chapter 2, there are three main forms of 'unauthorised access' that constitute criminal offences under the Computer Misuse Act, 1990. These are:

- Unauthorised access to computer material
- Unauthorised access with intent to commit further offences (such as blackmail)
- Unauthorised modification of computer material (for example, distributing viruses).

In Chapter 2 we also looked at some of the techniques for gaining unauthorised access, such as Trojan horses, as well as other malicious and destructive programs, such as viruses and worms. Other techniques of gaining unauthorised access include 'piggybacking', which refers to tapping into communication lines, and 'riding' into a system, behind a legitimate user with a password.

Theft of goods, information or money

Computer technology has enabled new kinds of theft, for example theft of goods (e.g. diverting goods to the wrong destination) and theft of information (e.g. unauthorised tapping into data transmission lines or databases). Commonly used techniques include data 'diddling', swapping one piece of data for another, so it is, for example, almost impossible to tell that funds have been stolen; and scavenging for stray data or garbage, for clues that might unlock the secrets of a system or information that might be used for criminal purposes.

Theft of money can take various forms, such as transferring payments to a bogus bank account. Embezzlement is one of the most common crimes, and refers to the fraudulent appropriation of funds by a person to whom those funds have been entrusted.

With the use of a computer, trusted employees can steal hundreds of thousands, and in some cases, millions of pounds from their employers. The victims are banks, brokerage houses, insurance companies and other large financial institutions. A common technique here is the 'salami', which involves theft of tiny sums of money from many thousands of accounts. For example, a bank clerk might shave a few pennies off many customers' bank accounts (like slices of salami) depositing them in their own account. The haul is thus spread over a large number of transactions and eventually accumulates as a large sum. For example, Forester and Morrison [1990] describe the 'Flying Dutchman':

> On Christmas Eve, 1987, a 26 year old clerk at Lloyds Bank in Amsterdam, Frans Noe, ordered that sums of $8.4m and $6.7m be transferred from the Lloyds branch in New York to an account he had opened with the Swiss Bank Corporation in Zurich. The young Dutchman then flew to Switzerland to collect the money. But owing to an unforeseen computer malfunction, the transfer failed to go through. Returning after Christmas, fellow employees saw the failed transaction on their screens and reported it. Noe was subsequently arrested and returned to Amsterdam. In May 1988 the "flying" Dutchman was jailed for 18 months for breaking into a computer system and his two accomplices received 12 months each.

Theft of computer time

Theft of computer time involves the use of an employer's computer resources for personal work. This is something of a grey area, however. Although some unauthorised use of computer resources is technically theft of processing and storage power, most employers turn a blind eye to employees using a company's computers in moderation for such purposes. Using company computers for financial gain, however, such as private consulting work, is unethical, unless permitted by the employee's employment contract.

Computer fraud

Con artists and criminals of many sorts have found new opportunities on the Internet to cheat unsuspecting users. Some scams are almost unchanged from their pre-Internet forms – for example, pyramid schemes, chain letters, sales of counterfeit goods, and phoney business investment opportunities.

Stock fraud is an area of criminal activity that has been adapted to the Internet. In one particular case, an employee of a US company called PairGain Technologies created a fake web page to look like the site of the Bloomberg financial news service. The site featured a positive but false announcement about PairGain. The employee also posted messages about the 'news', with a link to the fake site.

People copied and e-mailed the link, spreading the false information quickly, and causing PairGain stock to rise more than 30%. The perpetrator was traced and caught within a week.

Another area of fraudulent activity has been web auction sites, like eBay, founded in 1995, and perhaps the largest and best-known online auction site. Approximately $400 million of goods were sold on eBay in 2000. In one month in 2001, 24 million people visited the site. But problems soon arose. Some sellers did not send the items people paid for, or they sent inferior goods that did not meet the online description. Dishonest sellers also engaged in 'shill bidding', that is, bidding on one's own goods to drive up the price.

Some 'old' crimes, like extortion, have been given a new lease of life in the electronic environment. Len Hynds of the National Hi-Tech Crime Unit (discussed later) cites the example of hackers accessing companies' systems, for the purpose of downloading databases, then contacting their victims to offer security patches for their software in order to put things right again.

Corporate espionage

Corporate computer systems contain a great deal of information of interest to competitors, including product development plans, customer contact lists, product specifications, manufacturing process knowledge, and strategic plans. Corporate espionage and theft is a rapidly growing area of computer crime which involves the theft of these corporate assets or trade secrets from competitors.

Identity theft

One of the fastest-growing computer crimes is identity theft which involves not just the theft of credit card numbers, but also national insurance or social security numbers, bank account details, addresses and any other personal data that a person might use to verify their identity. This data can be pieced together to either form a fake identity or to impersonate someone by usurping their identity, whether for purposes of theft, fraud or other malicious activities.

It has been suggested that identity theft is the fastest-growing white-collar crime in the UK, generating a criminal cash flow of £10 million a day. In 1999, there were 20,264 reported cases of identity theft in the UK; by 2002, that figure had reached 74,766, an increase of 50% from the year before. These figures accounted only for reported cases. It is estimated that approximately 80% of this type of fraud goes unrecognised, is kept quiet, or is written off as bad debt (*Guardian Weekend*, 25 Oct, 2003).

Forgery and piracy

Computers have been employed to assist forgery, using desktop publishing software, high-resolution scanners and laser printers to produce counterfeit money, fake cheques, passports, visas, birth certificates, identity cards, degree certificates and corporate stationery, to name but a few examples. Software piracy is a major area of criminal activity, involving the distribution of illegal software and other intellectual products. This matter will be discussed in greater detail in Chapter 4.

Harassment and sexually related material

Computer technology, and the Internet specifically, have assisted a range of sexual crimes, from the distribution and consumption of child pornography via paedophile rings, to electronic forms of sexual harassment and cyber stalking (the use of e-mail and other electronic media to harass or threaten a person repeatedly).

Activity 3.2

Researching a computer crime case

Using the additional reading or a suitable online search engine, research a particular case of computer crime. Answer the following questions:

- What *type* of computer crime does this case fall under?

- Was the computer *incidental* or *essential* to the crime?

- What were the motives for this crime?

- How was the perpetrator caught?

- What prosecutions were brought, under what legislation?

Computer criminals

There is a commonly held view that the typical computer criminal is something of a 'whizz kid', with highly developed computing skills and a compulsive desire to 'beat the system'. However, not many crimes demonstrate high technical ingenuity on the part of the perpetrator. Most exhibit an opportunistic exploitation of an inherent weakness in the computer system being used.

Early research into computer crime showed that the vast majority of crimes involving computers were carried out by employees or insiders from within an organisation or business. These were invariably opportunist crimes perpetrated by managers, supervisors, clerks or cashiers who had little in the way of technical skills and were mostly first-time offenders (Hynds [2002]). This picture is changing, however, and the trend is away from insider crimes, towards crimes committed by outsiders – from external, remote, locations. This has been accompanied by a general rise in new types of 'high-tech' cyber crime committed by organised criminals, working across national borders.

The motives of computer criminals are many and varied, ranging from crimes committed as a means of easy financial gain, to those motivated by vengeance or grudges. As with hacking, some crimes are committed purely for the intellectual challenge. One of the attractions of computer crimes is that they involve very little physical risk, compared to crimes such as bank robbery. Most computer crimes can be committed anonymously, without having to confront the victims; this touches on the 'invisibility factor' of computing technology that was discussed in Chapter 1. Moreover, computer crimes can often appear not to be 'criminal' acts – shuffling numbers around in a remote and abstract way is not quite the same as handling huge piles of paper money. This partly explains why many perpetrators do not consider their crimes to be 'dishonest'.

A number of factors have contributed to the general increase in the amount of computer crime. Hynds argues that these include the availability of point and click interfaces, that are much easier to use by the technically less competent, and the availability of software which can be easily downloaded from the Internet and used for criminal purposes.

In addition, there has been a general increase in computer literacy in the wider population, and greater access to computer technology.

Computer crimes are increasingly carried out from remote locations, like Internet cafes, and from mobile sites, with the greater availability and power of laptop computers, personal digital assistants (PDAs) and mobile phones. This, and the fact that crimes are committed across national borders, increases problems of detection for law enforcement agencies. Computer crimes can be also be committed alone, without talkative associates, thus further reducing the risk of detection.

Another factor that has contributed to computer crime is the fact that the Internet is above all a network and, as such, facilitates connections between like-minded people. On the Internet it is possible to inhabit a niche world populated solely by others whose experiences, values and beliefs are approximately the same as one's own. The benign aspect of this is the plethora of newsgroups, websites and chat rooms tailored to specific interests and hobbies, from 'hip-hop' to gardening. The malevolent side is that these technologies allow networking and communication among various kinds of criminals, from fraudsters to terrorists. This has, arguably, encouraged crimes such as paedophilia by facilitating the growth of networks of sex offenders which would be far more difficult to form in the physical world Hynds [2002].

Why is there more computer crime than we realise? In 2001–2002 nearly half of all UK businesses suffered at least one malicious security breach, according to a Department of Trade and Industry survey, and the average cost was £30,000. One in five incidents caused disruption lasting more than a week. A British Chamber of Commerce survey in 2002 showed that 60% of small-to-medium-sized enterprises had been victims of computer-related crime and 75% were worried about doing business online (www.iee.org, Feb 2004).

Although it is generally agreed that computer crime is a large and growing problem, many experts believe that the amount of computer crime is much greater than is estimated. There are two main reasons for this:

- Firstly, many crimes go completely undetected and are often only discovered by accident. This is because computer crimes, by their nature, are very hard to detect – it is not always easy to know when someone has gained unauthorised access to a computer system. This is compounded by the problems of tracing and tracking down computer criminals because of the anonymous, remote and increasingly transnational nature of the crimes concerned

- Secondly, many crimes go unreported. This is partly because there is often very little perceived benefit for the victim. The law is unlikely to be able to undo the damage caused, and the criminal is unlikely to be convicted. In addition, much staff time is likely to be tied up assembling evidence – even if it can be collected at all. More importantly, perhaps, wider knowledge of the crime is likely to harm the future prospects of the organisation that has been the victim of the crime. Very few computer frauds, for example, are made public because companies, especially banks and other financial institutions, are loath to admit that their security systems are fallible. Such bad publicity makes them look less than competent. Publicity of this nature is disastrous for public relations and could lead to a major loss of customer confidence.

Combating computer crime: the Hi-Tech Crime Unit and the Serious Organised Crime Agency

To counteract the rapid growth in computer crime in the UK, the National Hi-Tech Crime Unit (NHTCU) was launched in April 2001 as a specialised agency within the National Crime Squad. Its brief was to combat serious and organised hi-tech crime both within the UK, and outside (in cases where crimes have an impact upon the UK).

Crimes targeted include software piracy, hacking and virus attacks, fraud, blackmail and extortion, online paedophilia, and identity theft. Although a relatively small unit, the NHTCU, within two years of being launched, had already accumulated over 3 terabytes of evidence (BBCi, 3 Oct, 2003). The NHTCU comprised four sections:

- **Investigations**, which gathered evidence and secures prosecutions
- **Intelligence**, which delivered tactical and strategic information
- **Tactical and technical support,** which acted in a consulting capacity alongside local law enforcement
- **Digital evidence recovery**, which undertook forensic work.

Note that the NHTCU was incorporated into the Serious Organised Crime Agency (SOCA) (**www.soca.gov.uk**) in 2006, as a part of a wide-ranging reform of policing activity.

Computers present new challenges for the detection and prosecution of computer crimes. To prove that a criminal act has been committed (for example, that a suspect has downloaded child porn images) requires the gathering and processing of new kinds of evidence. The field of collecting evidence from computers is called computer forensics. Computers seized from suspects act as a virtual crime scene. Computer forensics specialists retrieve evidence from the hard disks of such computers. Many offenders are unaware that Internet usage leaves footprints that can be traced, and that files, e-mails and images can be recovered even after they have been 'deleted'.

Seizure of computers, however, presents particular problems for both law enforcement and suspects because of a computer's multipurpose use. For a computer to be seized and removed from a suspect's premises, a warrant is required; but such warrants can only be granted to search for specific material on a computer. Investigators may suspect that a hard disk contains files of illegally obscene material, material that infringes copyrights, stolen credit card numbers or evidence of other crimes. The problem is that a computer also contains many legitimate, legal files, many of which belong to other people.

Crime detection work often involves the use of similar kinds of technologies to those used by hackers, in order to apprehend suspects. In France, 74 suspected paedophiles were apprehended using Internet technology and networking tools. Police managed to access a registry of 150,000 paedophile websites, a move that would be impossible to achieve in an offline context. Another strategy employed by security professionals and law enforcement agents is to set up 'honeypots', websites that look attractive to hackers, but are closely monitored so that everything a hacker does at the site is recorded and studied in order to trap suspects.

3.3 Computer security measures

In this section we briefly discuss various measures that may be taken in order to enhance computer security. The topics covered are indicated in Figure 3.3.

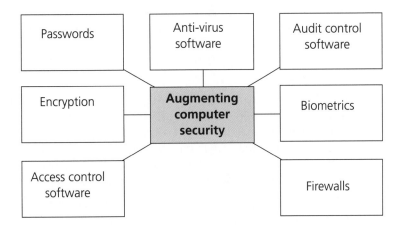

Figure 3.3: Various security measures that are discussed in this section

Passwords

One of the simplest and most widely used computer security measures involves the use of passwords which authenticate authorised users and allow access to a system or network. Passwords represent the first line of defence in network security. However, they have a number of inherent weaknesses. Perhaps the most serious of these is that passwords are often too obvious and easy to guess. People tend to choose the names of their partners, spouses or family pets, or a favourite hobby. If a password cannot be guessed, then password-cracking software is relatively easy to obtain.

To counteract these weaknesses, rigorously enforced password policies need to be adhered to. Passwords can be made less obvious and memorable by avoiding the use of partner's names. They should include at least eight characters, with a mixture of numbers and lower- and upper-case letters, and should not be words found in any conventional dictionary. Passwords should be issued only to the minimum number of people requiring access. Passwords, moreover, must be kept confidential at all times and should not be disclosed to anyone else. They must be changed on a regular basis (every two to four weeks). A password policy should also include the monitoring of logins (to see the date and time of recent logins, and all unsuccessful login attempts since the previous successful login). This is in order to see whether an unauthorised user has been attempting to gain access to an authorised user's account. Another important measure in any password policy is to secure the password database – a crucial area of vulnerability in a computer network.

Encryption

In computer networks, whether local area networks or the wider Internet, one of the more complicated problems is to secure information in transit between the server and the end user, and between sender and receiver. This is important in the transmission of any kind of sensitive or confidential information which must be protected adequately from the risk of being intercepted. It applies to eCommerce transactions and submission of credit card numbers, private e-mails, or any kind of security, military or business communication. One way to secure this data is through encryption.

Encryption is the conversion of data into a form (called a cipher) that cannot be easily understood by unauthorised receivers. Decryption is the process of converting encrypted data back into its original form, so it can be understood. Simple ciphers include the substitution of letters for numbers, the rotation of letters in the alphabet, and the 'scrambling' of voice signals. More complex ciphers work according to sophisticated computer algorithms that rearrange the data bits in digital signals.

When a message or piece of data is encrypted, it is effectively 'locked' and can only be decrypted (or deciphered) by someone with the correct password or key. In order to easily recover the contents of an encrypted signal, the correct decryption 'key' is required. This key is an algorithm that 'undoes' the work of the encryption algorithm. Alternatively, a computer can be used in an attempt to 'break' the cipher. The more complex the encryption algorithm, the more difficult it becomes to infiltrate communications without access to the key.

Encryption/decryption is used when carrying out any kind of sensitive transaction, such as a credit card purchase online, or confidential communication, such as the discussion of a company secret between different departments of an organisation.

In the US banking system, for obvious security reasons, the Treasury Department already requires that all electronic fund transfers be encrypted. For those of us doing commerce at a somewhat smaller level(!), or simply e-mail or information transfers, security is equally important.

There are many different protocols, or standards, used in encryption. The SET (Secure Electronic Transactions) standard is used to encrypt credit card information being transmitted over the Internet. An alternative protocol is a Secure Socket Layer (SSL) which automatically encrypts information sent to websites and then decrypts it before the recipient reads it. Websites that request credit card details carry a padlock sign denoting a secure socket layer, which means the link between the user and the web server is encrypted. Encryption devices in the form of DSPs (Digital Signal Processors) are also used to scramble voice and data messages over telephone networks. Voice encryption is especially important in military and security communication, but is also used in many other fields.

Other encryption technologies include digital signatures which are used to verify the identities of both the senders and the recipients of a message, or the authenticity of electronic documents. This technology also relies on the use of encryption keys to encode and decode a message. In this case, a private key is used to sign one's signature to a message or file, and a public key is used to verify the signature after it has been sent. The public key might be published in a directory or made available to other users. Spinello [2000] presents a scenario to best describe the functioning of digital signatures:

> Assume that John and Mary are exchanging e-mail, and Mary wants to verify John's identity. Mary can send John a letter with a random number, requesting that he digitally sign that number and send it back. John receives the letter, and digitally signs the random number with his private key. When the letter is sent back to Mary, she verifies that signature with her copy of John's public key. If the signature matches, she knows that she is communicating with John, assuming that John has been careful with his private key.

The drawbacks of encryption, however, are the security of the keys or ciphers themselves, which can be stolen or hacked.

The level of encryption is another major issue. In general, the stronger the cipher (that is, the harder it is for unauthorised people to break) the better. However, as the strength of encryption/decryption increases, so does the cost. The strength of encryption is measured by the number of bits used in the key to encode the message or data. It is generally recognised within the computer security field that the default 40-bit encryption used by web browsers is inadequate. The SSL used by browsers when purchasing goods online, for example, can easily be hacked into. For adequate levels of protection, 128-bit encryption, at least, is needed.

Access control software

Access control software assigns access rights and privileges in a computer network to different users. It restricts users, individually identified by password, to only those files they are authorised to use. Even then, the software permits the users to perform only authorised functions, such as appending or deleting information, and prevents them from accessing parts of the system which they are not entitled to enter.

However, one obvious limitation with access control software, is that it does not protect an organisation against frauds committed by employees while going about their legitimate tasks; as we mentioned earlier, a high proportion of computer crimes occurs this way. Most networks provide system administrators with 'superuser status', enabling them to access and modify virtually any file on the network. A further problem with access control software is that if intruders are able to obtain this status, they can obtain access to all parts of the system.

Another technology used to authenticate user access to a network, and to protect an organisation's assets, is dial back or black box systems. When a user dials into a computer, a black box intercepts the call and demands a password. The unit then disconnects the call, looks up the password in the directory and calls the user back at their listed telephone number. Fraudsters dialling from another telephone number will be screened out. A server may have hundreds of ports of entry from remote stations and each one has to be protected.

Firewalls

A firewall consists of hardware and/or software that is designed to insulate an organisation's internal network (or 'intranet') from the wider Internet, by putting a boundary around it (a 'firewall'). Firewall software gives access only to trusted Internet (IP) addresses and scrutinises data for irregularities or signs of danger. Ideally, firewalls are configured so that all connections to an internal network go through relatively few, well-monitored locations. A firewall cannot only serve to protect against hacking from outside, but also to restrict access to the Internet from inside a network, for example by blocking access to certain websites. The main shortcoming of firewalls, however, is that they provide no protection against crimes by insiders.

Firewalls are used to achieve a basic level of security for commercial websites, by firstly, securing the web server and the files that it contains, and secondly, guaranteeing the integrity of the information that travels between web server and the end user. This includes user names, passwords and credit card numbers. Securing the web server itself can also be accomplished by using standard computer security techniques, such as authentication mechanisms and intrusion protection devices. Gatekeepers and digital locks can also secure networks on which these servers reside. Although firewalls can be used to protect web servers, most companies set up public websites outside their firewalls to make them more easily accessible to those trying to buy their products.

Biometrics

Another weapon in the fight against computer crime is biometrics, or the digitising of biological characteristics. These technologies work by sampling 'unique' biological features, such as the voice, the pattern of blood vessels in the retina, or fingerprints. They then extract and convert these features into a mathematical code and store them as a biometric template. To confirm a user's identity, the user interacts with the system, for example by an iris or fingerprint scan. The sample is then compared to the template for a match, and access is accordingly granted or denied. Some computer systems, for example, require a thumbprint match to log onto to a computer, either physically or over the Internet. The main applications of biometrics are in security and fraud prevention. Biometric scanning devices can control access to computer rooms, bank vaults and military bases.

To reduce the risks of terrorism, several US airports now use fingerprint identification systems to ensure that only authorised employees enter restricted areas. Following trials at Heathrow Airport, it was reported in 2004 that the UK Home Office was planning to introduce an iris recognition system at five UK airports to verify identities of selected overseas travellers. These were part of wider plans to roll out biometric technology in the use of visas, passports and eventually ID cards (*Computer Weekly*, 22 June, 2004)

Whereas the use of biometrics seems set to increase dramatically, there are some serious practical, social and political problems with this technology. When a credit card number is stolen, we can get a new account with a new number, but if a hacker gets a copy of the file with our digitised thumbprint or retina scan, we cannot get a new one. Given the weak security of the Internet, it is likely that hackers will be able to steal biometric files as easily as they now steal files of credit cards. Another problem is reliability. The two most developed forms of biometric identification, fingerprints and iris scanning, can produce false results, especially when used for mass identification purposes. This could mean that someone who was a legitimate owner of a passport or a credit card, or someone with authorised access, could be rejected by the identification system. Biometric systems have to be completely robust and carefully tested before being introduced – and at present this is certainly not the case.

A third area of concern is that the increased use of biometrics can also lead to increased surveillance and tracking of our activities by government agencies. The potential for loss of privacy and civil liberties is considerable. These issues will be addressed in greater detail in Chapter 6.

Audit control software

Audit control software is used to closely monitor the use of a computer. This enables auditors to trace and identify any operator who gains access to a system, and the exact time that this occurred – such as after working hours. This type of software can also be used specifically to browse through vast amounts of financial transactions, looking for signs of any abnormal activity, such as a high number of 'correction entries', which often indicates the trial-and-error approach of fraud. Such systems are often used in the financial sector, to identify insider trading and stock or foreign exchange fraud.

Anti-virus software

In the previous chapter, we explained that computer viruses are malicious programs with enormous destructive potential. Anti-virus programs are therefore an essential aspect of computer security. Anti-virus software works by searching the computer's hard disk and storage media for virus patterns and signatures, and matching them against its own database of virus definitions. If a match is found, and an existing virus is detected, an appropriate course of action is suggested to remove the virus. Anti-virus programs also prevent infected files from being downloaded (whether from a disk or an e-mail attachment) and prevent viruses from inserting themselves into a computer system.

However, since new viruses are appearing all the time, the application's database has to be constantly updated. Some viruses also change their pattern as they replicate, so the software must also scan for suspicious code as well as known virus patterns.

The market for this kind of software has expanded rapidly with the increasing use of the Internet by organisations and individuals, and the increasingly destructive potential of computer viruses. Some forms of virus protection include isolation of the infected system(s), or the use of non-writable system disks so that viruses cannot copy themselves there. Other anti-virus measures include testing of unknown software (particularly public domain software downloaded from bulletin boards) on a minimal, isolated system.

Management issues

Security is not only a technical issue, it is also a management issue that involves educating staff and increasing employee awareness of security issues. As IT security consultant, Gary Hinson (2004) argues:

> 'Computers alone don't implement information security policies and standards – human beings purchase and configure the systems, switch on the control functions, monitor the alarms and run them. Whatever way you look at the problems, it is just as important to invest in your people as your technology.'

Security policies also need to include management policies for checking employees – for example, undertaking thorough reference and background checks when recruiting staff. This is especially important in the case of personnel whose jobs involve access to confidential or sensitive data. Security policies also involve decisions about appropriate levels of network access and authority, and the implementation of password systems, disaster recovery plans and other security procedures.

Activity 3.3

Researching security technologies

Using the additional reading, or a suitable online search engine, research one of the following security technologies, focusing on a particular application or example. Discuss some of the problems of implementing this technology, and its strengths and weaknesses .

- Biometrics

- Encryption

- Access control software

- Firewalls.

Activity 3.4

Recommending security measures

Imagine that you are a computer security consultant. What security measures would you advise the four customers in the list below to take, bearing in mind the type of organisation, and their business or activities. For each case, answer the following questions:

- What are the likely crimes to be committed?

- Who, and where, are the threats coming from, both internally and externally?

- What technical security measures would be most appropriate, and why?

1. An online company who accepts credit card details wants to secure its customers' details, and safeguard against damage.

2. A communications company employing a lot of young, technically able people, wants to ensure its online facilities are not being abused.

3. A high-security establishment needs to ensure that only authorised users can access certain parts of the system.

4. A private consultant has a contract with a research organisation working on highly sensitive issues. He needs to be sure his communications are secure, and some of the documents he sends might be used as legal proof of his recommendations.

3.4 The Computer Misuse Act, 1990

Computer crime in the form of unauthorised access to computer systems, in any of the three main categories discussed in Chapter 2, is covered by the Computer Misuse Act, as amended by the Police and Justice Act 2006. We saw how an individual can be prosecuted in the UK under the Computer Misuse Act as long as there is at least one 'significant link' with the UK. This is especially important with new kinds of cybercrime which are committed across national borders. International jurisdiction of the law, however, also represents a problem in the apprehension and prosecution of computer criminals. The individual suspected of writing and releasing the ILOVEYOU computer virus in 2000, for example, which jammed computers and destroyed files worldwide, was not prosecuted because he lived in the Philippines, which had no law that applied to his actions.

There are a number of additional legal problems when prosecuting suspected computer criminals. One general area of concern about the current legislation on computer misuse is that the law is out of step with the rapidly changing nature of computer crime. Legal experts, security consultants, and law enforcement agencies have argued that the Computer Misuse Act needs urgently updating to take into account the growth of the Internet and the emergence of new kinds of offences. The Police Justice Act 2006 moves towards this, with its amendments to the Computer Misuse Act; the Fraud Act 2006 (introduced in January 2007) covers areas of technology-related crime, such as phishing and spoofing.

Another problem is that there are no statutory provisions relating specifically to computer evidence in trials involving computer crimes. Evidence from computers that have been attacked may not be admissible in court proceedings, because, under common law, it has been taken from mechanical instruments which are not in 'working order' (Hill, Shelley, Dec 2003/ Jan 2004, Computer Misuse, C & L, **www.scl.org**).

The question of intention has been another sticking point. Section 3 of the Computer Misuse Act, 1990 states that an offender is guilty of an offence only if 'he has requisite intent and requisite knowledge'. The problem is then how to show and prove this intent, with evidence of responsibility. A key defence in many cases has been that 'the accused did not intend to cause any harm,' or that 'material had been placed on the computer of the accused without their knowledge'. In the case of Aaron Caffrey, the accused had allegedly launched a denial-of-service attack against the Port of Houston's (US) computer system which prevented access to the port's information by shipping, mooring and support services. The port is one of the busiest in the world. Caffrey alleged that a Trojan horse was responsible and that it installed itself on his computer without his knowledge. There was no trace of the Trojan found on his machine, but he argued that it deleted itself after committing the acts of which he was accused. Despite the prosecution arguing that this technology did not exist, the jury acquitted Caffrey. (Hill, Shelley, Dec 2003/Jan 2004, Computer Misuse, C & L, www.scl.org).

In another case in 2002, computer experts found 11 Trojan horse programs on the computer of Julian Green which had been downloaded as a result of his opening unsolicited e-mails. After receiving this expert evidence, prosecutors dropped charges against Green for possession of 172 indecent images of children.

Commentators suggested that one of the key reasons for these acquittals was that the juries were confused by the technical evidence put before them – a further key problem in the prosecution of computer crime cases. In both cases, the defence argued that Trojan horses could delete themselves after they had infected a machine, and that this was the reason for the absence of infection when the machine was inspected. The prosecution on the other hand argued that this technology did not exist. Some reports suggest that one juror developed a migraine after hearing the technical evidence! (Hill, Shelley, Dec 2003/Jan 2004, Computer Misuse, C & L, www.scl.org).

Another concern voiced by law enforcement agencies, and victims of computer crime, is that the sentences for computer crimes are simply too lenient. All too often, such criminal activities attract light sentences or avoid prosecution altogether as the Crown Prosecution Service and the judiciary fail to recognise their damaging nature. Computer theft, fraud and vandalism, it is argued, deserve to be treated as seriously as more traditional areas of law and order such as crimes against the person, crimes against property and the maintenance of public order.

Activity 3.5

Researching security technologies

Download a copy of "Good Practice for Computer Based Electronic Evidence" authored by the Association of Chief Police Officers (ACPO) from:
www.7safe.com/electronic_evidence/ACPO_guidelines_computer_evidence.pdf

What are the four principles of good practice for computer-based electronic evidence discussed in the report?

3.5 Professional duties and obligations

Other legislation relevant to the field of computer security is the Data Protection Act, 1998. We will be exploring this Act in greater detail in Chapter 6 in relation to privacy issues. However, one of the Act's key principles has a direct bearing on the issue of computer security. This principle requires that companies and organisations take 'appropriate security measures … against unauthorised access to, or alteration, disclosure or destruction of, personal data, and against accidental loss or destruction of personal data'. This means that organisations have a legal obligation to protect any personal data that they may hold, and to take appropriate security measures against the destruction, alteration or disclosure of that data.

This also raises issues of professional responsibility. It can be argued that computer professionals, individually, and organisations, collectively, have ethical and professional duties to implement adequate security measures. While security techniques and practices have improved dramatically in the past few decades, there are still gaping holes. Attitudes to security in many businesses, organisations and government agencies have not caught up with the new risks. New technologies and applications are introduced – new vulnerabilities ensue.

Professional duty can also be taken to include responsibility to incorporate security features when designing new software. In the rush to get products online, to develop the potential of the Web, and to use the newest technologies, security issues are repeatedly ignored until systems are vandalised, robbed or shut down. Many computer viruses, worms and intrusions use well-known security flaws that have not been fixed on the victim's systems. Known corrections for loopholes are not implemented, out of carelessness, lack of management support, or lack of knowledge (of the problem, the risks or the solution). Many computer system administrators, particularly in small businesses and organisations, do not have adequate security training or knowledge of the systems they administer.

Economic considerations also come into play here. To implement extra security measures and features costs organisations' time and money, and many companies have other spending priorities. However, this short-sighted view may backfire on businesses. Customers may punish companies who have a cavalier attitude about their personal data and credit card numbers by shunning their websites. By damaging customer confidence and trust, and denting a company's public image, security breaches can also damage business. The longer-term view is that sound security measures are an important investment – one that will repay itself by bolstering consumer confidence that the Internet is a safe place to do business.

Many of these professional duties and obligations, with regard to security, crime and the law, are stated in the codes of conduct of bodies like the British Computer Society (BCS). There are a number of clauses in the BCS Code of Conduct, and in the codes of professional computing bodies in other countries, that allude to such responsibilities. Some of these we have noted already in the previous chapter. In particular, they are that 'members shall have due regard to the legitimate rights of third parties' and that they '… have knowledge and understanding of relevant legislation, regulations and standards … and … comply with such requirements' (British Computer Society, *Code of Conduct* 2006).

3.6 An ethical dilemma

The current major NHS-IT initiative in the UK is intended to allow patient records to be accessed from any authorised geographic location in the UK. Thus, patient records no longer reside with, for example, the local general practitioner or specialist, but can be accessed remotely.

Traditionally, the doctor/patient relationship has been deemed to be confidential and, naturally, patients often expect conversations with a doctor to be sacrosanct. One argument for moving away from this traditional approach is that people entering a hospital following an accident, for example, can be better accommodated as medical staff can gain immediate access to their medical histories. On the other hand, there can be no doubt that insurance companies and other bodies would very much like to obtain such information, as this can be used in a number of ways. For example, armed with such material, an insurance company can take a past history of ill-health into account when defining insurance premiums. Furthermore, when such a system has been in place over several generations, insurance companies can use historical information concerning ill-health and life-expectancy trends within, for example, a family, not only to define premiums for medical insurance, but also to determine life insurance premiums. These are very simple examples of how such data may be of use to third parties.

Without doubt a great deal of the major investment that has been made in the NHS-IT project will have been targeted at security – an attempt to ensure that only authorised people can gain access to online medical records. However, the relatively brief history of computing shows us that the security of practically all computer systems has been, or can be, breached. As we have discussed in this chapter, there are many ways of breaching security and one of the simplest and most straightforward approaches is through the human operators of computer systems. Although governments and organisations are generally willing to spend enormous amounts of money on computer technologies, they are far more reluctant to spend an appropriate amount of money paying the staff who are needed to run and maintain the systems. As a result, staff undertaking this sort of work are often underpaid – particularly in view of the complexity of the work they often carry out, and the responsibility of their role.

It is most likely that either the computer-based security systems that have been put in place to protect medical records stored on the NHS system will be breached or that a staff member who has access to these records via the network may be coerced into making records available to third parties.

This raises a number of ethical issues and dilemmas for those who have been involved in this undertaking. The traditional system involving the doctor/patient relationship – which over time has proved to work quite well – has been significantly altered. Given the history of experience within the computing community, can we be sure that our medical records will not be made available (without our knowledge/permission) to third parties? Does the introduction of this technology have an ethical basis, or does it simply reflect a government wishing to demonstrate its willingness to embrace state-of-the-art systems? Over time, how will the system develop? Are we now laying the foundations of a system whose ultimate purpose we cannot define?

The ultimate ramifications of the NHS-IT project are enormous, but this system has been introduced with only relatively minor debate. To what extent do you believe that those involved within the computing community should have exercised their ethical responsibility in making clear to the general public the implications and ramifications of this system?

3.7 Summary

This chapter has briefly examined some of the key issues raised by computer crime. We began by defining computer crime, and thinking about the extent to which computer crimes are 'new' kinds of crimes. We then outlined some of the different forms that computer crime takes, and examined some of the perpetrators of these crimes and their motives. We also described government initiatives (specifically in the UK) to detect and tackle computer crime, and explained some of the difficulties of this work. In particular, we explained why there is more computer crime than is realised or publicly known.

This chapter also looked at the legislation that exists to address computer crime, and the role of computer security in preventing computer crime, especially technical measures that can be implemented to protect computer systems.

We provided an overview of the security measures that can be implemented to prevent the threat of computer crime, including passwords, encryption, biometrics, firewalls and access control software. Finally, we addressed some of the professional and ethical issues raised by computer crime both for organisations and for computing professionals as individuals.

One over-riding point to note – no computer system is 100% secure and whatever security measures are taken, people will always find a way around them!

3.8 Review questions

Review question 3.1

Give a brief definition of computer crime, distinguishing between crimes where the computer is incidental, and crimes where computers are essential.

Review question 3.2

Give brief explanations of each of the following terms:

- Piggybacking
- Data diddling
- Salami
- Corporate espionage.

Review question 3.3

What is 'theft of computer time' and why is it considered a 'grey area', ethically?

Review question 3.4

What factors have contributed to the general increase in the amount of computer crime?

Review question 3.5

Why is there more computer crime than we realise?

Review question 3.6

What are the main elements of a password policy, in the context of network security?

Review question 3.7

What are the main limitations of encryption as a security measure in the context of eCommerce?

3.9 Feedback on activities

Feedback on activity 3.1

Examples you might have chosen include:

- Bank fraud (or theft)

- Distributing obscene material

- Extortion

- Forgery.

In all these cases, computers have made a difference in the scale of the crime (increasing it), the physical engagement with the victims and the execution of the crime (decreasing it) and the likelihood of being caught (lessening it).

Feedback on activity 3.4

1. The likely crimes and threats here are hacking, theft of credit card numbers and passwords, and possibly viruses. The threats are mainly external from hackers and fraudsters, though there may also be internal threats from dishonest employees. Security measures would need to be implemented to protect the transmission of data between the end user and the web server, and to protect the database files on the servers. For these reasons, encryption of personal or confidential data (credit card numbers, passwords etc) would be essential, along with the installation of firewalls, and anti-virus software.

2. Likely crimes in this case might include abuse of company time and resources, illegal downloading of software or inappropriate material from the Internet, and possibly hacking from within the company into restricted areas. The threats would be mostly internal from the employees themselves, the key words in this case being 'young, technically able'. Security measures might include installation of workplace monitoring and auditing software, and the use of firewalls to restrict access to the Internet from inside the company.

3. The likely crimes in this case are security breaches and hacking into restricted parts of the network by unauthorised personnel from both internal and external sources. Accordingly, the most appropriate security measures would be access control software, to set access rights and privileges across the network, a rigorously enforced password system, and possibly the use of biometric identification for the most sensitive parts of the system.

4. In this case, the most likely crimes are theft of documents for the purpose of corporate espionage, fraud or blackmail. The threats are most likely to come from external sources – rivals, or competitors. Appropriate security measures would include technologies such as strong encryption and digital signatures.

References

Baase, S (2003), A Gift of Fire: Social, *Legal and Ethical Issues for Computers and the Internet,* Pearson.

Forester, T & Morrison, P (1990), *Computer Ethics: Cautionary Tales and Ethical Dilemmas in Computing*, MIT Press.

Hinson, G (2004), *Human factors in information security*, www.sci.org, Dec 2003/Jan 2004.

Hynds, L (2002), 'Hacker cracker' (edited version of lecture to the Royal Society of Arts, 27 November 2001), *RSA Journal* 1/6/2002.

Spinello, RA (2000), *CyberEthics: Morality and Law*, Jones & Bartlett.

Further reading

Baase, S (2003), *A Gift of Fire: Social, Legal and Ethical Issues for Computers and the Internet*, (Chapter 3), Pearson.

Langford, D (1995), *Practical Computer Ethics*, (Appendices B and C), McGraw-Hill.

References

Further reading

CHAPTER 4

Intellectual property rights

Overview

This chapter explores one of the most topical issues in the computing field, that of intellectual property. The mass downloading of 'free' music from the Internet, the rampant software piracy that exists in many countries – these issues have dominated the news in the computing field in recent years. Computing technology, and specifically the Internet, has transformed the way intellectual property is distributed and consumed, raising a number of important ethical, legal and professional questions, some of which we review in this chapter. In particular, we shall be looking at what constitutes intellectual property in the computing field, and what legislation exists to protect it. The issue of software piracy will be examined, including arguments for and against the copying of software, as well as the related issues of free software and open source code. The issue of intellectual property touches on a number of long-standing philosophical and ethical debates about ownership of ideas, and we shall be looking at opposing viewpoints in this debate.

Learning outcomes	At the end of this chapter you should be able to:

- Define intellectual property

- Have an overview knowledge of copyright, patent and trademark law

- Appreciate the debate between intellectual ownership and shared knowledge

- Understand the application and implications of technical approaches to protecting intellectual property.

4.1 Introduction

This chapter explores the issue of intellectual property. We begin by defining and looking at some examples of intellectual objects. Subsequently, we look at the impact of computing technology on intellectual property, particularly in the area of digital rights management. We outline the existing forms of legal protection for intellectual property, in the form of copyrights, patents and trademarks, and the role of fair use provisions. In Section 4.4, we investigate the issue of software piracy and copyright infringement in fields such as music. We look at the evidence on the nature and extent of software piracy, then present the arguments for and against the practice of copying software. We briefly discuss the position of the free software movement, and its advocacy of open source code. Professional duties to honour intellectual property rights will also be highlighted. Finally, we outline some of the philosophical and ethical debates surrounding the ownership of ideas and the nature of intellectual creativity.

4.2 The nature of intellectual property

According to the United Nations' World Intellectual Property Organization (WIPO), intellectual property is defined as: 'the rights to, among other things, the results of intellectual activity in the industrial, scientific, literary or artistic fields'. Intellectual property takes the form of 'intellectual objects', such as original musical compositions, poems, novels, inventions, and product formulas. Intellectual objects are non-exclusive because many people can use them simultaneously and their use by some does not preclude their use by others. Furthermore, although the initial development of intellectual property objects may be time-consuming and costly, the cost and effort associated with the reproduction of intellectual objects is usually marginal. These non-exclusive and reproducible features of intellectual objects have made the issue of ownership rights especially problematic and all the more difficult to define. Protecting intellectual property from unauthorised copying, defining who are the creators and who are owners (as two distinct parties), deciding how their interests should be protected legally, and balancing these interests with those of the public, are contentious issues.

But what has been the impact of computing technology on intellectual property? Certainly computing technologies, and the Internet specially, have made the copying and distribution of intellectual objects much easier, but they have also raised a number of new legal and ethical issues about intellectual property rights in general.

Computing technology and intellectual property

Computer technologies have made high-quality copying and high-quantity distribution of intellectual property extremely easy and cheap. Some of these technologies are as follows:

* Storage of all sorts of information (text, sound, graphics) in standard digitised formats
* High-volume, relatively inexpensive digital storage media, such as hard disks, CD-ROMs, and DVDs (digital versatile discs, also called digital video discs)
* Character scanners and image scanners, which simplify converting printed text, photos, and artwork to digitised electronic form
* Compression formats, such as MP3, that make music and movie files small enough to download, copy, and store
* The ease of copying digitised material and the fact that each copy is a 'perfect' copy
* The ease of distributing digitised material over computer networks
* The World Wide Web, which makes it easy to find and download material
* Peer-to-peer technology, which permits easy transfer and exchange of files among large numbers of people over the Internet, without any centralised system or service.

In response to these new challenges to intellectual property protection, the entertainment and software industries have implemented a number of technical measures to protect their interests. These fall under the general heading of digital rights management technologies which attempt to prevent or deter unauthorised copying and distribution of films, music, software and other products. Many of these technologies attempt to use encryption, with varying degrees of success, to prevent copying of DVDs and CDs. For example, music and films are released in 'protected' formats that can only be played on particular hardware, or will not play on older or incompatible machines. These measures have included attempts to create copy-protected CDs, using 'digital watermarks' that prevent unauthorised copying of audio files. They have also included content scrambling systems which prevent DVDs from being copied or viewed on any other hardware than DVD players.

In 2001, Microsoft irritated customers with its 'activation' feature which required users installing Windows XP to undergo an intrusive registration process in order to prevent the operating system being installed on other machines. Future software in Microsoft operating systems will automatically detect 'unauthorised' media files and check their copyright status. Many of these measures have failed, partly because of consumer resistance, and because software has quickly been produced that has 'cracked' these anti-copying protections.

Digital rights management has also involved a move away from a 'sale' paradigm where an intellectual product, once sold, is the property of the owner to do with as they wish, to a 'licensing' paradigm, where the user enters into a licensing agreement with the owner of the copyright. In this paradigm, a licensing contract places restrictions on uses, such as time limits. Some critics of this trend have argued that it is a restrictive tool that prevents fair uses of intellectual property, for example in educational institutions and libraries.

Activity 4.1

What happened to SDMI?

Using the recommended texts shown under 'further reading' at the end of this section, or a suitable search engine, research the Secure Digital Music Initiative (SDMI). What was SDMI, what did it attempt to do (in the context of digital rights management) and why did it fail?

4.3 Intellectual property legislation

As summarised in Figure 4.1, three main categories for which legal protection of intellectual property exists are:

- **Copyrights**
- **Patents**
- **Trademarks.**

The relevant legislation governing intellectual property in the UK is the Copyright, Designs and Patents Act, 1988. The US equivalents are the Copyright Act, 1976 and 1980, and Digital Millennium Copyright Act, 1998.

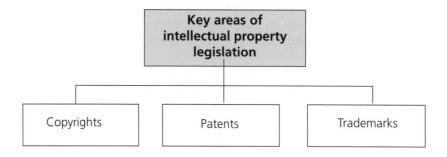

Figure 4.1: Three key areas of intellectual legislation

Copyright and copyright protection

In principle, copyright can be used to protect literary, musical, dramatic, artistic, architectural, audio or audio-visual works from being reproduced without the permission of the copyright holder. Copyright literally means the right to make and distribute copies to perform or display the work in public, and to produce derivative works, such as translations into other languages.

Changes to copyright law were implemented on 31 October 2003. These amended the Copyright, Designs and Patents Act, 1988 to comply with an EU Directive on the harmonisation of certain aspects of copyright and related rights in the information society.

To be eligible for copyright protection, the work in question must be original; in other words, independently created by its author. The work must also be embodied in some tangible medium of expression. When thinking about intellectual property, an important distinction needs to be made between the idea and the expression of that idea. In most cases, copyright protection is granted to the expression of an idea, but not the idea itself. Thus, a musical sound cannot be copyrighted, unless it is written down as sheet music, or recorded in a specific medium.

Copyright laws do not protect concepts or principles. Copyright is easier to obtain than patents (discussed below) and has a much longer duration, usually lasting for an author's lifetime plus seventy years. In the US the copyright law was revised in 1980 to cover some forms of computer software.

Works protected by copyright law include computer databases and computer programs that exhibit 'authorship'; that is, they contain original expressions of ideas.

The Copyright Licensing Agency (CLA)

The CLA was established in 1982 to protect the rights of copyright holders, by allowing organisations which are likely to need to make copies (such as business, education and the government) to purchase a licence to reproduce material from books, journals, periodicals and magazines. (**www.cla.co.uk**)

Federation Against Software Theft (FAST)

FAST was the world's first anti-piracy organisation, working to protect the intellectual property of software publishers. It was formed in 1984. (**www.fast.org.uk**)

Patents and patent protection

The primary candidates for patent protection are original, useful and non-obvious inventions such as mechanical processes and designs, or compositions of matter such as a new pharmaceutical product. Examples of patented technologies in the computer field include hardware components (e.g. circuits, sound cards and microprocessors) and some forms of software (such as online shopping systems). In principle, patented designs or inventions are legally protected, and cannot be used by other manufacturers without a licence, or payment of royalties to the patent owner. A patent is generally awarded for a period of seventeen years and usually after this time the invention will become 'public domain'. Formulas and scientific principles, however, belong in the public domain and cannot be patented.

The UK Patent Act, 1977 requires the following conditions to be satisfied for a patent to be granted for an invention:

- The invention is new
- It involves an inventive step
- It is capable of industrial application.

In addition, the Patent Act 1977 states that anything that consists of the following is *not* an invention for the purposes of the Act:

- A discovery, scientific theory or mathematical method
- A literary, dramatic, musical or artistic work, or any other aesthetic creation whatsoever
- A scheme, rule or method for performing any mental act, playing a game or doing business, or a program for a computer
- The presentation of information.

In some industries, patents have been the object of much criticism, because they are seen as giving a virtual monopoly on a product or invention, enabling the producer to benefit from that monopoly by charging high licensing fees. There has also been a prolonged legal debate over whether software programs, and the algorithms that they incorporate, should be eligible for patent protection.

In the 1972 decision *Gottschalk v Benson*, the US Supreme Court ruled that algorithms could not be patented. This ruling was reversed in the 1981 landmark case *Diamond v Diehr*, when the court ruled that a patent claim for a process should not be rejected merely because it includes a mathematical algorithm or computer program. The process itself must be original and hence patentable, and if computer calculations are part of the process, then they are included in the patent protection.

Trademarks and trademark protection

Another type of legal protection for intellectual property objects are trademarks. These are words, phrases, or symbols, which uniquely identify a product or a service. Examples include logos such as the famous bitten apple image crafted by Apple Computer, or the Microsoft Windows logo. To qualify as a trademark, the mark or name must be truly distinctive and, strictly speaking, the names should always be accompanied by the official trademark symbol, such as Microsoft Windows™. A trademark is acquired when someone is either the first to use the mark publicly or registers it with the Patent Office.

Trademarks are generally violated in one of two ways: they can be infringed upon, or they can be diluted.

- **Infringement** occurs when someone else uses the trademark in connection with the sale of its goods or services.
- **Dilution** is applicable only to famous trademarks that are distinctive, of long duration, and usually known to the public through extensive advertising and publicity. Dilution is the result of either *blurring* or *tarnishment*.
  - *blurring* occurs when the trademark is associated with dissimilar products; we can encounter descriptions such as a 'Rolls Royce product', meaning 'high quality'.
  - *tarnishment* occurs when the mark is portrayed in a negative or compromising way or associated with products or services of questionable value or reputation; Hoover (vacuum cleaners) and Bic (ballpoint pens) are regularly (incorrectly) used generically rather than with reference to each specific manufacturer's products. In the field of computing, Google takes pains to remind users that the word is a registered mark and should not be used generically with the meaning of 'to search the web'.

The Digital Millennium Copyright Act

The Digital Millennium Copyright Act (DMCA) of 1998 was designed to implement the treaties signed in 1996 at the World Intellectual Property Organization's (WIPO) Geneva conference.

Provisions in the DMCA significantly curtail fair use of copyrighted material, and increase the penalties for copyright infringement. For example, the Act makes it illegal for consumers to make copies of any digitally recorded work for any purpose. In addition, the Act:

- Makes it a crime to circumvent anti-piracy measures built into most commercial software
- Outlaws the manufacture, sale or distribution of code-cracking devices to illegally copy software (except for the purposes of encryption research, or to test the security of systems)
- Requires that 'webcasters' pay licensing fees to record companies.

Some of the practical consequences of the Act are that Internet service providers that misuse copyrighted materials, or host websites that do the same, face severe penalties. This means, for example, that a university which knows students are exchanging MP3 files on the campus network – and does nothing to stop them – can be sued. It also means that copyright protection is now extended to music broadcast over the Internet, requiring royalty payments to be made to copyright holders.

The Act has been the focus of some controversy. On the whole, the software and entertainment industries have supported it, for protecting their economic and legal interests. However, librarians, universities and other organisations have opposed the Act's ban on circumvention methods because it criminalises such actions which can be interpreted as 'fair use' of copyrighted material for research and education. Researchers, in particular, oppose the ban because it hinders open discussion of technologies such as encryption.

Fair use provision

US and UK copyright laws both contain important 'exception clauses' which allow for the reproduction and use of copyrighted works, under certain conditions. These are the provisions for 'fair use' of copyrighted material. Fair use provisions attempt to balance the intellectual property interests of authors, publishers and copyright owners with society's need for the free exchange and free flow of ideas.

The fair use provision of the US Copyright Act, 1976 and the fair dealing exception to copyright infringement in the UK Copyright, Designs and Patents Act, 1988 both allow reproduction and other use of copyrighted works for purposes such as those summarised in Figure 4.2.

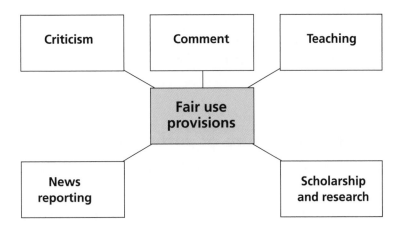

Figure 4.2: Examples of 'Fair Use' provisions in the US Copyright Act and the UK Copyright, Designs and Patents Act

Other factors are taken into account in defining what constitutes 'fair use'. These include the purpose and nature of the use (whether it is for commercial, non-profit or educational use); the amount and significance of the portion being used; and the effect of the use on the potential market for, or value of, the copyrighted work.

The UK copyright legislation also lists the following exceptions, where use of copyrighted material is permissible:

* Parliamentary and judiciary proceedings
* Royal commissions and statutory inquiries
* Material open to public inspection or on official register
* Material communicated to the Crown in the course of public business
* Public records and acts done under statutory authority.

In the US, additional provisions of the law allow uses specifically permitted to further educational and library activities. Representatives of libraries and educational institutions argue that the preservation and continuation of 'fair use' is essential to the free flow of information and to the development of an information infrastructure that serves the public interest. Taken together, fair use and other public rights to use copyrighted works promote the dissemination of knowledge, while ensuring authors, publishers and copyright owners appropriate protection of their creative works and economic investments.

Activity 4.2

Fair use

Consider the following scenario:

A lecturer puts some journal articles on reserve in the library and makes them assigned reading for her class. These articles are copyrighted material. Some students in the class complain that they cannot get access to the articles because they are always on loan to other students. The professor scans them and posts them on her website. The professor gives the students in the class the password they need to access the articles. What factors need to be considered in deciding whether this constitutes 'fair use' of copyrighted material?

4.4 The extent and nature of software piracy

Software piracy refers to the large-scale and organised copying and distribution of counterfeit software. There now exists a vast international trade involving the production, transport and sale of illegal software, along with counterfeit documentation and packaging. Millions of web pages now exist, offering links to, or providing downloads of 'warez', the Internet code word for illegal software; or 'appz' a term for pirated applications. Hacker sites offer serial numbers, access codes and software 'patches' (known as 'cracks'). These bypass or circumvent encryption or other technical protections that the copyright owner may have applied to its products. Virtually every software product now available on the market can be located on one or other of these sites, from games to operating systems and popular desktop applications, many of which appear before their official release.

Illegal software is advertised, posted or made available for downloading on websites, newsgroups, IRC channels, and other bulletin board areas. Some of these sites operate free of charge, while others require a form of barter, a person first has to offer a product for others to take in order to have the right to download products already posted. Many sites fund themselves by providing advertising space to advertisers of pornography. Today, it is the norm for pirate software web pages to be crowded with advertising (usually in the form of pop-up banners) for various forms of pornographic materials.

Illegal software has also become the core business of some auction sites. Items are offered for sale on such sites for a fraction of their legal retail price. When a sale is made, the pirate simply makes a copy of the software, and ships it to the buyer. Some key statistics on the extent of software piracy are as follows:

- In 2000, Microsoft found that 90% of its products offered for sale on auction sites in Europe, the Middle East and Africa were illegal copies
- The Business Software Alliance (**www.bsa.org**) estimated the value of pirated software worldwide to be between 11 and 13 million dollars per year
- In the United States, pirated software is estimated to be 35% of the total software market, and industry losses are estimated at $2.3 billion per year
- Many European countries have a higher piracy rate than in the US (57% in Germany and 80% in Italy, for example)
- The highest piracy rates are in Asia. It has been estimated, for example, that 99% of the software sold in Vietnam is illegal.

Copying software: the case against

Predictably, the most vocal campaigners against software piracy are representatives of the software industry, particularly bodies such as the Business Software Alliance (BSA) and the Software and Information Industry Association (SIIA). The main argument of the software industry is that software piracy is in every respect a criminal and unethical activity, sometimes engaged in by misguided students, but increasingly engaged in for substantial profit by professional thieves. The impact of software piracy extends far beyond the confines of the software industry. It harms economies worldwide in the form of greatly diminished tax revenues and leads to substantial numbers of lost jobs.

The time and trouble involved in producing good software, the industry argues, is far greater than the average user may appreciate. If developers do not make a profit, they can no longer develop software, and this may have adverse consequences for the user. Software companies will not want to invest as much in developing new products, because they cannot expect any return on their investment in certain parts of the world. The argument can be summarised as: 'remove the income from software sales, and you remove the incentive for developing the software in the first place'. The continuing loss of revenue will, it is claimed, result in software of declining quality as there will be diminished resources for development.

Copying software: the case for

The copying of software remains an area of considerable conflict and disagreement. Stealing may be morally wrong but, if software suppliers are to be believed, most consumers have used bootleg software at one time or another. Possibly because of the physical and emotional distance of the application from its real owner, to most users the copying of software seldom appears to be stealing. People who would never dream of shoplifting are prepared to casually borrow and duplicate copyright disks and to photocopy manuals.

Software is still largely seen as 'overpriced' by many consumers, perhaps because the sale price does not always bear an obvious relationship to development costs. The situation is complicated further by the escalating cost of software – some commercial packages for personal computers cost up to a thousand pounds. If buying a single package involves such high expenditure, users may understandably want to sample it first. Small groups of users may justify clubbing together to buy a single copy of software in order to share it between themselves.

Software may therefore be pirated because it is seen as unnecessarily expensive, hard to evaluate, more troublesome to buy, and perhaps because to do so is seen as challenging. Using pirated software certainly lowers the cost of personal computing, and realistically, there is little likelihood of being caught.

There is also an important international dimension to this debate. Piracy rates in most Asian countries, such as Indonesia, Thailand, China and Vietnam, are estimated to be nearly 100%. In these countries, pirated software is sold openly on the streets, along with photocopied manuals, for a few dollars. Explaining why there are such high piracy rates in these countries remains a matter of debate. Poverty and economic development are certainly one set of factors, but in a number of reports, the Software Publishers Association and others have connected software piracy directly to culture and attitude. They argue that people in some countries regard the practice as less unethical than inhabitants of other countries.

Some countries view copyright as simply a means for companies in richer nations, such as the US, to protect their global economic and technological dominance in the computing industry. Copyright is no more than a legal veil to protect what are virtually global monopolies in the hardware and software fields.

In the late 1980s, Brazil led a group of countries who opposed US moves to extend copyright protection for US software. The US, through GATT (the General Agreement on Tariffs and Trade), attempted to extend copyright protection for US software in a number of developing countries, including Thailand, South Korea and Brazil. These countries opposed the US on the basis that extending copyright protection would only strengthen the hands of transnational computer companies. It would also inhibit countries like Brazil from building up their own IT industries. The effect, these countries, argued, would be to restrict people's access to software in poorer countries, especially for education and training.

In 1988 the US government responded by imposing 100% import duties on $39m worth of Brazilian goods Forester and Morrison (1990). Under similar pressure from the US in 1991, China passed laws to protect intellectual property rights, particularly for foreign works, but the laws were not enforced. Some of the copying of software was reportedly undertaken in government factories, Baase (2003).

These cases highlight the global inequities of access to computing technology, and the uneven development of IT industries in different countries. In particular, they suggest that notions of copyright and intellectual property cannot be assumed as universal legal and ethical principles.

Activity 4.3

Debating software piracy

Assume the position of one of the following:

* A representative of the Business Software Alliance

* A computer science student in a developing country.

What is your position on 'software piracy'? Provide at least three major arguments, backing them up with ethical theories, the law, codes of conduct, and any other appropriate principles.

Activity 4.4

Representing developing countries

You have been chosen to be the representative leading a group of developing nations who oppose US moves through GATT (the General Agreement on Tariffs and Trade) and the WTO (World Trade Organization) to extend international copyright protection to US software.

Prepare a case for your decision to refuse copyright protection to US software. Assume that you are to introduce your reasons to all the member states present at the talks, justifying your stance.

Digital music: from Napster to KaZaA

The late 1990s saw the emergence in the computing market of a new standard for compressing audio signals that had previously been used in the film industry: MP3. This is a file compression format that reduces the size of audio files by a factor of 10 to 12, making it possible to download a song via the Internet in a matter of minutes. By 1999, MP3 players were being manufactured and sold, and hundreds of websites had appeared making thousands of songs available for download in the MP3 format.

By far the most well-known of these was Napster.

Napster opened on the Web in 1999 as a service allowing users to copy songs in MP3 files from the hard disks of other users. By late 2000, an average of 98 million MP3 files were available via the service. There were a number of reasons for Napster's popularity (Baase, 2003). These are indicated in Figure 4.3 and are summarised below:

- Free music
- The opportunity to download individual songs, without having to buy a whole CD
- The opportunity to sample music and so determine personal appeal
- Access to a huge database of songs, including songs that were not commercially available
- Convenience of online access to music and being able to download and play a song from anywhere without the need to a use physical CD
- Ease of download: users could chat online while downloading music in the background.

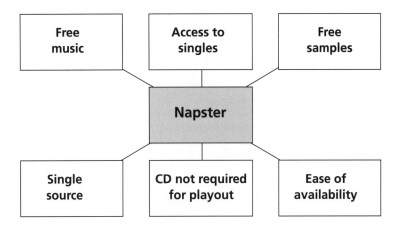

Figure 4.3: Napster's key features

Needless to say, the record industry was not happy with this state of affairs, and the major record companies, through their trade organisation, the Record Industry Association of America (RIAA), issued Napster with a lawsuit. At issue in the legal case was a) whether the copying and distribution of music by Napster users was legal under the 'fair use' guidelines, and b) whether Napster was responsible for the actions of its users.

Many legal observers thought the large-scale copying on Napster was indeed illegal copyright infringement – not fair use – and after a lengthy case that is how the court ruled. On the second issue, Napster argued that it did not keep copies of songs on its computers. It provided lists of available songs and lists of users logged on at any time; users transferred songs from each other's hard disks using peer-to-peer software downloaded from Napster. Napster's defence was that it was not responsible for users of its software who infringed copyrights. The court, however, ruled that Napster 'knowingly encourages and assists in the infringement of copyrights'. Napster was ordered to remove, from its listings, song titles which infringed copyright. It faced civil suits that would require payments of billions of dollars in damages. After some ineffective attempts to manage its song lists, Napster closed.

However, the death of Napster did not signal the end of free file-sharing on the Internet. Other peer-to-peer networks took Napster's place. One of the most popular peer-to-peer networks was KaZaA. Because of the way KaZaA was designed, with a different implementation of peer-to-peer file sharing, it proved much more difficult to shut down than Napster. Whereas Napster relied upon a central computer to maintain a global index of all files available for sharing, KaZaA distributed the index of available files among a large number of 'supernode' computers. Any computer with a high-speed Internet connection running KaZaA Media Desktop had the potential to become a supernode. The use of multiple supernodes made searching for content slower, but it also made it much more difficult for legal authorities to shut down the file-sharing network, because the creators of KaZaA argued that they were unable to control, and hence should not be held responsible for, the actions of the people who were using KaZaA.

KaZaA proved to be highly popular. By mid-2006, nearly 240 million copies of KaZaA Media Desktop had been downloaded, and by the third quarter of 2002 its monthly user base was about 9.4 million.

The RIAA's response was to identify the IP addresses of the most active KaZaA supernodes, leading it to the ISPs of users who had stored large numbers of copyrighted files. It then either sued the ISPs or forced them to identify the names of customers suspected of running these KaZaA supernodes. A new tactic was adopted by the RIAA in September 2003 when it sued 261 individuals for distributing copyrighted music over the Internet. A month later the RIAA sent letters to 204 people who had downloaded at least 1,000 music files, giving them an opportunity to settle before being taken to court.

In the wake of recent lawsuits and unfavourable publicity, the number of users of such sites has fallen considerably.

4.5 Ethical and professional issues

Professional codes of conduct

We have previously noted the clause in the BCS code of conduct (see Chapter 1) which states that 'members shall ensure they have knowledge of and understanding of relevant legislation … and that they comply with such requirements'.

In the section on Duty to Employers and Clients, the BCS Code of Conduct also states that 'members should seek to avoid being put in a position where they may become privy to or party to activities or information concerning activities which would conflict with their responsibilities'. In any broad interpretation of these responsibilities, such activities could be taken to refer to copyright infringement.

It is difficult to reconcile unauthorised copying of software, in either a private or professional context, with the professional codes of conduct defined by bodies such as the BCS or its US equivalent, the Association for Computing Machinery (ACM). The ACM Code of Ethics and Professional Conduct contains a number of general moral imperatives that refer specifically to the issue of intellectual property. General Moral Imperative 1.5, for example, states 'Honor property rights including copyrights and patent' and goes on to say:

> Violation of copyrights, patents, trade secrets and the terms of license agreements is prohibited by law in most circumstances. Even when software is not so protected, such violations are contrary to professional behaviour. Copies of software should be made only with proper authorization. Unauthorized duplication of materials must not be condoned.

General Moral Imperative 1.6 states 'Give proper credit for intellectual property' and adds:

> Computing professionals are obligated to protect the integrity of intellectual property. Specifically, one must not take credit for other's ideas or work, even in cases where the work has not been explicitly protected by copyright, patent, etc.

There are sound reasons why companies buy software legitimately, rather than copying it, or using illegal software. First and foremost, they need to keep within the bounds of the law in their business practices and day-to-day operations, in order to maintain their professional and business reputation. Otherwise they risk fines, expensive settlements or serious legal action. More than this, legitimately purchased software comes with important benefits; technical support, patches, upgrades and documentation, things that do not generally accompany pirated software.

In defence of intellectual property

Many countries (at least in principle) have a tradition that defends the notions of private ownership and property. Probably the most famous justification of property in general comes from John Locke (1632–1704), who argued that people have a natural right to the things they have removed from nature through their own labour.

The philosopher Hegel (1770–1831) argued that property enables an individual to put their will into something. For Hegel, property was an expression of an individual's personality in the world. As human beings freely externalise their will in various things, such as novels, works of arts and craftsmanship, they create property to which they are entitled because it is an expression of their 'being', and as such belongs to them.

These arguments have even more force when applied to intellectual objects, which are seen as an expression of the author's or creator's personality. Surely the author should have the right to control his or her individual expression, to prevent its misappropriation and misuse? Hegel's conception of property provides a rationale for why the end product should belong to its creator. Labourers are entitled to the fruits of their intellectual labour.

Another argument that has frequently been used in support of intellectual property is the notion that private ownership is necessary as an incentive to create and to work. This idea dates back to David Hume (1711–1776), who argued that a person's creations should be owned by them to encourage 'useful habits and accomplishments'. Intellectual work adds value to the end product. Incentive to add value is greatly enhanced if some of that value is attributed to the creator of the work, personally.

Another justification for property is based on the notion of reward. In this argument, a producer or creator deserves to be rewarded for their production or creation in return for their effort. This argument does not necessarily imply ownership, but ownership is often thought to be a just reward. It can be time-consuming and costly to generate and develop ideas, so there must be some reward for those who do this. If there is not, nobody will bother to create. If we assume the most important reward is financial, then without financial reward, society's supply of new ideas will dry up. It follows that there must be some system of copyright and patent regulations that protects intellectual property. At the very least, to enjoy the financial fruits of one's creative work means being able to support oneself, providing an income, and a means of doing further creative work. How else would artists, musicians and writers survive?

James DeLong (1997) puts forward another point of view, defending ownership rights in terms of value. He observes that unless we have clear ownership rights, and unless we pay for the goods that we need, those goods will become devalued and abused.

Having to pay for things forces us to think about what is really valuable and what is not. If all goods were free, these goods would be abused and diluted. History and experience has taught us that people do not value things that do not have 'value' (that is, which are cheap or free). The abuse of free things, such as land, air, and water has already led to serious environmental degradation. Similar tragedies could arise if property rights are diluted and ownership shifts too dramatically from the private to the common.

Against intellectual property

There is an equally long tradition of philosophical and ethical arguments against the notion of the private ownership of ideas. One key argument has been to question the assumption that an idea can be 'owned' by solely one individual. Probably any idea that we have is not ours alone. Most of our ideas come from someone or somewhere else. What is originality if not the combining of existing ideas in new ways? At best, when someone is 'original', they are expressing an idea in a new way, perhaps seeing new associations between ideas that were not noticed before. Anything creative that is achieved is the adding of something to pre-existing ideas, which have been obtained from others.

On this point, the renowned scientist and philosopher Sir Isaac Newton, referring to his original idea on gravity, wrote: 'If I have seen further it is by standing on the shoulders of giants', thereby acknowledging all those scientists who had come before him, and upon whose knowledge and discoveries his own contribution to science had drawn.

It can be argued that if all ideas were in the public domain, and if anyone could work on and develop anything, regardless of where the idea originated, we would all be better off because more would be developed. To say that the source of new and innovative ideas would dry up without copyright and patent protection to facilitate financial reward is little more than an article of faith. Artists, academics and scientists frequently create without such reward. They do so for other reasons; acknowledgement, recognition, gratitude, fame and improving the lives of others. Perhaps, in some circumstances, creation is its own reward.

Like physical property rights, intellectual property rights imply that someone has the right to certain concepts, knowledge, or information. But there are obvious difficulties with the notion that one has property rights in an idea because this would mean the right to exclude others from using and building upon those ideas. By placing a monetary value on intellectual property are we not controlling who can use and enjoy it?

In a more fundamental sense, assigning property rights to intellectual objects seems to go against many of the goals and traditions of a free society. Ownership of ideas can be seen to restrict progress and the free exchange of ideas in the scientific or artistic fields, by withholding new knowledge and preventing the free dissemination of ideas to the public.

At the heart of the issue, perhaps, is finding a balance between ensuring that innovators are duly acknowledged and rewarded for their creative ideas, while still allowing those ideas to be shared for the benefit of the community and for human progress.

Activity 4.5

Counter-arguments to copying

Consider the following scenario:

A friend of yours has downloaded a 'cracked' (that is, pirated) version of a moderately expensive image-editing application called PictureShop, and is now circulating copies of the software, free, among his friends and fellow students. You have to convince your friend that what he is doing is unethical.

He uses the following arguments; how would you counter each one?

- I cannot afford to buy the product

- The company is a large, wealthy corporation that can afford the losses

- I wouldn't buy it at the retail price anyway

- Making a copy for a friend is just an act of generosity

- This violation is insignificant compared to the billions of dollars lost to piracy by dishonest resellers making big profits

- Everyone does it. You would be foolish not to.

4.6 Free software and open source code

Free software is a concept and ethic that is advocated by a loose-knit, but large group of computer programmers who let people copy and modify their software, often without charge, and encourage others to do so. The 'free' in free software implies freedom – not necessarily lack of cost – although there is often no charge. Free software enthusiasts advocate the unrestricted copying of programs and making the source code (the human-readable form of a program) available to everyone. Software distributed or made public in source code is called 'open source', and the open source movement is closely related to the free software movement. Perhaps the best-known advocate of free software, and open source code is Richard Stallman, president and founder of the Free Software Foundation.

Richard Stallman has argued, with great insistence, that all software should be free. Stallman claims that ownership of software programs is obstructive and counterproductive. Hence, software should be in the public domain, freely available to anyone who wants to use it, modify it, or customise it. He regards software licensing fees as an enormous disincentive to using programs because it excludes many worthy users from enjoying many popular programs. Ownership also interferes with the evolution and incremental improvement of software products. According to Stallman, software development should be an evolutionary process, where a person takes a program and rewrites parts of it for one new feature, and then another person rewrites parts to add another feature. Software development could continue in this manner over a period of several years. The existence of 'owners' prevents this kind of evolution, making it necessary to start from scratch when developing a program. If information is distributed openly, it is argued, developers will not have to reinvent the wheel, or needlessly design from scratch something that already exists elsewhere. Software development, for Stallman, works best when programmers pool their knowledge to create better quality software. Stallman concludes that because the ownership of programs is so obstructive and yields such negative consequences, this practice should be abolished.

During the past few years, there has been a noticeable trend among major software vendors to make their code more openly accessible on the Internet. In 1998, Netscape surprised the software industry when it released the source code for its Navigator web browser. In addition, the open source code movement has been energised by the limited success of programs such as PERL and LINUX operating systems, a variation of UNIX that runs on personal computers. Any user can download LINUX free of charge.

Open source code gives computer users direct access to the software's source code, enabling them to fix bugs or develop incremental enhancements. The premise is that the collective programming wisdom available on the Internet will help create software that is of better quality than any single individual or group of individuals working within a company could construct.

Activity 4.6

Researching open source software

Visit the Linux website at **www.linux.org**

Using the information available on this site, describe the key features of Linux, briefly explaining how it developed and evolved. Try to find some other examples of open source software.

4.7 An ethical dilemma

As we have discussed, the law relating to copyright provides – at least in principle – a way in which a creative person can gain recompense for their original work. Let us now take a simple example of how this can operate in practice.

Consider the case of Alice who was writing a textbook. She wishes to include in her book material from various sources – particularly a few key diagrams that have previously been published in other books. Some of these books are quite old, dating back to the 1930s and 1940s.

In the intervening years, the original publishers of these books have been taken over several times but , following some fairly extensive research, she is finally able to track down the names of companies who currently own the rights to the books from which she wishes to reproduce diagrams. Following this exercise, she contacts these companies, and asks for permission to reproduce diagrams from these works.

The majority of companies respond and indicate that she can reproduce the diagrams – providing that she pays a fee (ranging from £40 through to £2,000 per diagram reproduced). Payment is deemed necessary because, although the diagrams are quite old, the copyright has not expired (typically, copyright for material that is published in a book continues for 70 years after the death of the book's author). Alice decides that she cannot afford the permissions costs (these total an amount which is far in excess of the revenue that she will get from her book once it is published).

Although copyright serves to reward people for their creative work, in practice this does not always happen. For example, only relatively recently have authors' contracts with publishers contained clauses to the effect that they will receive royalty payments for materials reproduced from their work. Consequently, in the case of old books, there is little, if any, chance that an author (or their estate) will receive any remuneration when original material from their book is reproduced.

With this in mind, Alice decides to scan the relevant diagrams, make a few alterations to them – so they looked a little different – and then use them in her book without having obtained any permissions to reproduce them.

This raises a number of ethical issues. In the case of older books, should publishers require significant fees to be paid to them if material from one of their books is reproduced elsewhere? To what extent should this be underpinned by consideration of fair use? Is it reasonable for publishers to require significant amounts of money to be paid in relation to the reproduction of material from an old book – particularly when they know that this will not be passed on to the author, or their estate? To what extent is it appropriate to simply make modifications of diagrams, and therefore avoid the payment of permissions fees? By way of a simple example, consider Figure 4.3. Let us suppose that this is 'edited' by Alice and reproduced in her book in the form illustrated in Figure 4.4. To what extent (if any) is Alice guilty of plagiarism? One point to note: by not paying permissions fees, it follows that the author will not acknowledge the original source of the diagram – thus, the original creative person does not receive any credit.

To what extent do such considerations apply to software? For example, is it permissible to take another person's code, make limited modifications to it, and represent it as one's own work?

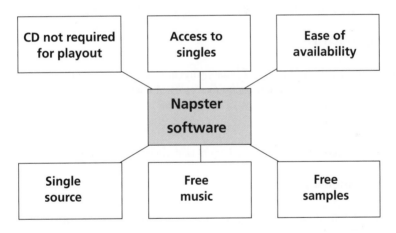

Figure 4.4: Alice 'edits' Figure 4.3 and represents the diagram as her own work. See the 'Ethical Dilemma' for discussion

4.8 Summary

In this chapter we have explored the issue of intellectual property, particularly focusing on issues that relate to the field of computing.

We began by defining intellectual property and looking at some examples of intellectual objects. Subsequently, we briefly considered the impact of computing technology on intellectual property, particularly in the area of digital rights management, focusing on the manner in which the Internet has transformed the way intellectual property is distributed and consumed.

We outlined the existing forms of legal protection for intellectual property, in the form of copyright, patent and trademarks, and the role of fair use provisions. We then explored the issue of software piracy and copyright infringement in fields such as music. In this context, we looked at some of the evidence on the nature and extent of software piracy, then we presented the arguments for and against the practice of copying software. We have outlined some of the philosophical and ethical debates relating to the ownership of ideas and the nature of intellectual creativity. Finally, we briefly discussed the position of the free software movement, and its advocacy of open source code.

4.9 Review questions

 **Review question 4.1**

Give examples of intellectual property and explain what is meant by the non-exclusive and reproducible features of intellectual objects.

Review question 4.2

Name three computer technologies that have enabled relatively cheap and simple high-quality copying and high-quantity distribution of intellectual property.

Review question 4.3

Name the three principal forms of legal protection for intellectual property, explaining the differences between them, and giving examples of each from the computing field.

Review question 4.4

Which groups generally oppose the Digital Millennium Copyright Act and why?

Review question 4.5

List the conditions under which the 'fair use' provision of the US Copyright Act allows copying. What is the purpose of the fair use provision?

Review question 4.6

What technical aspects of peer-to-peer file sharing used by KaZaA have made it more difficult to shut down by the authorities – as compared to Napster?

Review question 4.7

List the main philosophical arguments against intellectual property and the private ownership of ideas.

Review question 4.8

Give four reasons why the open source movement is considered to be better for the computing industry than commercially protected software.

4.10 Feedback on activities

Feedback on activity 4.1

The Secure Digital Music Initiative (SDMI) was an effort to create copy-protected CDs and secure digital music downloads that would play only on SDMI-compliant devices. About 200 entertainment and technology companies joined together in a consortium, which worked for three years to develop 'digital watermarks' that would make unauthorised copying of audio files impossible. The SDMI was unsuccessful for three reasons.

- First, before any copy-protection technologies could be put in place, the number of music files being copied on the Internet mushroomed

- Second, some of the sponsors of the SDMI (consumer electronics companies) started making a lot of money selling devices that became more attractive to customers as access to free MP3 files got easier. Their sales could be hurt by restrictions on copying

- Third, the digital watermarking scheme was cracked. In September 2000, SDMI issued a 'Hack SDMI' challenge. It released some digitally watermarked audio files and offered a $10,000 prize to the first person to crack them. Princeton computer science professor Edward Felten and eight colleagues picked up the gauntlet. Three weeks later the team had successfully read the audio files.

Feedback on activity 4.2

Factors to consider include:

- Purpose of the use (whether it is educational or commercial)

- Nature of the work being copied (whether it is fictional, or factual news)

- Amount of material being copied (whether the whole articles have been copied, or portions of those articles, and whether students are able to make multiple copies)

- The effect the copying will have on the market for journal sales. Will it infringe the market for the journals from which these articles are taken?

- Has permission been sought from the authors or publishers of the articles? In this instance, such permission must be granted for the use of any copyrighted material.

Feedback on activity 4.3

Possible arguments for a representative of the Business Software Alliance:

- Legal: software piracy is a criminal activity under international law and copyright agreements

- Economic: the time and trouble involved in producing good software is far greater than the computer student may appreciate. If developers do not make a profit, they can no longer develop software. Software companies will not want to invest as much in developing new products, because they cannot expect any return on their investment in certain parts of the world

- The impact of software piracy extends far beyond the confines of the software industry. It harms economies worldwide in the form of greatly diminished tax revenues and leads to substantial numbers of lost jobs. The continuing loss of revenue will result in software of declining quality as there will be diminished resources for development

- Ethical: copying software is not seen as 'unethical' in many developing countries, and these attitudes need to be changed.

Possible arguments for a computer science student in a developing country:

- Economic: software is overpriced. The full (western) price of most commercially available software is way beyond the reach of most ordinary citizens in this country. Software can be obtained for a tiny fraction of this cost in the local market

- Educational: the students need the software in order to study for their degrees, take courses, pass assignments etc. This is essential if the country's fledgling IT industry is to grow

- Legal: copyright legislation is very weak in this country, and is not generally enforced. The US has tried to encourage the enforcement of copyright legislation, but this has had little effect. These laws are seen as 'foreign' and imposed for economic and political purposes. Copying software is therefore not seen as 'illegal'

- Ethical: there is no strong ethical opposition to the copying and sharing of intellectual property. Copying software is not generally seen as 'unethical'.

Feedback on activity 4.4

The decision could be based on the following grounds:

- Copyright protection interferes with the evolution and incremental improvement that programmers in developing countries can offer to US software

- Copyright protection strengthens the hands of monopolies, leading to artificially high price fixing

- It inhibits developing and poorer countries from building up their own IT industries and economies

- It excludes a worthy population from using and enjoying the benefits of US software

- The reward for US programmers should not be monetary via copyright protection, but the recognition and satisfaction of helping poorer nations develop

- US software is being used for teaching, research and scholarship purposes in developing countries

- Considering that programmers from around the globe and of numerous nationalities have contributed towards developing US software, can the US claim sole ownership?

Feedback on activity 4.5

Below are some examples of the ways these arguments could be countered. There could be many other arguments:

- I cannot afford to buy the product. *There are many things we cannot afford; not being able to afford something is not an excuse for taking it*

- The company is a large, wealthy corporation that can afford the losses. *The size and success of the company do not justify taking from it. Individual programmers, writers, and artists lose income too when copying is common*

- Making a copy for a friend is just an act of generosity. *Do we have the right to be generous when giving something that is not ours? Is copying the software an act of generosity on our part, or an act that compels involuntary generosity from the programmer?*

- This violation is insignificant compared to the billions of dollars lost to piracy by dishonest resellers making big profits. *Yes, large-scale commercial piracy is worse, but that does not imply that individual copying is ethical. And, if the practice is widespread, the losses become significant*

- Everyone does it. You would be foolish not to. *The number of people doing something does not determine whether it is right or ethical.*

References

Baase, S (2003), *A Gift of Fire: Social, Legal and Ethical Issues for Computers and the Internet,* Pearson.

DeLong, J (1997), *Property Matters: How Property Rights Are Under Assault—and Why You Should Care*, Simon & Schuster.

Forester, T & Morrison, P (1990), *Computer Ethics: Cautionary Tales and Ethical Dilemmas in Computing*, MIT Press.

Further reading

Ayres, R (1999) *The Essence of Professional issues in Computing*, (Chapter 6), Prentice-Hall.

Baase, S (2003), *A Gift of Fire: Social, Legal and Ethical Issues for Computers and the Internet,* (Chapter 6), Pearson.

de George, RT (2003), *The ethics of information technology and business*, Oxford.

Quinn, M (2004), *Ethics for the Information Age*, Addison Wesley.

Tavani, HT (2004), *Ethics and technology: ethical issues in an age of information and communication technology*, John Wiley and Sons.

CHAPTER 5

Regulating Internet content

OVERVIEW

The regulation of content on the Internet poses some interesting but somewhat difficult questions. What content, if any, should be prohibited? Who should decide what is prohibited and what is not? Some people believe there should be no regulation and put forward the argument that they are protecting the right to free speech and expression. These are rights protected by law in many countries. Others believe that some content should be banned because it is, for example, immoral, anti-government, racist or pro-terrorist. Even in the case of unrestricted content, we must also consider the issue of surveillance – for instance, government agencies monitoring who accesses and contributes to Internet sites. In this chapter we highlight issues relating to freedom of speech, freedom of expression and censorship.

Freedom of speech and censorship have long been contentious issues. The right to free speech is a precious entitlement in many societies. The purpose of this chapter is to examine these issues within the context of computer technology, and specifically in terms of the Internet. How do computer technologies enable and/or encourage freedom of expression? Alternatively, in what ways can such technologies be used to censor or restrict free speech? How do we maintain a balance between the need to restrict some forms of expression in certain circumstances, and the desire to protect our basic human right to freedom of speech? This chapter looks at some of the legal, professional and ethical issues invoked by these questions.

Learning outcomes	At the end of this chapter you should be able to:

- Understand the rationale for free speech

- Understand the principles of freedom of expression embodied in national or international law

- Appreciate the balance between free speech and censorship

- Appreciate the impact of computer technology on free speech.

5.1 Introduction

The Internet is arguably the most effective publishing and broadcasting medium that has ever been available to the general population. It is difficult to regulate – with the result that anyone can publish anything and, in theory, anyone can view anything. It is this aspect of the Internet – the content that is transmitted – that is the subject of this chapter. What content should, or should not, be allowed, and who should make such decisions? Is free expression to be protected at all costs, or should Internet content be regulated? How do we strike the balance between freedom of expression and personal responsibility – can one exist without the other?

We begin by looking at some of the arguments and philosophies that defend the notion of free expression. We give examples of how the suppression of free thought has, historically, curtailed the speed of human advancement in science and the arts. We then look at the case for censorship, citing the ideas of Plato in *The Republic* in which he argues for the control of music and poetry in the education of the young. The principal forms of legislation that uphold or restrict free speech are briefly examined. We then discuss the impact of computer technology on freedom of expression, looking at those Internet technologies that have enabled free speech, and those which have tended to restrict it. We also outline arguments for and against anonymous expression in cyberspace. Finally, we explore the professional duties of those working in the computing industry to uphold the principles of free speech, we look at censorship as a global issue, and we conclude with some models for regulating the Internet.

5.2 In defence of freedom of expression

Free speech is generally understood to mean all forms of expression across all media (not just the spoken word) and in all fields of knowledge – scientific, religious and artistic. It has been taken to broadly include openness in literature, art and music, as well as religious tolerance, the allowing of political dissent, and the right to question the existing social order. The defence of free thought and expression has a long tradition in western thought. Free speech is generally accepted as a foundation of an open, democratic society, and, as such, has come to be seen as a basic human right – unfortunately, it is a right that we often take for granted.

In his famous essay *On Liberty,* the philosopher John Stuart Mill (1806–1873) advocated the importance of free speech and thought. He argued that only by open discussion could truth emerge, and falsity be revealed. He insisted that engagement in discussion encouraged people to think for themselves rather than simply accept ideas promoted by others. The suppression of political ideas, in particular, can mean that citizens no longer have the freedom to choose their political representatives, leading to a one-party, or totalitarian, state.

The denial of free speech, and the free exchange of ideas, can also have intellectual consequences. Free speech and open discussion of ideas stimulates thinking, and the questioning of ideas. So, it can be argued that the consequence of denying free expression is the suppression of intellectual activity. History has taught us that the suppression of free thought can curtail the speed of human advancement and prevent progress – holding back artistic development and scientific discovery. The right to speak freely promotes creative thinking and stimulates intellectual activity. Often, ideas that are non-mainstream and conflict with orthodox belief are initially rejected, scorned and silenced. History is full of examples of proponents of radical or new ideas that were originally banned or discredited, but later accepted. The following are just some examples.

- The Polish astronomer Nicolas Copernicus (1473–1543) challenged the established church's view that the Earth was at the centre of the universe. He suggested that observational evidence showed that the Earth orbited the sun. The dethronement of the Earth from the centre of the universe caused profound shock. In 1632, the Italian astronomer and physicist Galileo Galilei (1564–1642) having conducted his own experiments, dared to agree with Copernicus. For this, Galileo was hauled up before the Inquisition, the church tribunal to combat heresy. His subsequent house arrest and recantation negatively impacted on scientific discovery in Italy for many years

- A young woman's sensual awakening is at the heart of the book, *Lady Chatterley's Lover*, which D H Lawrence (1885–1930) called 'the most improper novel in the world'. Because of its frank depiction of sex, the book was, for many years, banned. When it was finally first published in England in 1960, it was the centre of a sensational obscenity trial at the Old Bailey. Yet the author attempted, via the literature, to 'urge men and women to live, to honour the quick of themselves, to glory in the exhilarating terror of this brief life'

- Charles Darwin (1809–1882) proposed that all present species were derived from earlier species by the process of natural selection. Thus all species on Earth are related by descent from common ancestors. Many found this concept difficult to accept – especially because it does not demonstrate that the path of evolution has a direction towards the emergence of 'higher forms' – humans in particular. Instead it is determined by the particular circumstances of time and place, that is, nature favours particular characteristics under particular environmental conditions. The idea alarmed Victorian society and the church, with their strictly biblical explanation of the origins of humanity

- The British writer Salman Rushdie (1947–) was born in India of a Muslim family. His 1988 novel *The Satanic Verses* (the title refers to verses deleted from the Koran) offended many Muslims with alleged blasphemy. In 1989 Ayatollah Khomeini of Iran called for Rushdie and his publishers to be killed. The furore caused by the publication of the book led to the withdrawal of British diplomats from Iran. In India and elsewhere, people were killed in demonstrations against the book and Rushdie was forced to go into hiding

- Martin Scorsese (1942–), US film director, screenwriter, and producer, often deals with the notion of sin and redemption. Among his most influential and forceful films is the 1988 film *The Last Temptation of Christ*. The film offended many Christians with its alleged blasphemy by controversially depicting the sexual thoughts and actions of Christ.

These last two examples highlight an important issue. As we depict in Figure 5.1(a), freedom of expression and personal responsibility are closely linked – and we must continually strike a balance between the two. In this sense we cherish and guard freedom of expression and at the same time use this freedom wisely. If, for example, we use freedom of expression to ferment religious hatred, then we are not acting with wisdom and the motives behind our actions need to be considered. In cases in which we seek to use freedom of expression to cause outrage (and so perhaps make a financial gain via the sales of a film or article) then we are exploiting freedom of expression for our own ends.

5.3 Censorship

There is another, equally long, tradition of thought in which it has been argued that freedom of speech is not absolute and unlimited, and should be subject to certain restrictions. These arguments have been used to support various forms of censorship. Censorship is defined as the suppression or regulation of speech (in its broadest definition) that is considered immoral, heretical, subversive, libellous, damaging to state security, or otherwise offensive. It is the control and regulation both of what people can and cannot say or express, and what they are permitted to see, read and view. Censorship tends to be more stringent in times of war, and under totalitarian regimes. However, in many societies, there is a constant struggle over what material ought to be censored, and who should decide. In the US, for example, government agencies and various groups continually make attempts at imposing censorship. The question is often tested in the courts, especially with respect to sexually explicit material. Recently, efforts have been made to suppress certain pieces of music and works of art on the grounds of obscenity.

As we shall see later in the chapter, laws relating to obscenity, libel and national security act as a form of censorship. The media also exercise a degree of self-censorship deciding to report some stories, and not others, sometimes for legal reasons, and at other times for political or ideological reasons.

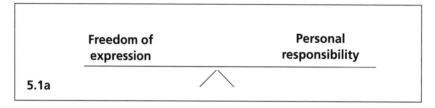

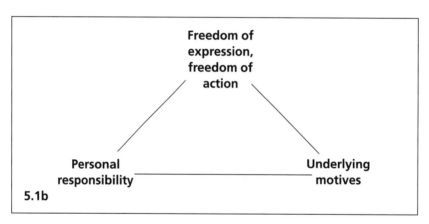

Figure 5.1: As indicated in 5.1a, freedom of expression is generally tempered by our sense of personal responsibility – and a careful balance (at least in principle) maintained between the two. In addition, when we make use of our right of free expression, we need to continually examine the motives that underpin our actions – see 5.1b.

Activity 5.1

Defending free speech and expression

Describe the main arguments in favour of freedom of expression in the fields of politics and science, citing specific historical examples.

Plato

One of the most renowned philosophical allies of censorship advocates is the Greek thinker Plato. The best known of Plato's dialogues, *The Republic*, lays out Plato's visions of the ideal state. It covers a wide range of topics, including education. The influence of the environment on growing minds is emphasised by Plato, in that he calls for a rigid control of music and poetry in education:

> We must start to educate the mind before training the body. And the first step, as you know, is always what matters most, particularly when we are dealing with those who are young and tender. That is the time when they are easily moulded and when any impression we choose to make leaves a permanent mark. Shall we therefore readily allow our children to listen to any stories made up by anyone, and to form opinions that are for the most part the opposite of those we think they should have when they grow up? ... Then it seems that our first business is to supervise the production of stories, and choose only those we think suitable, and reject the rest.

For Plato, carefully selecting the sorts of stories that we ought (or ought not) to hear from our earliest childhood would produce citizens who honoured the gods, their parents and would know how important it was to love one another. Plato continues:

> It is not only to the poets therefore that we must issue orders requiring them to portray good character in their poems or not to write at all; we must issue similar orders to all artists and craftsman, and prevent them from portraying bad character, ill discipline, meanness and ugliness in pictures of living things, in sculpture, architecture, or any work of art, and if they are unable to comply they must be forbidden to practice their art among us.... We must look for artists and craftsman capable of perceiving the real nature of what is beautiful, and then our young men, living as it were in a healthy climate, will benefit because all the works of art they see and hear influence them for good, like breezes from some healthy country....

Plato's arguments still have a remarkable contemporary resonance if we transpose his ideas to the 21st-century world of the Internet and mass media. Pro-censorship advocates identify forms of expression in music, art, film and computer games that are deemed unfit for consumption by minors. They point to examples of 'speech' which violate obscenity laws, and where individuals utter racial, ethnic, sexist or homophobic slurs. The question can then be asked – does this type of speech fit in with Plato's idea of the 'sorts of stories which men ought to hear from their earliest childhood'? Are these stories that will produce 'citizens who show tolerance, respect and love to one another'? Arguably not, say the censorship advocates.

Should we influence 'the environment' that has an impact on young, impressionable, undeveloped minds? Do we restrict the right to freedom of speech to include only those educated by Plato's methods, who can in adulthood distinguish between good and evil works of art? Many of these questions continue to be relevant when applied to the debate between free speech and censorship, particularly in the context of pornography and hate speech. We shall be returning to some of these issues later in the chapter.

5.4 Laws upholding free speech

Articles 18 and 19 of the United Nations' Universal Declaration of Human Rights, 1948 affirm the value and importance of free speech, internationally.

Protection of the right to freedom of speech is also enshrined in the legislation of individual countries. Perhaps the most well-known and widely cited of these is the First Amendment to the US Constitution, 1791. One of ten amendments made to the original US Constitution, which were designed to protect the rights of US citizens (known as the Bill of Rights), the First Amendment guarantees freedom of speech and the press, in the following terms:

> Congress shall make no law respecting an establishment of religion, or prohibiting the free exercise thereof; or abridging the freedom of speech, or of the press; or the right of the people peaceably to assemble, and to petition the Government for a redress of grievances.

Similarly, in the UK the more recent Human Rights Act, 1998 states, in Article 10, that:

> Everyone has the right of freedom of expression. This right shall include freedom to hold opinions and to receive and impart information and ideas without interference by public authority and regardless of frontiers.

Laws restricting free speech

In both the US and the UK there are some categories of speech not protected by free speech legislation. In the US the most important of these is obscene speech. US obscenity laws are complex, and there have been several cases where the meaning of the law has been tested – with different outcomes. However, the basic framework for determining 'obscene speech' is provided by the landmark case of *Miller v California* (1973). In this case, the US Supreme Court established a three-part test to determine whether or not speech was considered 'obscene'. Obscene speech, or expression, is anything that falls within all of the following three categories:

- Depicts sexual (or excretory) acts explicitly prohibited by state law
- Appeals to prurient interests as judged by a reasonable person using community standards, and
- Has no serious literary, artistic, social political or scientific value.

Under these conditions, the depiction of child pornography is a clear example of obscene speech, and is illegal under US federal law.

A second class of 'obscene' speech, often called indecent speech, is that which is permissible for adults, but to which children under the age of seventeen should not be exposed. Indecent speech is considered speech that is harmful to minors. Sale of such speech to anyone under the age of seventeen is illegal. In the landmark case of *Ginsberg v New York*, 'harmful to minors' was defined as follows:

> 'That quality of any description or representation, in whatever form, of nudity, sexual conduct, sexual excitement, or sado-masochistic abuse, when it:
> - Predominantly appeals to prurient, shameful, or morbid interests of minors, *and*
> - Is patently offensive to prevailing standards in the adult community as a whole with what is suitable for minors, *and*
> - Is utterly without redeeming social importance for minors.'

Although state legislatures and local communities have applied these standards of 'obscenity' and 'indecency' differently, these criteria have served as a general guide to what speech should be 'off limits' to everyone, and what should be 'off limits' to children under the age of seventeen.

More recent legislation introduced by the US Congress, includes the Children's Internet Protection Act, 2000 which targets Internet terminals in schools and libraries. The Act applies only to schools and libraries that participate in certain federal programmes, receiving federal money for technology. It requires that such schools and libraries install filtering software on all Internet terminals to block access to sites with child pornography, obscene material and material 'harmful to minors'.

In the United States there is no legislation that specifically prohibits hate speech directed at a particular racial, ethnic or social group. There are, however, related laws in most communities which can apply – for example, slander, conspiracy, incitement to riot and disturbing the peace, among others. Whereas an individual may be able to stand up and say that ethnic group 'X' is composed of thieves and criminals, they may be breaking the law if they name specific members of that race as thieves and criminals. They may also be prosecuted for specifically attempting to plan a criminal activity, and to incite a crowd to commit acts of violence against members of an ethnic group. In other words, to say hateful things is permissible, as long as there is no overt effort to encourage expressions of that hate beyond speech and into specific actions.

The UK Official Secrets Act, 1989 prohibits the disclosure of confidential material from government sources by employees. It is an offence for a member or former member of the security and intelligence services, or those working closely with them, to disclose information about their work. There is no defence according to the 'public interest', and disclosure of information already in the public domain is still a crime. Journalists who repeat such disclosures may also be prosecuted.

The British government also uses the DA (Defence Advisory) Notice – a notice to the media strongly recommending the withholding of publication of certain material that is deemed to be of importance to national security. This is, however, only a voluntary code.

We saw above that the Human Rights Act, 1998, upholds the right to freedom of expression in Article 10. The second part of this Article goes on to make a number of important exceptions to this right, stating that:

> 'The exercise of these freedoms, since it carries with it duties and responsibilities, may be subject to such formalities, conditions, restrictions or penalties as are prescribed by law and are necessary in a democratic society, in the interests of national security, territorial integrity or public safety, for the prevention of disorder or crime, for the protection of health or morals, for the protection of the reputation or rights of others, for preventing the disclosure of information received in confidence, or for maintaining the authority and impartiality of the judiciary.'

Activity 5.2

The Human Rights Act

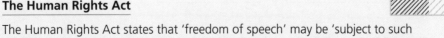

The Human Rights Act states that 'freedom of speech' may be 'subject to such formalities, conditions, restrictions or penalties as are prescribed by law and are necessary in a democratic society'. Describe each of the conditions mentioned by the Act, and illustrate each instance with a scenario or case that you have found in textbooks, journals or from the Internet.

5.5 Free speech and the Internet

The Internet has raised a whole range of new questions and issues regarding appropriate content and appropriate regulation of that content in different contexts. Among the most problematic forms of speech on the Internet have been pornography, hate speech and forms of expression connected with terrorism or political dissent. However, many of the challenges posed by the Internet are the result of the characteristics of the Internet itself. Quinn (2004) suggests that there are five such characteristics (see Figure 5.2) which have made censorship more difficult:

- **Many-to-many communications:** unlike traditional one-to-many broadcast media, the Internet supports many-to-many communications. Whereas it is relatively easy for a government to shut down a newspaper or a radio station, it is very difficult for a government to prevent an idea from being published on the Internet, where millions of people have the ability to post web pages

- **Dynamic:** the Internet is dynamic: millions of new computers are being connected to the Internet each year

- **Scale and size of the Internet:** the Internet is huge. There is no way for a team of human censors to keep track of everything that is posted on the Web. While automated tools are available, they are fallible. Hence any attempt to control access to material stored on the Internet cannot be 100% effective

- **Global:** the Internet is global. National governments have limited authority to restrict activities happening outside their borders

- **Users – adults and children:** it is hard to distinguish between children and adults on the Internet, and it is difficult for 'adult' websites to verify the age of someone attempting to enter their site. In the early days of the Web, young children were not likely to come upon pornography by accident. Search engines and web browsers changed this. Pornography now arrives in e-mail, and porn sites turn up in lists found by search engines for many innocent topics.

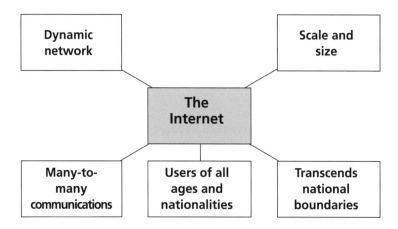

Figure 5.2: Quinn [2004] suggests five facets of the Internet that make it difficult to effectively introduce censorship. This is not an exhaustive list and you may wish to spend a little time considering other aspects of the Internet that impact on the ability of governments to impose censorship.

Internet technologies supporting free expression

In addition to the foregoing characteristics, specific Internet technologies can enable free expression.

Those Internet technologies that tend to enhance free expression are as follows:

- Electronic mail. The Internet essentially started with electronic mail as its primary communications medium, and has historically fought hard to keep this free from censorship. By its very nature, electronic mail is extremely hard to censor, especially simple, point-to-point mail, because of the distributed and robust nature of routing protocols
- Newsgroups and usenet technologies are widespread and difficult to censor
- Internet chat facilities can also enable free expression, where unregulated, and provide the opportunity for anonymity (though this can have its own drawbacks as we shall see in the following section)
- The Web is a democratic publishing medium where there are few restrictions. Any business, organisation or individual can set up a home page on the Web
- Cryptography has protected free expression by allowing people to express their opinions with some degree of confidentiality and privacy. As discussed in Chapter 2, encryption scrambles messages so that only the legitimate recipient, or intended parties, can understand them.

Activity 5.3

Internet technologies and free expression

Describe three computer or Internet technologies that support free expression. Use examples to demonstrate how they do this and whom they benefit.

Internet technologies as tools for censorship

The three technologies that effectively act as 'censorship tools', are indicated in Figure 5.3 and are briefly discussed below:

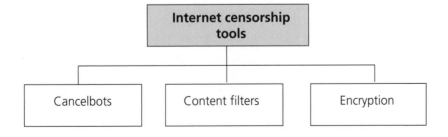

Figure 5.3: Exemplar tools that may be used to impose degrees of Internet censorship

Cancelbots

Certain Internet technologies, such as Usenet news, have shown themselves vulnerable to cancellation of previously published information, for example through the use of cancelbots. A cancelbot is a robot program that sends a message to one or more Usenet newsgroups to cancel, or remove from posting, a certain type of message. It searches for messages matching a certain pattern, whether it is a duplicate message or offensive material, and sends out cancels for them. When a message has been cancelled, its status is changed to 'cancel,' and the Usenet servers will no longer post them.

Encryption

We have seen that encryption technology protects confidentiality and privacy and can thereby enable freedom of expression. However, control of, and access to, the same technology can undermine free speech. Examples are the intercepting of e-mail and other forms of electronic communication by governments and state agencies, and the monitoring of employees in workplaces (this issue will be discussed in greater detail in subsequent chapters). In the mid-1990s, for example, the US government demanded limits on encryption technology and access to all encrypted messages. The government's efforts took the form of proposals for a 'clipper chip' in 1993, a technology that would have been installed in all electronic communications devices, and which would have required encryption users to submit their encryption keys to a government database. The proposals met with such a hail of objections from technical and civil liberties groups that they were never implemented.

Content filters

A web filter is a piece of software that prevents certain web pages from being displayed by a browser. While a browser application is running, the filter runs as a background process, checking every page your browser attempts to load. If the filter determines the page is objectionable, it prevents the browser from displaying it.

Filters can be installed on individual computers, or an ISP may provide filtering services for its customers. Programs designed to be installed on individual computers, such as Cyber Sentinel, eBlaster, and Spector PRO can be set up to e-mail parents as soon as they detect an inappropriate web page. They enable parents to set the level of filtering on their children's accounts. It also allows parents to look at logs showing the pages their children have visited. Filtering software is also used in libraries, educational institutions and other areas of public Internet use, especially those to which children have access.

Typical filters use two different methods to determine if a page should be blocked. The first method is to check the URL of the page against a blacklist of objectionable sites. If the web page comes from a blacklisted site, it is not displayed. The second method is to look for combinations of letters or words that may indicate a site has objectionable content.

Neither of these methods is foolproof. The Web contains millions of pages containing pornography, and new sites continue to be created at a high rate. Hence any blacklist of pornographic sites will be incomplete by definition. The algorithms used to identify objectionable words and phrases can cause web filters to block out perfectly innocent and legitimate web pages for no apparent reason. For example, the websites of Middlesex, Essex or Sussex universities might be blocked by some web filters simply because they contain the word 'sex', one of the words most commonly entered into search engines!

ISPs can also implement their own restrictions on the content of websites, newsgroups and e-mails that are hosted on their servers. Some of these content regulations might be self-imposed by the ISP, as specified in their acceptable use policies. Others may be imposed by legal restraints – for example, the case of Yahoo.

The case of Yahoo!

In 2000 a French court ordered Yahoo! to block access by French people to Yahoo!'s US-based auction sites where Nazi memorabilia were sold. Display and sale of Nazi memorabilia is illegal in France and Germany (with some exceptions for historical purposes).

The order raised several technical and legal issues, and was widely viewed as a threat to freedom of speech.

- It was technically not feasible to block access by all French people because they could access Yahoo!'s sites from outside France or use anonymising services that obscured their location

    One of the basic characteristics of the Internet is that one's physical location is irrelevant, in terms of access. One's physical location is also difficult to determine

- The use of filters to screen out Nazi material has the problems we discussed earlier. Yahoo! said filters would be less than 50% effective and could not distinguish references to Nazis in hate material and from references in, for example, *The Diary of Anne Frank* or Holocaust memorials (Baase, 2003)

- Free speech advocates worried that the policy changes demonstrated the power of one government to impose its censorship standards on other countries. Others saw it as adoption of a responsible policy, discouraging the spread of Nazi material.

Activity 5.4

The public library scenario

Consider the following scenario (this is adapted from Spinello [2000]):

Assume you have just taken over the IT department of a large inner-city library. You discover that the main library building has ten computers, but this library's many patrons use them only sporadically. This is partly because the computers lack any interesting software and do not have Internet connectivity. Many of the people who live in the local area do not have a computer at home. As one of your first tasks, you decide to purchase some popular software packages and to provide Internet access. The computer area soon becomes a big success. The computers are in constant use, and the most popular activity is browsing the Web. You are pleased with this decision because this is an excellent way for those in the community who cannot afford computer systems to gain access to the Internet

Problems begin to emerge. Some young teenagers (probably about twelve or thirteen years old) are seen downloading highly graphic sexual material. A shocked staff member tells you that these young boys were looking at obscene images, and were asked to leave the library. About ten days later, an old man was noticed looking at child pornography for several hours. Every few weeks, there are similar incidents.

The senior librarian, and several other staff members, recommend that you purchase and immediately install some type of filtering software. Other librarians remind you that this violates the Library Association's code of responsibility. You re-read that code and are struck by the following sentence:

'The selection and development of library resources should not be diluted because of minors having the same access to library resources as adult users.'　　**...cont/**

They urge you to resist the temptation to filter, an activity they equate with censorship. One staff member urges that filtering is equivalent to purchasing an encyclopaedia and cutting out articles that do not meet certain standards. Another librarian points out that the library does not put pornographic material in its collection, so why should it allow access to such material on the Internet? As word spreads about this problem, there is also public pressure emerging from community leaders to do something about these computers. Even the city's mayor has joined in – she, too, is uncomfortable with unfettered access.

- Outline the practical options that are open to you

- What course of action would you take?

- Defend your decision using appropriate ethical principles and arguments.

Anonymous expression: for and against

Anonymous communication in cyberspace is enabled largely through the use of anonymous re-mailers, which strip off the identifying information on an e-mail message and substitute an anonymous code or a random number. By encrypting a message and then routing that message through a series of anonymous re-mailers, a user can assume that their message will remain anonymous and confidential. This process is called 'chained re-mailing'. The process is effective because none of the re-mailers will have the key to read the encrypted message; neither the recipient nor any re-mailers (except the first) in the chain can identify the sender. The recipient cannot connect the sender to the message unless every single re-mailer in the chain cooperates. This would assume that each re-mailer kept a log of their incoming and outgoing mail, which is highly unlikely.

There are many specific examples in support of the argument that anonymous free expression deserves protection. Social intolerance may require some individuals to rely on anonymity to communicate openly about an embarrassing medical condition or an awkward disability. Computer-mediated communication, in a more general sense, enables a degree of social anonymity by removing status cues such as sitting at the head of a table, or body language. Computer-mediated communication may be attractive to those who feel less competent in face-to-face settings where the subtleties of voice, dress, mannerisms and vocabulary are mixed in complex ways. In fact, investigations into computer conferencing and e-mail have highlighted that group decision-making discussions using computers exhibit more equal participation and a larger coverage of issues.

Whistle-blowers are another group that can benefit from anonymity. People who wish to publicise what they see as 'wrongdoing', but are wary of repercussions (e.g. from employers) may understandably be reluctant to come forward with information unless they can remain anonymous. Such information might include exposure of corruption, wrongdoing or abuses of power within an organisation. Political dissent, even in democratic societies that prize free speech, may be impeded unless it can be voiced anonymously. Anonymity has an incontestable value in the struggle against repression, and even against the more routine corporate and government abuses of power. In the Kosovo conflict, for example, some individuals relied on anonymous programs (such as Anonymizer) to describe atrocities perpetrated by Serbians against ethnic Albanians. If the Serbians were able to trace the identity of these individuals, their lives would have been in grave danger.

Anonymous communication, whether facilitated by re-mailers or by other means, does of course have drawbacks. For example, it can be abused by criminals or terrorists seeking to communicate anonymously when plotting the crimes. It also permits cowardly users to communicate without civility, or to libel someone without accountability and with little likelihood of apprehension by law enforcement authorities. Anonymity can also be used to reveal trade secrets or violate intellectual property laws. There are also a number of documented cases where anonymity has been abused by sexual predators, to conceal their identity, in online chatrooms. For example:

> In 1995, Katie Tarbox, a 13-year-old swimmer from New Canaan, Connecticut, met a man in an AOL chat room. He said his name was Mark and his age was 23. His grammar and vocabulary were good, and he made her feel special. Katie agreed to meet Mark at a hotel in Texas, where her swim team was competing. Soon after she entered his hotel room, he molested her. 'Mark' turned out to be 41-year-old Francis Kufrovich from Calabasas, California – a man with a history of preying on children. In March 1998, Kufrovich was the first person in the United States to be sentenced for Internet paedophilia. After pleading guilty, he served 18 months in prison. (Quinn, 2004)

5.6 Ethical and professional issues

What are the responsibilities and duties of computing professionals on matters to do with free speech? Many professional computing bodies echo the proclamations about free speech in the legislation cited earlier. Rule 4 of the British Computer Society Code of Conduct, for example, states that members 'shall conduct … professional activities without discrimination against clients or colleagues..' and that they 'should adhere to relevant law within the jurisdiction where [they] are working and, if appropriate, the European Convention on Human Rights'. The Association for Computing Machinery (ACM), meanwhile, states that '… as a professional you have a professional duty to safeguard the basic human right to freedom of speech'.

In a broader sense, freedom of expression can also be taken to entail thinking about questions of social responsibility in the design of technology and software. For example, when designing new Internet technologies, computing professionals arguably have an ethical responsibility to think about how the uses and functions of those technologies might allow certain actions, and restrict others. Clearly, some computer technologies can be designed to enable freedom of expression, whereas others can be designed to more easily enable censorship and control of expression.

The Internet was founded on the principles of sharing programming ideas. Early web technology was placed in the public domain. The technological infrastructure of the Internet was deliberately designed to make the centralised control of the network difficult. It could easily have been designed another way.

Global censorship issues

The vibrant communication made possible by the Internet threatens governments in countries that lack political and cultural freedom. Many governments took steps to cut, or seriously reduce, the flow of information and opinion on the Internet. In 2000, Burma (Myanmar) banned the use of the Internet or creation of web pages without official permission, the posting of material about politics, and the posting of any material deemed by the government to be harmful to its policies. Under an earlier law, possession of an unauthorised modem or satellite dish was punishable by a jail term of up to 15 years (Baase, 2003).

Saudi Arabians only gained access to the Internet in 1999, after the government installed a centralised control centre outside Riyadh.

Virtually all Internet traffic flows through this control centre, which blocks pornography and gambling sites, and many other pages deemed to be offensive to Islam or to the government of Saudi Arabia. Blocked sites and pages typically include those concerned with non-Islamic religious organisations, women's health and sexuality issues, certain music and films, gay rights, Middle Eastern politics, and information about ways to circumvent web filtering.

Vietnam uses filtering software to find and block anticommunist messages coming from other countries. In some countries, governments are struggling with the dilemma of modernising their economy and technology while trying to maintain tight control over information. In contrast to Saudi Arabia, the government of the People's Republic of China does not direct all Internet traffic through a single control centre. Instead, it allows many Internet service providers to make their own connections outside China. However, all Internet service providers (ISPs), including Yahoo!, have agreed to abide by a 'self-discipline' agreement forbidding them from forwarding politically or morally objectionable web pages. Besides blocking many sites containing sexually explicit material, Chinese ISPs typically block sites concerned with Chinese dissidents, sites related to Taiwan and Tibet, and many news sites, such as BBC News and CNN. The government monitors ISPs to ensure sites that should be blocked are, in fact, unavailable to web surfers. Users of the Internet and other international computer networks are required to register with the police – even to use terminals in Internet cafes. Regulations prohibit 'producing, retrieving, duplicating and spreading information that may hinder public order'.

Some observers point out that such regulations are better than blocking Internet access totally, and that, in practice, the government cannot monitor all users, so the regulation is actually a step towards more freedom and information access than was previously available.

Singapore required that online political and religious groups register with the government. Content providers were prohibited from distributing material that could 'undermine public morals, political stability or religious harmony'. In 1996, the government of Singapore justified its censorship attempts in part by citing the censorship efforts in the United States. In 1999, Singapore, which made a great effort to build a high-tech economy, relaxed enforcement of Internet censorship laws but did not change them.

All of these examples raise the crucial question of whether online services should bar people in other countries from news, political discussions and other material that is banned in those countries. If websites must comply with the laws of 150 other countries, what would happen to the openness and global information flow of the Web? This rises yet another pressing issue within the international computing field, and that is how the Internet should be governed and regulated and, indeed, whether it should be regulated at all.

Internet governance

The Web and the Internet have created many opportunities for data sharing and eCommerce, but, as we have seen, they have also posed some formidable problems for lawmakers of national governments. The Internet has traditionally been decentralised and self-governing, and it has so far evaded strict or systemic regulations. However, there will always be a need for some type of stability imposed from above, that is, from the government or other centralised authorities. At a minimum, there must be a central body to manage Internet domain name distribution and to handle trademark disputes.

But what exactly is the right mix of top-down regulations and bottom-up control? There are at least three basic top-down models that have some plausibility and are worth a cursory review:

- **Direct state intervention:** the existing laws of each nation could govern the Internet; thus, the state could amend or extend its current laws so that they apply to pertinent activities in cyberspace

- **Coordinated international intervention:** a new intergovernmental organisation composed of representatives from countries that use the Internet could establish new rules and regulations for cyberspace that will have international jurisdiction

- **Self-governance:** the Internet would develop its own semi-official political structure; it would be governed by charters established by non-profit organisations that represent the Internet's stakeholders.

Activity 5.5

Researching the EFF

Log onto the website of the Electronic Frontier Foundation website at: **www.eff.org**

- What is the EFF?

- What are their core ideas on freedom of speech?

Read about, and make notes on, one of the main topics on the EFF's website.

5.7 An ethical dilemma

Let us suppose that you are employed by a company that develops websites for clients. One day your boss presents you with a new project. In brief, your company has obtained a contract from a law enforcement agency to develop several websites. These are to act in line with the 'honeypot' scenario mentioned in the previous chapter. The project being undertaken by the law enforcement agency is to gather information in relation to individuals who may be 'interested' in extreme forms of violence. By developing this website you will be assisting the law enforcement agencies who will gather material in relation to people who peruse the site.

What is your ethical position? Do you think this is an appropriate agenda in terms of invisibly policing the Internet? Since your boss has presented you with this brief, in the case that you do not agree with the ramifications of policing the Internet in this way, do you have any practical alternative but to undertake the work? (Here we assume that your boss is insistent that the work should be carried out by you.) What – if any – real objections do you have? Do you feel this is encroaching upon the liberty of the individual? Are your views influenced by the nature of the content of the website? For example, would your views be any different if the website related directly to terrorism or other forms of political extremism? To what extent do you think that the Internet is currently being policed – not only in terms of monitoring those who enter particular websites or who enter contentious chat room areas or the like?

5.8 Summary

In this chapter we have briefly examined the issue of freedom of expression within the context of computer technology, and specifically in terms of the Internet. We began by looking at some of the arguments and philosophies in defence of the notion of free expression. We have provided examples showing how the suppression of free thought has, historically, curtailed the speed of human advancement in science and the arts. Subsequently, we considered the case for censorship, citing the ideas of Plato in *The Republic*. The principal forms of legislation which uphold or restrict free speech were examined. We then discussed the impact of computer technology on freedom of expression, looking at those Internet technologies that have enabled free speech, and those which have tended to restrict it. We also outlined the arguments in favour of, and against, anonymous expression in cyberspace. We have explored the professional duties of those working in the computing industry to uphold the principles of free speech. Finally, we considered Internet censorship in global terms and provided brief discussion of possible models for regulating the Internet.

5.9 Review questions

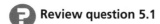 **Review question 5.1**

What is meant by the term 'censorship'?

Review question 5.2

How might Plato be seen as an early advocate of censorship?

Review question 5.3

What laws uphold the principle of 'free speech' in the US and UK?

Review question 5.4

What are the restrictions on speech outlined in the Official Secrets Act?

Review question 5.5

According to Quinn, what are the five characteristics of the Internet that have made censorship more difficult?

Review question 5.6

How might anonymous expression be seen to encourage free expression? Give three instances where anonymous expression might be for the public good.

Review question 5.7

What are the three possible models of Internet governance?

5.10 Feedback on activities

Feedback on activity 5.1

- **Politics:** Free speech is a basic human right, and one of the key, underlying principles of an open, democratic society. Genuine debate and criticism is necessary in any political process, to test assumptions, and expose false ideas, and to enable people to chose their political representatives freely. Censorship can lead to the suppression of opposition, the loss of freedom, and, ultimately, totalitarianism (as in Nazi Germany or the Soviet Union)

- **Science:** Freedom of thought encourages openness, and the exchange of ideas, in research and discovery. The dethronement of the Earth from the centre of the universe caused profound shock in 1632, when Italian astronomer and physicist Galileo (1564–1642) suggested that the Earth orbited the sun, thereby challenging the established church's view that the Earth was at the centre of the universe. Galileo was hauled up before the Inquisition, the church tribunal to combat heresy. His subsequent house arrest and recantation hindered scientific discovery in Italy for 100 years.

Feedback on activity 5.2

- For the interests of national security. For example, talking about military secrets, or the work of intelligence services, such as the case of David Shayler, a former MI5 agent

- To maintain public safety. For example, any expression that might cause widespread panic, thereby threatening public safety (a bomb hoax, perhaps)

- For the prevention of disorder or crime. An example would be speech that incites people to civic unrest (to riot, perhaps) or to commit crimes

- For the protection of health or morals. Restricting the distribution or consumption of pornographic material that involves minors

- For the protection of the reputation or rights of others. Restricting speech that is slanderous or libellous, or results in an invasion of someone's privacy (press stories, for example)

- For preventing the disclosure of information received in confidence. Examples might be 'protected' confidential communication between doctors and their patents, solicitors and their clients, or religious advisers and members of a faith or church

- For maintaining the authority and impartiality of the judiciary. For example, reporting restrictions on the press during court cases – naming witnesses, the accused, or anything that might affect the outcome of a case.

Feedback on activity 5.3

- E-mail: by its very nature, extremely hard to censor, especially simple, point-to-point mail, because of the distributed and robust nature of routing protocols

- Usenet news: widespread and difficult to censor. There are thousands of newsgroups that exist on every imaginable topic, where contributors are generally able to say what they like

- The World Wide Web: a democratic publishing medium par excellence, where there are few restrictions. Any business, organisation or individual can set up a web home page

- Cryptography: protects free expression by allowing people to express their opinions with some degree of confidentiality and privacy

- Internet chat: allows communication in real-time between two parties. Has many of the same advantages as e-mail.

Feedback on activity 5.4

The practical options open to you are many.

- You could install polarising filters on terminals, or walls around terminals, so that the screens were visible only from directly in front (both to protect the privacy of the user and to shield other users and employees from material they find objectionable)

- You could set time limits on the use of terminals

- You could ask patrons to stop viewing pornography, just as they would ask someone to stop making noise

- You could revoke borrowing privileges of people viewing pornography or obscene material

- You could install filtering software on all terminals, allowing those filters to be turned off for those over the age of 18

- You could create a separate computer room for adults, with no filtering software, and one for children, with filtering software installed

- You could require parental supervision for children using the Internet, or written parental permission.

Decisions to allow all patrons unrestricted access to the Internet, whatever their age could be justified on the basis of an unlimited, absolute definition of free speech. However, this might harm minors, and other patrons of the library. It might be difficult to justify to others in terms of serving the greater 'public good'.

For some adults, public libraries represent their only opportunity to access the Web at no cost. In order to be treated as free and equal citizens, they should have the same web access as people who have Internet access from their homes. Limiting this access could be seen as undemocratic and discriminatory.

You could defend any decision to install filtering software, by citing Plato and the need to protect and mould young minds, and shape their moral development. But this could be seen as somewhat patronising as a public defence of such filtering.

Above all, you would need to pay close attention to the law – is there legislation on this issue that can help you make a decision? You also need to take into account the library's code of conduct and ethics, if it exists, and think carefully about the duties and obligations of public libraries in general.

Activity 5.5

The EFF is an civil liberties group in the US which considers free speech to be a fundamental building block of a free society. It regards intellectual freedom (including freedom to think, believe, read, speak, write, publish, perform, produce software, and protest) as one of the most fundamental of basic human rights, protected by the UN Universal Declaration of Human Rights, as well as national and state constitutions, amendments, and case law. The EFF was founded in July of 1990. Based in San Francisco, it is a donor-supported membership organisation, working to:

- Protect the public's fundamental rights

- Educate the press, policymakers and general public about civil liberties issues related to technology

- Act as a defender of those liberties

- Oppose what they see as 'misguided' legislation

- Initiate and defend court cases preserving individuals' rights

- Launch global public campaigns

- Introduce leading-edge proposals and papers

- Host frequent educational events

- Engage the press

- Publish a comprehensive archive of digital civil liberties information.

References

Baase, S (2003), *A Gift of Fire: Social, Legal and Ethical Issues for Computers and the Internet*, Pearson.

Mill, JS (1998), *On Liberty and Other Essays*, Oxford Paperbacks.

Plato (2003), *The Republic*, Penguin Books.

Quinn, M (2004), *Ethics for the Information Age*, Addison Wesley.

Spinello, R (2000), *Cyber ethics: morality and law in cyberspace*, Jones and Bartlett.

Further reading

Ayres, R (1999), *The Essence of Professional issues in Computing*, (Chapter 3), Prentice-Hall.

Baase, S (2003), *A Gift of Fire: Social, Legal and Ethical Issues for Computers and the Internet*, (Chapter 5), Pearson.

Talbott, SL (1995), *The Future Does Not Compute*, O'Reilly and Associates, Inc. (general reading, also available to read online at **http://netfuture.org/fdnc/index.html**)

CHAPTER 6

Personal privacy and computer technologies

OVERVIEW

When thinking about the social and ethical issues of computing, privacy is perhaps the single issue that concerns people the most. The purpose of this chapter is to explore this area – particularly the implications of computer technology. But what do we mean by 'privacy,' and why do we value our privacy? How is our privacy affected by what other people know about us? One of the areas of greatest concern is how information about us is collected, held and used by different organisations, from government departments to private companies. What kind of information is held about us, and who should have the rights to access and use this information? We will be addressing these questions in this chapter. We will also be looking at some of the computing and Internet technologies that pose a threat to our privacy, and what legislation exists to protect that privacy. One of the key themes will be how to balance civil liberties and privacy rights with commercial interests and the duties and obligations of the state.

Learning outcomes	At the end of this chapter you should be able to:

- Understand the concept of privacy in relation to personal information

- Understand the impact of particular computer technologies on privacy

- Understand the principles of the right to privacy embodied in national/international law

- Understand the application of the Data Protection Act (UK)

- Appreciate the conflict between civil liberties and state interests.

6.1 Introduction

We begin this chapter by thinking about the notion of privacy, how to define it, and why we value it. We then explore the implications of computer technology on privacy, particularly for the collection, analysis and use of personal information by different organisations and government bodies. We examine specific computer and Internet technologies that pose a threat to our privacy, including cookies, spam and RFID (radio frequency identification). We shall be looking at some of the legislation that affirms the right to privacy. In particular, we devote a section to the main UK legislation regarding privacy issues – the Data Protection Act. We highlight the key principles and provisions of the Act, and how it covers the processing, use and misuse of personal data. Subsequently we explore some of the professional and ethical issues raised in connection with privacy, particularly debates about how to balance our privacy rights and civil liberties with commercial interests and the duties of the state.

6.2 Valuing privacy

The right to privacy is arguably a basic human right – like that of freedom of speech. It includes the right to confidentiality (to limit the spread of knowledge about oneself); the right to anonymity (to be free from unwanted attention); and the right to solitude (a lack of physical proximity to others, in other words the right to one's own space). When we take away someone's privacy, we take away essential elements of their freedom and autonomy as human beings. It has often been said that 'knowledge is power' and, to a large extent, the more someone knows about us, the more vulnerable we are to manipulation and control.

One of the main contemporary privacy issues is the disclosure and use of our personal information. Personal information includes any information relating to, or traceable to, an individual person. Personal information includes information which identifies us (our name, address and age) and information which says something about us and our lifestyles (for example, our interests and shopping habits). Personal information can be defined by contrasting it with public information – however, the boundaries between the two are increasingly blurred. Public information is information that someone has provided to an organisation that has the right to share it with other organisations. An example of public information is a listing in a telephone directory. Most of us allow our name, address, and phone number to appear in telephone directories. Personal information is information that is not public, nor part of a public record. You may rightly consider your religion to be personal information. It remains personal information as long as you never disclose it to an organisation that has the right to share it. However, if you do disclose your religious affiliation to such an organisation, it then becomes public information.

In the UK, the office of the Information Commissioner (**www.ico.gov.uk**) has been established to protect personal information. Their mission is stated as:

> We shall develop respect for the private lives of individuals and encourage the openness and accountability of public authorities:
>
> - By promoting good information handling practice and enforcing data protection and freedom of information legislation
>
> - By seeking to influence national and international thinking on privacy on information access issues. (**www.informationcommissioner.gov.uk**)

The impact of computer technology

Computer technology has had a profound impact on what information is collected about us, the quantity of that information, who has access to it, and how it is used. In general terms, information technology has made possible the collection and the exchange of personal data on an unprecedented scale, such that there is now a computerised record concerning practically every aspect of our lives. Computerised data is easier to collect than paper data. More importantly perhaps, it is easier to collate, manipulate, and analyse. Taken together, computer databases, the Internet and the Web make the collection, searching, analysis, access to, and distribution of, large amounts of information easier, cheaper and faster than before. Some of this information, such as our specific purchases at supermarkets and bookshops, was simply not recorded before. Our communications by e-mail and discussion groups, and our online activities (where we went, what we did, and how long we stayed on a particular page) can all be recorded, logged, distributed and read by others – even years later.

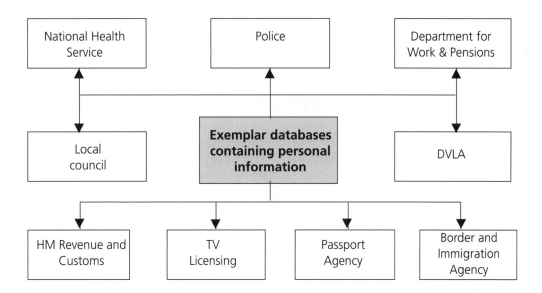

Figure 6.1: Examples of UK government departments that employ databases storing personal information in relation to UK citizens

Today there are thousands of databases, both government and private, containing personal information about us. For example, in the UK, records for most citizens will exist in many of the following government or local state databases: the National Health Service, the local council, the Inland Revenue, the Passport Office, Immigration, the Driver and Vehicle Licensing Agency, the Department of Social Security, the TV Licensing Office and the Police. See Figure 6.1.

Some of the most extensive databases of personal information, however, are held by private corporations, such as credit-checking companies. One of the world's biggest credit-checking companies is Experian. Experian has detailed records of over 40 million people in the UK and carries out checks for the police, various government departments, private companies and other organisations. The kinds of personal information held by credit-checking companies will include names and addresses, former addresses, and current credit ratings, among many other items of information. The information in these databases has invariably been collected from a wide range of sources, and organised so that it constitutes a history, and an assessment, of our trustworthiness as debtors.

Supermarkets are now also compiling vast databases of information about their customers. They do this through their loyalty cards, in conjunction with records of credit card transactions at their stores. British supermarket chain Tesco, for example, has over 10 million names on its Clubcard database. Information in these databases is used to analyse the shopping patterns of customers and to target them with specific advertising based on their demographic profile and spending patterns.

The foregoing are all examples of the secondary use of personal information, that is, the use of information for a purpose other than the one for which it was supplied. It is difficult for individuals to control their personal information if it is collected by one business, organisation or government agency and shared with or sold to others. This information is gathered from a number of different sources, from product guarantee cards, customer details recorded when purchasing a product, and increasingly through online transactions. A number of private companies now exist with the sole purpose of buying and selling databases of personal information. In 2003 the list industry in the UK was valued at £2bn. These databases are sold particularly to marketing companies and used in profiling, where the data in computer files is used to determine characteristics of people most likely to engage in certain behaviour. Businesses use profiling to find people who are likely customers for particular products and services.

Another trend in the use of personal information is that of data matching. Data matching involves combining and comparing information from different databases. Personal information that is supplied or collected for one purpose, and stored in a particular database, is cross-referenced to information in other databases, where data may have been gathered for an entirely different purpose. An individual's details can thus be searched across a number of different databases, enabling a fairly detailed picture to be built up about that person. This is a trend that has concerned privacy advocates and civil liberties groups, because of the potential misuses of such information. Health data, for example, in the form of people's medical records, constitutes highly sensitive information. What if this data were to find its way into the hands of drugs companies, insurance companies or potential employers? The possibilities for abuse of such information are endless – vetting people for jobs, or denying someone a bank loan, based on their current health, their propensity to certain health conditions, or their family medical history.

6.3 Internet technologies and privacy

In this section, we briefly consider the following concepts:

- **Cookies**
- **Spam**
- **Encryption**
- **Radio frequency identification (RFID).**

Cookies

Cookies are text files that websites store on the hard drive of the user's computer. They may store passwords and user names, so that the user does not have to keep retyping them every time they revisit the site that issued the cookie. However, the function of some cookies may not be readily apparent, especially those which redirect the user to sites other than the one they are trying to visit, or which reside permanently on the user's hard disk.

Cookies can be used for 'data mining' purposes, to track the user's motions through a website, the time they spend there, what links or advertising banners they click on and other details that the company wants to record, usually for marketing purposes. As the user visits other sites, previously stored cookies are detected, read, and matched with a profile of the user's previous browsing activity. On this basis, an advertising network selects and displays a 'banner ad', a rectangular advertisement which is not actually part of the web page the user is viewing, but is instead separately supplied by the advertising network.

Most cookies can be read only by the party that created them. However, some companies that manage online banner advertising are, in essence, cookie-sharing rings. The information that they collect about different users is shared with all of their client websites (who may number in the hundreds, or even thousands). The kind of information that is transmitted to these client sites or companies might include someone's name, their e-mail addresses, their home address and telephone phone number, and transactional data – for example, the names of products they purchased online, details of plane trip reservations and phrases typed into search engines.

The use of cookies to gather data and track a user's online activities has raised a number of concerns about possible violations of privacy. Chief among these is the fact that data collected about Internet users can be recorded and shared with third-party companies for marketing purposes, without knowledge or consent.

Activity 6.1

The case of DoubleClick

Research the case of 'DoubleClick'. How did DoubleClick use cookies and why was this controversial? What privacy issues are raised by this case?

Spam

Spam is unsolicited bulk e-mail consisting of marketing and advertising e-mails, junk mail (such as get-rich-quick scams and pornography), chain letters, and occupational spam (inter-office memos and global e-mails within an organisation). The term 'spam' can be traced back to a *Monty Python* sketch, in which a group of Vikings drown out a cafe conversation by loudly and continuously chanting the word 'spam'!

Dealing with spam has become one of the Internet's biggest problems. As recently as 2001, spam accounted for only about eight per cent of all e-mail. By 2003, about 40 per cent of all e-mails were spam (Quinn, [2004]). Spam consumes a large percentage of the Internet's bandwidth and huge amounts of storage space on mail servers and individual computers. The fact that most spam is unsolicited (that is unwanted or unasked for), and that it clogs up the inbox of a user's e-mail program has led to it being seen as an intrusive invasion of privacy.

The volume of spam is increasing because companies have found it to be effective. Its principal advantage is its low cost compared to other forms of advertising. A company can hire an Internet marketing firm to send an advertisement to a million different e-mail addresses. An e-mail advertisement is estimated to be more than 100 times cheaper than a traditional flyer sent via regular post.

Direct marketing firms build up e-mail lists with millions of addresses. They do this using 'robot' software that collects e-mail addresses from websites, message boards and newsgroups. One way that spammers collect e-mail addresses is through 'dictionary attacks'. The term comes from programs that try to guess passwords by trying every entry in an online dictionary of e-mail addresses. Spammers bombard Internet service providers (ISPs) with millions of e-mails sent to made-up or guessed e-mail addresses. Most of these e-mails will bounce back, because the addresses are not valid. However, if an e-mail does not bounce, the spammer knows there is a user with that e-mail address and adds it to their mailing list. To keep networks from being flooded with spam, ISPs have installed spam filters to block spam from reaching users' mailboxes. These filters look for a large number of messages coming from the same e-mail address, messages with suspicious subject lines, or messages with spam-like content. However, spammers are changing their tactics to confound the efforts of spam blockers, by changing e-mail and IP addresses to disguise the sending machine.

Another way spammers can obtain e-mail addresses is through opt-in lists. In order to make a purchase online, very often the user has to agree to the terms and conditions of the vendor, which include agreeing to be sent promotional e-mails, both from the company and their 'marketing partners'. This is known as 'opting in' on the part of the consumer.

By law, customers should be given a choice about whether data collected about them is distributed to other businesses or organisations and is used to send advertisements (see Section 6.5). The two most common ways of providing such choices are called opt out and opt in. Under an opt-out policy, one must check a box on a contract, membership form, or agreement, or call or write to the organisation to request removal from distribution lists. If the consumer does not take action, the presumption is that his or her information may be used. Under an opt-in policy, personal information is not distributed to other businesses or organisations unless the consumer has explicitly checked a box or signed a form permitting disclosure.

The UK follows the 'opt-in' scheme, under the provisions of The Privacy and Electronic Communications (EC Directive) Regulations, 2003. In essence it states:

- Senders cannot send marketing messages unless they have the recipient's prior consent unless the recipient's e-mail address was collected in the course of a sale, or negotiations for a sale
- The sender sends only mail related to similar services or products
- And when the address was collected, the recipient was given the opportunity to opt out, which they did not take.

It also provides two new rules for e-mail marketing:

- The sender must not conceal their identity
- The sender must provide a valid address for opt-out requests.

The sending of unsolicited marketing material also applies to the mobile phone industry; since 11 December 2003 it has been unlawful to send an unsolicited SMS marketing message to an individual.

Complaints regarding the receipt of such messages can be made via the Office of the Information Commissioner at their website (**www.informationcommissioner.gov.uk**). This website gives advice on what to do if the message contains a premium rate number, and links to the Telephone Preference Service where individuals or businesses can register to 'opt out' (**www.tpsonline.org.uk**).

Encryption

As discussed in Chapters 3 and 5, encryption concerns the conversion of data into a form that cannot be understood without the correct decryption 'key'. We saw that encryption/ decryption is especially important in any kind of confidential communication or sensitive transaction, such as a credit card purchase online, or the discussion of company secrets inside an organisation. Encryption is thus one way to ensure privacy in communication. Relatively easy to use e-mail and file encryption software is available, such as Pretty Good Privacy (PGP) which runs on almost all computers and integrates with most major e-mail software. PGP is the most widely used privacy-ensuring program by individuals and is also used by many corporations.

Access to, and control of, encryption technology touches on a number of privacy issues. We saw in the previous chapter how the potential intrusiveness of the clipper chip raised fears about unwarranted invasions of individual privacy by the US government. In its efforts to balance national security needs with privacy rights, this technology put too much emphasis on national security by creating a system in which the risks to privacy invasions were unacceptable, and unnecessarily high. As a result of this overwhelming criticism and negative publicity, the original clipper chip proposal was soon defunct.

Controversy has continued over so-called 'strong encryption'. This refers to ciphers that are essentially unbreakable without the correct decryption keys. Some governments view strong encryption as a potential vehicle by which terrorists might evade authorities. These governments, including the US, want to set up a key escrow arrangement. This means everyone who uses a cipher would be required to provide the government with a copy of the key. Decryption keys would be stored in a supposedly secure place, used only by authorities, and used only if supported by a court order.

Opponents of this scheme argue that criminals could hack into the key escrow database and illegally obtain, steal, or alter the keys. Supporters claim that while this is a possibility, implementing the key escrow scheme would be better than doing nothing to prevent criminals from freely using encryption/decryption. The use of encryption, and the control of encryption technologies, continues to be a highly controversial issue in the wake of the terrorist attacks on the US in September, 2001. (See Section 6.4: Privacy legislation – The Regulation of Investigatory Powers Act, 2000, and The USA Patriot Act, 2001.)

RFID

RFID (radio frequency identification) is a wireless transmitter technology. RFID tags are tiny microchips attached to an antenna that receive and transmit location information by means of radio waves. Some manufacturers have started to replace barcodes with RFIDs, because they give more information about a particular product and are easier to scan. An RFID can contain specific information about the particular item to which it is attached, or in which it is embedded. Proponents of the technology argue that by replacing barcodes with RFIDs, checkouts are quicker and companies can track their inventory more accurately, such as where the product was manufactured, where it was shipped to, and in which store it was sold. RFIDs can also help reduce shoplifting in retail outlets.

However, because RFIDs are not turned off when an item is purchased, the new technology has raised privacy concerns. RFID tags can be read from a distance so that if there are enough sites outside a shop capable of reading the signals given off by the RFID tags, retailers and manufacturers would be able to track the location of the RFID tag as the consumer carried the product from place to place. It is this aspect that has caused most concern. In particular, campaigners are concerned about the use of RFID tags within clothing since this opens up the possibility of retailers and manufacturers being able to track the movements of consumers. Some privacy advocates say consumers should have a way to remove or disable RFIDs in the products they purchase.

One of the legal questions that has arisen from the use of RFIDs is whether the data that is gathered from RFIDs constitutes 'personal data' under the provisions of the Data Protection Act. This Act defines personal data as 'data which relates to a living individual who can be identified from those data', and some legal experts have argued that RFID does indeed constitute personal data. If this is the case, it means that the data that is processed as a result of using RFIDs should conform to the principles of the Data Protection Act. (Brown, (2003).

Figure 6.2: The RFID dilemma?

6.4 Privacy legislation

Legislation relating to privacy can be broadly categorised into those laws which uphold the notion of privacy and protect privacy rights, and those which tend to serve the interests of the state in the name of national security, crime detection or counter-terrorism. As summarised in Figure 6.3 in this section we briefly discuss:

- **Upholding the notion of privacy**
  - The 4th Amendment to the US Constitution, 1791
  - The Human Rights Act, 1998
- **Protecting individual privacy**
  - The Data Protection Act, 1998
  - The Freedom of Information Act, 2000
- **Serving the interests of the state**
  - The Regulation of Investigatory Powers Act, 2000
  - The USA Patriot Act, 2001.

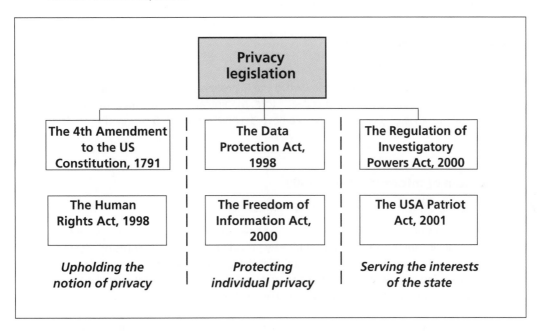

Figure 6.3: Acts in the UK and US that relate to privacy

Upholding the notion of privacy

The following two pieces of legislation set out in concrete terms the value of privacy to individuals.

- **The 4th Amendment to the US Constitution, 1791**

  The right of personal privacy is implicit in the Fourth Amendment to the US Constitution, 1791 which states that:

  > The right of the people to be secure in their persons, houses, papers, and effects, against unreasonable searches and seizures, shall not be violated, and no warrants shall issue, but upon probable cause, supported by oath or affirmation, and particularly describing the place to be searched, and the persons or things to be seized.

- **The Human Rights Act, 1998**

    Article 8 of the UK Human Rights Act, 1998 also upholds the right to privacy, affirming that:

    > Everyone has the right to respect for his private and family life, his home and his correspondence.

    However, Part Two of the same Article goes on to state some important exceptions to this right:

    > There shall be no interference by a public authority with the exercise of this right except such as is in accordance with the law and is necessary in a democratic society in the interests of national security, public safety or the economic well-being of the country, for the prevention of disorder or crime, for the protection of health or morals, or for the protection of the rights and freedoms of others.

    These are similar, in most regards, to the free speech exemptions that we saw in the previous chapter. We shall see that many of these phrases appear in the Regulation of Investigatory Powers Act (RIPA) discussed shortly. RIPA is the law that gives the UK government the right to intercept and view private communications.

Protecting privacy rights

The Data Protection Act, 1998

This piece of legislation is particularly relevant to the IT professional because computer technology has made it much easier to collect, store, manipulate, collate and disseminate personal data. Because of its importance, we have devoted Section 6.5 of this chapter to this Act

The Freedom of Information Act, 2000

According to the Office of the Information Commissioner:

> The Freedom of Information Act 2000 is intended to promote a culture of openness and accountability amongst public authorities by providing people with rights of access to the information held by them. It is expected that these rights will facilitate better public understanding of how public authorities carry out their duties, why they make the decisions they do and how they spend public money.

The Act creates two principal obligations for public authorities, from which other obligations stem:

> 1. Each public authority must adopt and maintain a publication scheme, setting out details of information it will routinely make available, how the information can be obtained and whether there is any charge for it. The date by which public authorities are required to have their schemes in place varies. Public authorities should consult the timetable in approval process to confirm the submission and scheme active dates that will apply to them.

> 2. From 1 January 2005 each public authority must comply with requests for the information that it holds unless an exemption from disclosure applies. Public authorities will normally have a maximum of twenty working days to respond to the request; however, there are circumstances when this time limit can be extended.
> **www.informationcommissioner.gov.uk**

In the context of personal information, this Act gives individuals the opportunity to find out from organisations what information is being held about them.

As with the Human Rights Act, there are a number of exemptions to the provisions of the Freedom of Information Act. Various categories of information are exempt from disclosure, such as information which would prejudicially affect the sovereignty and integrity of the country, security of the state, strategic scientific or economic interest of the state, or conduct of international relations. Also exempt is information which would prejudicially affect public safety and order, detection and investigation of an offence or which may lead to an incitement to commit an offence or prejudicially affect fair trial, or adjudication of a pending case.

Serving the interests of the state

The following two pieces of legislation have caused some concern with privacy and civil liberties groups because of their impact on individual privacy. Essentially, they give governments (UK and US) the right of access to personal communications.

- **The Regulation of Investigatory Powers Act, 2000**
- **The USA Patriot Act, 2001.**

We'll now look at each in a little more depth.

The Regulation of Investigatory Powers Act, 2000

The Regulation of Investigatory Powers Act (RIPA) was passed in July 2000. The Act enables the government to demand that a 'public telecommunications service' provides access to a customer's communications in secret. The definition of public telecommunications services is broad and could apply to Internet services providers, phone companies, or even someone running a website.

Under certain circumstances the Home Secretary can order that the 'external communications' of a telecommunications service be intercepted (for example, all the Internet traffic flowing through a particular ISP's machines). The Home Secretary can serve 'interception warrants' to perform mass surveillance and can require ISPs to fit equipment that enables them to do perform such surveillance. When an ISP is served with an interception warrant, it has to comply and it may not reveal this fact to anyone – ever. Sections 1 to 5 define unlawful and authorised interceptions, and Sections 6 to 11 define interception warrants and associated powers and duties. The Act's 'interception warrants' can be served for purposes of 'national security, preventing or detecting serious crime, safeguarding the economic well-being of the UK, in the interests of public safety, for protecting public health, for tax assessment or collection, for preventing death/injury or damage to a person's health in the event of an emergency, and for any reason the Secretary of State deems fit'. (Note that many of these are phrases appearing in the 'exemptions' list of the Human Rights Act discussed previously.)

The government can demand that decryption keys be handed over in order to access protected information. It is an offence not to hand over such a key – on pain of two years' imprisonment. An individual is deemed to have possessed the key if they possessed it at any time before the disclosure notice was served, unless they can show that they did not have it after the time the notice was served and before the time they were required to disclose it. (Note that if an individual ever had the key, they would have to produce evidence that they no longer possess it.) Also, if the notice requiring disclosure demands secrecy it is an offence to let anyone know that they had been asked to hand over the key(s) in question on pain of five years' imprisonment.

Under the Act, surveillance data that is obtained illegally cannot be used in legal proceedings. This means that were the government to illegitimately intercept an individual's communications, the data cannot be used in a court of law, the existence of surveillance data cannot be mentioned in a court of law, and that data cannot be used to provide evidence in a court of law.

Overall, critics have argued that RIPA allows the government to access a person's electronic communications in a highly unrestricted manner, thus infringing the privacy of their correspondence in a manner, which many would not tolerate regarding their postal communications. The terms under which 'warranted interception' is justified are sufficiently vague to permit electronic surveillance of anyone, under any circumstance. The state can thus gather information such as what websites you visit and when, who you e-mail, who e-mails you, what newsgroups you read, all the phone numbers you call, what software you have downloaded, what documents you have downloaded, where and when you log on to a machine and from where you logged on.

Specific concerns have also been raised about the government's powers to require ISPs to fit surveillance equipment. This could allow the government to require ISPs to install 'back doors' into their systems for the purposes of monitoring. Furthermore, there is no requirement that the design of such equipment be public. The history of computer network security demonstrates that such back doors are serious vulnerabilities and that the best way to remain secure is for one's security system to be publicly open to expert evaluation.

It is has been argued that the legal requirements to hand over decryption keys undermine the use of public key systems, such as PGP, to protect information that is communicated between people. It puts those who use PGP at risk of:

- Having to disclose their private keys (thus compromising the security of all the information sent to them) *or*
- Going to prison for destroying, forgetting or losing a key.

Others have questioned the restriction on the use of surveillance data in legal proceedings, the main objection being that if someone has illegitimately been the subject of an interception warrant there is no legal way for them to know about it (except through investigation by a tribunal, and very limited other circumstances).

The USA Patriot Act, 2001

Following the terrorists attacks of 11 September, 2001, the United States Congress passed the Uniting and Strengthening America by Providing Appropriate Tools Required to Intercept and Obstruct Terrorism (USA PATRIOT) Act of 2001. Some of key features of the Patriot Act are briefly outlined below:

> The Act expands the kinds of information that law enforcement officials can gather with pen registers (devices that display phone numbers being dialled by a suspect) and trap-and-trace devices (which display the phone numbers of calls made to a suspect). It allows police to use pen registers on the Internet to track e-mail addresses and URLs. The law does not require that 'probable cause' needs to be demonstrated for the use of such devices. To obtain a warrant, police simply certify that the information to be gained is relevant to an ongoing criminal investigation.

The Patriot Act extends the jurisdiction of court-ordered wiretaps to the entire country. A judge in New York can, for example, authorise the installation of a device in California.

The Patriot Act broadens the number of circumstances under which roving surveillance can take place (roving surveillance being wiretaps that move from phone to phone). The Act allows roving surveillance to be performed for the purpose of intelligence, and the government does not have to prove that the person under investigation actually uses the device to be tapped.

Under the Patriot Act, law enforcement officials wishing to intercept communications to and from a person who has illegally gained access to a computer system do not need a court order if they have the permission of the owner of the computer system.

The Patriot Act makes it easier for the FBI to collect business, medical, educational, library, and church/mosque/synagogue records. To obtain a search warrant authorising the collection of these records, the FBI merely needs to state that the records are related to an ongoing investigation. There is no need for the FBI to show 'probable cause'.

Critics of the Patriot Act warn that its provisions give too many powers to the federal government. Despite language in the Patriot Act to the contrary, civil libertarians are concerned that law enforcement agencies may use their new powers to reduce the rights of law-abiding citizens.

Critics are also concerned that some of its provisions undermine rights guaranteed US citizens under the Fourth Amendment to the Constitution.

6.5 The Data Protection Act, 1998

The present UK Data Protection Act became law in 1998 and superseded the original Act of 1984. The Act is administered and enforced by the Information Commissioner who is appointed by, and answerable to, Parliament. The meaning of data within the Act is:

> ... information relating to a living individual, known as the data subject, which is processed by a person or organisation, known as the data user, using equipment operating automatically in response to instructions – usually, but not necessarily, a computer.

Any organisation processing personal data must comply with the Act. Processing includes collecting, storing, accessing, reformatting, sharing and deleting of information.

The Act therefore applies to government departments, local councils, charities, private companies, the police, health authorities, schools, and many other organisations.

The Act requires that all data users are legally bound to notify or register relevant automated systems giving such information as: name and address of data user and for access requests, source and description of data held or to be held, intended or possible recipients, overseas locations and bureau services. Areas to be notified include personal data on payroll, pensions, personnel files, attendance records, absence, performance, customers, suppliers, accounting and credit control, maintenance and service, training, medical, mailing lists, membership records, data derived from an outside source and telephone monitoring systems.

Under the Act, certain data are exempt from notification. This means it is not necessary to always notify the Information Commissioner of the processing of personal data.

There are three categories of data that are exempt:

- **Text-only preparation:** that is, lists that are not 'processed', collated or manipulated
- **Data held for personal, household and family matters** (for example a Christmas card or CD list). This exemption, however, does not apply to individuals who hold personal data for business or professional purposes
- **National security data:** that is, data related to security and intelligence work that necessarily has to be kept secret.

The underlying principles

Any organisation processing personal data must comply with eight main principles, which state the circumstances under which it is lawful to process personal data. These principles are as given below.

The eight principles of the Data Protection Act, 1998

- **First principle:** Personal data shall be processed fairly and lawfully and, in particular, shall not be processed unless at least one of the conditions in Schedule 2 (see below) is met, and in the case of sensitive personal data, at least one of the conditions in Schedule 3 (see below) is also met.
- **Second principle:** Personal data shall be obtained only for one or more specified and lawful purposes, and shall not be further processed in any manner incompatible with that purpose or those purposes.
- **Third principle:** Personal data shall be adequate, relevant and not excessive in relation to the purpose or purposes for which they are processed.
- **Fourth principle:** Personal data shall be accurate and, where necessary, kept up to date.
- **Fifth principle:** Personal data processed for any purpose or purposes shall not be kept for longer than is necessary for that purpose or those purposes.
- **Sixth principle:** Personal data shall be processed in accordance with the rights of data subjects under this Act.
- **Seventh principle:** Appropriate technical and organisational measures shall be taken against unauthorised or unlawful processing of personal data and against accidental loss or destruction of, or damage to, personal data.
- **Eighth principle:** Personal data shall not be transferred to a country or territory outside the European Economic Area, unless that country or territory ensures an adequate level of protection for the rights and freedoms of data subjects in relation to the processing of personal data.

Organisations in the US are able to comply with the eighth principle by means of the safe harbour arrangement. Commitment to the safe harbour arrangement provides an adequate level of protection for transfers of personal data to the US from EU member states, whereby organisations in the US commit themselves to complying with a set of data protection principles. UK data controllers are also able to transfer personal data to any other non-EU country subject to an EU Community Finding, which considers the data protection laws of that country to ascertain whether they provide adequate protection for personal data transferred from the EU.

The Commission, for example, has adopted a decision to the effect that Switzerland and Hungary provide adequate protection for personal data transferred to those countries from the EU. Over time a number of other countries will appear on the Commission approved list.

Activity 6.2

The eight principles of the Data Protection Act

What is the rationale for the eight main principles of the Data Protection Act?

Explain the principles in your own words, giving specific examples that illustrate each principle.

Other provisions of the Act

There are further provisions in the Act that state the conditions under which the processing of data is allowed (Schedule 2) and special protection for data that is classed as 'sensitive' – such as political or religious affiliation (Schedule 3).

Conditions under which processing is allowed

Schedule 2

At least one of the following conditions must be met in the case of all processing of personal data (except where a relevant exemption applies):

- The data subject has given their consent to the processing
- The processing is necessary:
    1. For the performance of a contract to which the data subject is a party, or
    2. For the taking of steps at the request of the data subject with a view to entering into a contract
- The processing is necessary to comply with any legal obligation to which the data controller is subject, other than an obligation imposed by contract
- The processing is necessary in order to protect the vital interests of the data subject
- The processing is necessary:
    1. For the administration of justice
    2. For the exercise of any functions conferred by or under any enactment
    3. For the exercise of any functions of the Crown, a minister of the Crown or a government department, or
    4. For the exercise of any other functions of a public nature exercised in the public interest
- The processing is necessary for the purposes of legitimate interests pursued by the data controller or by the third party or parties to whom the data are disclosed. However, there is an exception where the processing is unwarranted in any particular case because of prejudice to the rights and freedoms or legitimate interests of the data subject.

Sensitive data

There are restrictions on the holding of sensitive data. If sensitive personal data is being collected, the data subject must give their explicit consent to anything which is done with that data.

Schedule 3

This section of the Act specifies the categories of sensitive personal data that should not be held, as follows:

- The racial or ethnic origin of the data subject
- Their political opinions
- Their religious beliefs or other beliefs of a similar nature
- Whether they are a member of a trade union
- Their physical or mental health or condition
- Their sexual life
- The commission or alleged commission by them of any offence
- Any proceedings for any offence committed or alleged to have been committed by them, the disposal of such proceedings or the sentence of any court in such proceedings.

Rights, and restrictions of rights, of the data subject

We have already briefly discussed the Freedom of Information Act (Section 6.4), whereby organisations are required to inform individuals, upon request, of information they may be holding about them. This right is specified in the Data Protection Act, in the clauses referring to the 'Rights of the Data Subject'.

Data subjects have the following rights:

- The right of information about the processing of their personal data, including the right to be informed either at the time the data is first processed or when that data is first disclosed to a third party
- The right of access to their personal data
- The right to prevent processing likely to cause damage or distress
- The right to prevent processing for the purposes of direct marketing
- The right to prevent decision making solely by automatic means
- The right of compensation for damage or distress arising from failure to comply with the Act
- The right of rectification, blocking, erasure or destruction of personal data where it is inaccurate or which contains an opinion which appears to be based on inaccurate data.

The data subject must make a written request to the data controller clearly specifying the requirement. The latter must respond within 40 days, but the data subject may be charged a nominal fee (currently £10) for all data. The data subject may request that any incorrect data is corrected or erased to comply with the eight principles. Failure can lead to a case before a tribunal or by court order. Compensation will be given, based on provable damages in the event of a breach of any one of the eight principles. Breaches of the law by companies may lead to liability of the 'body corporate'. However, an individual director may become liable if he/she is personally party to any offence under the Act.

There are also certain occasions when the data subject's rights of access are restricted. These are set out as follows.

Restrictions of access

Data to which access by the data subject is restricted include the following:

- Criminal, tax and immigration control
- Legal and professional privilege
- Physical, mental and social work data
- Employment by or under the Crown
- Confidential references
- Management forecasting and planning, and
- Intentions in negotiations with the data subject.

The Data Protection Act: a good idea – but is it good enough?

Some of the main criticisms of the Data Protection Act that have been voiced include the following:

- Whereas large companies, especially in regulated areas such as financial services, exhibit a high level of compliance with the Act, other companies do not. Many companies and organisations have yet to notify (register) under the Data Protection Act, and until all major organisations do, the effectiveness of the Act will be limited
- The Act has no 'teeth' – powers of enforcement and sanctions for non-compliance are weak
- The Act contains many exemptions and 'get-out' clauses; for example, the Home Secretary has the power to exempt any information from disclosure, and such exemptions do not have to be justified
- The Official Secrets Act overrides the Data Protection Act in many instances, for example by forbidding unauthorised disclosure of information handled by the government
- Individuals have no right of appeal to the Data Protection Tribunal
- The Act only covered manual, paper-based data with effect from October 2007 (an important omission, as such data could be sent overseas to be entered into computer databases, and thereby escape compliance with the Act)
- It is difficult for the data subject to find out what data is held about them, who has access to that data, and how it is used. To find out such information, the data subject is required to write to the data protection officer of an organisation, which can currently charge up to £10 for each request. Yet the responsibility to verify accuracy of any personal data that is held is the data subject's and not the data holder's
- Overall, the balance is firmly in favour of the data holder, for example companies and organisations, rather than the data subject.

Activity 6.3

RFID and the Data Protection Act

Imagine you are the owner of a chain of clothing stores, and you are planning to use RFID technology in your stores by embedding RFID chips inside all your product lines. What steps would you need to take as a retailer to ensure that your use of RFID complies with the Data Protection Act?

Activity 6.4

The case of Innovations

Read the following scenario (taken from Ayres [1999]):

> Innovations was a mail order company which also sold lists of its customers' names and addresses to other companies. It obtained a significant proportion of its revenue from this source. Innovations' advertising did not specify that customer details would be sold on to other companies. Instead, when customers ordered something from Innovations they would receive an acknowledgement slip. On the back of the slip there was a notice that the company sold address lists to other companies and that the customer could prevent their own details being sold on in this way by writing in.

Does the business practice of Innovations comply with the Data Protection Act?

6.6 Professional and ethical issues

In previous chapters we have discussed to role of the British Computer Society in connection with setting the professional standards of competence, conduct and ethical practice for computing in the UK. The BCS code of practice includes statements which address the issue of privacy. Accordingly, computing professionals must 'take all reasonable measures to protect confidential information from inadvertent or deliberate improper access or use'. Computing professionals must also 'ensure that competent people are assigned to be responsible for the accuracy and integrity of the data in the data file and each part of an organisation's database'.

The US Association for Computing Machinery (ACM) has similar codes that state that computing professionals have a general moral imperative to respect the privacy of others. Moral Imperative 1.7, *Respect the privacy of others* explicitly states that:

> Computing and communication technology enables the collection and exchange of personal information on a scale unprecedented in the history of civilization. Thus there is increased potential for violating the privacy of individuals and groups. It is the responsibility of professionals to maintain the privacy and integrity of data describing individuals. This includes taking precautions to ensure the accuracy of data, as well as protecting it from unauthorized access or accidental disclosure to inappropriate individuals. Furthermore, procedures must be established to allow individuals to review their records and correct inaccuracies.

www.acm.org/constitution/code.html#sect1 [Accessed 05/07]

> This imperative implies that only the necessary amount of personal information be collected in a system, that retention and disposal periods for that information be clearly defined and enforced, and that personal information gathered for a specific purpose not be used for other purposes without consent of the individual(s). These principles apply to all electronic communications, including e-mail, and prohibit procedures that capture or monitor electronic user data, including messages, without the permission of users or bona fide authorization related to system operation and maintenance. User data observed during the normal duties of system operation and maintenance must be treated with strictest confidentiality, except in cases where it is evidence for the violation of law or organisational regulations. In these cases, the nature or contents of that information must be disclosed only to proper authorities.

Civil liberties versus state duties

There has been a long tug of war over the issue of privacy, between the perceived duties of the state (to preserve law and order and national security) and the rights of individuals to fundamental democratic freedoms. Government and law enforcement agencies have consistently argued that in order to combat criminal and terrorist activity they need be able to view any information (either stored or in transmission).

In the US there is a long history of covert, and illegal, domestic surveillance by federal agencies. During the 1960s and 1970s, far-reaching efforts were made by the FBI and other government intelligence agencies to keep track of civil rights activists and many other Americans (many of whom were opponents of the Vietnam war). Abuses included wiretappings (interception of telephone conversations), bugging (use of hidden microphones for surveillance), mail openings, burglaries, harassment, and questionable use of personal records.

The National Security Agency, formed in 1952, has coordinated, directed, and performed highly specialised activities to protect US information systems and produce foreign intelligence information. A high-technology organisation, NSA has long been on the frontiers of communications and data processing. In 1990 it was reputed that it had the computing capability to intercept and analyse over 70 per cent of all telephone, telex, data and radio transmissions worldwide.

Similar security and intelligence agencies exist in the UK, such as MI5, MI6, GCHQ and others. There is a growing trend towards the consolidation and integration of different government databases holding data on UK citizens. Proposals for a central national database of all UK residents and a national identity card system are part of this trend. Such proposals have been taking shape for some years, but have been accelerated by the terrorists attacks on the US of 11 September, 2001 and the increasing concern about similar terrorist threats in the UK. The Home Secretary's White Paper proposed the setting up of a central national database of the 67.5 million people resident in Britain, combined with a computerised national identification card system.

The intention is to include on the identity register, such particulars as an individual's name, date and place of birth, home address, National Insurance number, passport and driving licence numbers, nationality, sex, digitised signature, employment status, together with a photograph and a unique personal identification number. There have also been proposals to include biometric information such as a fingerprint or retina scan. The card would allow accurate verification of a person's identity when interacting with government agencies and for transactions such as credit card purchases, medical treatment and banking. A more expansive identity card scheme has been proposed that would involve the use of a two-dimensional barcode or a memory chip to store additional information, such as details of a person's medical condition (such as epilepsy or diabetes) that might be helpful to an ambulance crew.

The threat to privacy

Concerns about the threats to individual privacy and freedom represented by growing state power are nothing new. George Orwell's novel, *Nineteen Eighty-Four*, published in 1949, was an elaborate satire on modern politics that prophesied a future world in which every aspect of life is controlled by an authoritarian state government, personified in the figure of Big Brother. In this world, citizens are watched every minute of the day via 'telescreens' installed in all homes and public places. One of that government's slogans is 'Big Brother is Watching You'. The book's hero, Winston Smith, tries to resist but is arrested and tortured by the Thought Police. Orwell attempted to warn of what might happen if a strong central government was taken to its logical extreme. Concerns about the encroachment of a Big Brother state have increased in recent years.

Various civil liberties groups have questioned whether governments require more powers, and have tried to highlight the accompanying cost of these powers, in terms of the loss of privacies and freedoms. Civil liberties groups such as *Privacy International* and the *Electronic Frontier Foundation* (EFF) attempt to ensure that privacy rights are protected as new communications technologies emerge.

With regard to identity cards, civil liberties groups have raised concerns about what kind of data, and how much data, will be stored on such cards. The fear is that of 'data creep' – what will start out as a basic identity card will end up as an all-purpose database on each of us. Opponents of national ID cards argue that they might be used to keep tabs on anyone considered a 'threat' to national security, to control immigration, or to prevent legitimate entrants from working and claiming social security benefits.

Civil liberties groups have been concerned about the threat to privacy posed not only by governments but also by private corporations. They question the right of a company to hold personal information about individuals, the right to deny access to that information, and the right to sell it to other organisations without the consent or knowledge of those individuals.

A key principle advocated by civil liberties groups, with regard to the collection and use of personal data, is that of informed consent, which means when an individual agrees to something, they should be 'informed' (based on accurate information and an understanding of the issues). If information is deliberately withheld or is incomplete, then consent is given under false pretences and is invalid.

In conclusion, many social commentators argue that society is a finely balanced equilibrium of the rights and obligations of the individual, versus the rights and obligations of the state. Privacy involves a balancing act between the power of the state, the interests of private companies, and the rights of individual citizens. Privacy scholar Alan Westin describes the factors to be balanced as follows (Baase, 2003):

- Safeguarding personal and group privacy, in order to protect individuality and freedom against unjustified intrusions by authorities
- Collecting relevant personal information essential for rational decision making in social, commercial, and governmental life
- Conducting the constitutionally limited government surveillance of people and activities necessary to protect public order and safety.

Activity 6.5

Restricted information

There is a long history of the state protecting people from information they ought not to possess. Based on the exemptions stated in the Human Rights Act and the Freedom of Information Act, make a list of the types of information that citizens ought not to be able to access.

6.7 An ethical dilemma

Consider the scenario in which a group of your fellow students approach you to see whether you are interested in participating in a project that is intended to be a commercial venture. The group has come up with a novel approach to obtaining large numbers of e-mail addresses. This requires the development of some software, and once this is used it will be possible to develop a very extensive e-mail address list. Subsequently, this information is to be sold to companies involved in spam advertising. You voice some initial reservations based upon your concern that this may not be entirely legal/ethical. However, you are assured that the software will only be used to obtain e-mail addresses for people who are normally based overseas – specifically in third world countries. Since the team is to be based in the UK and the software is going to be used to locate e-mail addresses that are normally based outside the UK, you are assured that you will be breaking no UK law.

How would you proceed? Do you consider that this is a legal/ethical undertaking? In the case that you are not entirely happy with the possible ethical aspects of this venture (but are satisfied that you will not be breaking UK law), would you still be willing to participate if the level of remuneration is sufficient? At what point would personal remuneration override any ethical reservations that you may have?

Let us suppose that you do become involved in this undertaking but that you subsequently find that the software that you helped to develop is not only being used to locate e-mail addresses that are normally based outside the UK, but in addition e-mail addresses within the UK, and these are being sold on to companies who specialise in spam advertising? Does this compromise your legal position?

6.8 Summary

This chapter has explored the issue of privacy within the context of computer technology. We began by thinking about the notion of privacy – how to define it, and why we value it? We then explored the implications of computer technology for privacy, particularly for the collection, analysis and use of personal information by different organisations and government bodies. We examined specific computer and Internet technologies that pose a threat to our privacy, including cookies, spam and RFID. Subsequently, we looked at some of the legislation that affirms the right to privacy. In particular, we focused on the main UK legislation regarding privacy issues – the Data Protection Act. We highlighted the key principles and provisions of the Act, specifically how it covers the processing, use and misuse of personal data. We then explored some of the professional and ethical issues raised around privacy, particularly debates about how to balance our privacy rights and civil liberties with commercial interests and the duties of the state.

6.9 Review questions

Review question 6.1

What are the three elements of 'privacy'?

Review question 6.2

Explain the following terms, giving specific examples:

- Secondary use of personal information
- Profiling
- Data matching.

Review question 6.3

Explain what 'cookies' are, and how they have an impact on our privacy.

Review question 6.4

What is 'spam'? Explain how it might be considered a threat to privacy.

Review question 6.5

What is the difference between an 'opt-in' and an 'opt-out' policy with regard to the use of personal data for marketing purposes?

Review question 6.6

Name the US and UK legislations which uphold the right to privacy.

Review question 6.7

What are some of the main concerns voiced by civil liberties groups and others about the Regulation of Investigatory Powers Act?

Review question 6.8

What are the categories of sensitive personal data under Schedule 3 of the Data Protection Act?

6.10 Feedback on activities

Feedback on activity 6.1

DoubleClick is an online advertising service that sells ads on over 1,500 websites. It became the centre of a highly publicised controversy in 2000. DoubleClick used cookies to track users' browsing actions across thousands of the most popular Internet sites. When someone visited a website that had contracted with one of these companies, a cookie containing a unique identification number was deposited on their computer's hard drive. This cookie was used to track the user's browsing habits and preferences as they moved among the hundreds of sites that contracted with the ad network.

Concerns were expressed that this kind of tracking was violating Internet users' privacy. In early 2000 these fears were confirmed when DoubleClick paid $1 billion for Abacus Direct, a marketing database company that possessed detailed information on 120 million US households. DoubleClick announced that it would begin a new programme to combine its Internet and Abacus databases. Consumers who disliked such monitoring could opt out of the tracking by visiting the company's website.

DoubleClick's announcement resulted in a massive public outcry, a series of lawsuits, and the threat of an investigation from the US Federal Trade Commission (FTC). Faced with strong criticism by privacy advocates and investigations by government agencies, DoubleClick dropped the plan.

In an about-face, a group of major online advertising companies, led by DoubleClick, agreed to give consumers advanced notice and choice about how marketers used their information collected online. The companies also agreed to ban the use of sensitive information, including medical information and sexual orientation, for marketing. They agreed to give consumers access to the information collected about them and to give consumers an opportunity to opt out before information collected online is combined with offline information.

Feedback on activity 6.2

First principle

Personal data shall be processed fairly and lawfully and shall not be processed unless one of the following conditions outlined in Schedule 2 is met:

- The data subject must give their consent to the processing

- The processing must be necessary for the performance of a contract to which the data subject is a party

- The data subject wishes to enter into a contract with the data controller

- The processing is necessary to comply with any legal obligation to which the data controller is subject

- The processing is necessary to protect the vital interests of the data subject.

Also note, however, the exceptions, where processing is unwarranted because of prejudice to the rights and freedoms or legitimate interests of the data subject.

The first principle also refers to Schedule 3 which lists the categories of 'sensitive' data that should not be processed (at least not without the explicit consent of the data subject).

Second principle

Personal data should be obtained only for one or more specified and lawful purposes, and shall not be further processed in any manner incompatible with that purpose or those purposes. This means that data cannot be obtained for one specified purpose and then used for a different, unspecified purpose, particularly if it is unlawful.

Third principle

Personal data should be adequate, relevant and not excessive in relation to the purpose or purposes for which they are processed. For example:

- A routine form (a request to be put on a mailing list perhaps) that requests personal data that is excessive and irrelevant (income, marital status)

- An online store which needs to know a credit card number and name in order to conduct business, but not necessarily a National Insurance number.

Fourth principle

If information is wrong, it gives a misleading picture of the person. For example, a debt from the past (which has now been paid) would affect future applications for credit.

Fifth principle

Records of transactions, job applications and other personal data should not be kept longer than necessary, and should, in many cases, be destroyed after a specified period of time.

Sixth principle

Personal data shall be processed in accordance with the rights of data subjects. This means that in any processing of data, data subjects have the following rights, among others:

- Right of access to one's personal data

- Right to rectify or erase personal data where inaccurate

- Right to be informed when data is first processed or disclosed to third party

- Right to prevent processing for purposes of direct marketing

- Right to prevent decision making solely by automatic means (for example, automated sifting of CVs of job applicants or for loan assessments)

- Right to compensation for damage or distress arising from failure to comply with Act.

Seventh principle

Appropriate technical and organisational measures shall be taken against unauthorised or unlawful processing of personal data and against accidental loss or destruction of, or damage to, personal data. To comply with this principle, computer professionals need to:

• Secure personal data from external and internal damage

• Secure personal data from unauthorised access (hacking, for example), with appropriate security measures

• Manage any personal data properly, with adequate back-ups, disaster recovery plans

• Have procedures for deleting old or irrelevant data.

Eighth principle

This maintains that if data is to be sold or transferred to another country outside the EU, that country must have a similar framework of data protection in place to that of the Data Protection Act. For example, if you worked for an international organisation (such as a charity) processing the personal data of UK citizens you would need to ensure that such data was not passed on or transferred to another country outside the EU which had no data protection legislation.

Feedback on activity 6.3

Assuming that the data gathered from RFID is 'personal data,' one of the key requirements of the first principle of the Data Protection Act is that any personal data must be obtained in a fair and lawful manner, and that there must be one of the statutory justifications for processing the personal data set out in Schedule 2 of the Act. The two justifications that seem most relevant are that either the individual has consented to the processing of the data or that processing of such data is 'necessary for the purposes of the retailer's legitimate interests'. However, there is also a question as to whether the legitimacy of the interests pursued by the retailer are warranted in the light of any prejudice that may be caused to the rights, freedoms or legitimate interests of the data subject.

If one looks at the primary usage of RFID tags – the processing of personal data in order to prevent shoplifting or to manage the supply chain – this would seem to constitute a legitimate interest. Also, an argument could be made that the processing of RFID data for marketing purposes is in the legitimate interests of the retailer. However, in the context of the use of the RFID data to track product location for marketing purposes, any related processing of personal data could be regarded as being unnecessarily prejudicial to the rights and freedoms of the individual.

The safest route for a retailer using RFID would be to obtain the individual's consent to the processing of RFID data. The retailer should be able to achieve this by clearly notifying the consumer that RFID tags will be used and therefore personal data will be processed. Also, as part of this process, the retailer will need to notify the consumer of the purposes for which the RFID data will be processed. All this information could be presented on the packaging of the goods or on a sign next to the goods. The consumer then faces a simple choice: either to buy the goods and thereby consent to the processing of RFID data or not to buy the goods.

However, if the retailer justifies the processing of the RFID data they will have to supply certain basic information to consumers about the use of such data, in particular the identity of the party who intends to process the RFID data, and the purposes for which the data will be processed. In order to comply with the DPA therefore, retailers should probably inform the consumers that the RFID data may be used to track the location of the product, or even the consumer, both within and outside the shop and may even be combined with other personal data such as credit card or loyalty card details.

Feedback on activity 6.4

To comply with the Data Protection Act, companies should state whether any personal data that is being gathered would be shared with third parties such as other companies, credit references agencies and direct marketing companies. Prior consent of the user must be obtained before sending any direct marketing material. Prior consent has not been sought in this case. In addition, data subjects have the right to be informed when data is first processed or disclosed to a third party. Again, this is not happening in this particular case. Having to write in to the company to prevent one's personal details from being passed on to other companies makes it difficult for the customer to 'opt out.' Innovations could also be seen as contravening the first principle of the Data Protection Act because the primary purpose for which the data is being gathered (to sell the data on to other companies) is different to the one specified (selling goods by mail order).

Feedback on activity 6.5

Information the citizen ought not to have could include the following:

- Classified and sensitive information pertaining to national defence and security

- Scientific or economic information serving the interests of the state

- Information which upon disclosure would prejudicially affect public safety and order

- Information which may lead to an incitement to commit an offence or prejudicially affect fair trial or adjudication of a pending case

- Trade or commercial secrets protected by law; or information, the disclosure of which would prejudicially affect the legitimate economic and commercial interests or the competitive position of the state

- Information which could prejudicially affect the conduct of central and state governments if disclosed, including information exchanged in confidence between them

- The minutes or records of advice including legal advice, opinions or recommendations made by state officials during the decision-making process prior to government decision or policy formulation.

References

Ayres, R (1999), *The Essence of Professional issues in Computing*, Prentice-Hall.

Baase, S (2003), *A Gift of Fire: Social, Legal and Ethical Issues for Computers and the Internet*, Pearson.

Brown, A (2003), RFID Tags, *Computers & Law*, Dec 2003/Jan 2004, **www.scl.org**

Quinn, M (2004), *Ethics for the Information Age*, Addison Wesley.

Further reading

Ayres, R (1999) *The Essence of Professional issues in Computing*, (Chapter 8), Prentice-Hall.

Baase, S (2003), *A Gift of Fire: Social, Legal and Ethical Issues for Computers and the Internet*, (Chapter 9), Pearson.

Robinson, D & Garratt, C (2004), *Introducing Ethics*, Icon Books Ltd.

CHAPTER 7

Computer technologies: accessibility issues

OVERVIEW

This chapter highlights issues relating to equitable access to computer technologies: that is, the right of any individual to have an equal opportunity to use such systems. A fundamental premise is that information and communication technology (ICT) forms the infrastructure of today's society – in the developed world it underpins almost every activity, and every business. Therefore, for the purposes of this chapter, we assume that anyone who is denied access is at a disadvantage.

There are a number of groups who, in one way or another, find access difficult. These are the poor, the illiterate (or computer-illiterate), people with disabilities, and those living in countries without the necessary technical infrastructure. This gap between those who have IT access and those who do not is often referred to as the 'digital divide'. The digital divide is a social issue. For some groups it is also a legal issue (where groups are legally entitled to equal opportunity – people with disabilities for example). It is also a professional issue, not least because of the design aspects. For example, depiction of content in a small font size can be disadvantageous to people with poor eyesight.

In this chapter we will be discussing the principle of equal access and will review the legislation that supports this principle. We will show, through studying the particular case of disabled people, the obstacles to equality and we also look at the means to overcome these obstacles. The role of the professional is a crucial one in addressing this issue, and throughout the chapter we highlight areas where professionals working within the computer industry can make a difference.

Learning outcomes   At the end of this chapter you should be able to:

- Understand the principle of equal access

- Have knowledge of relevant legislation and international initiatives for equal rights

- Recognise the distinction between the medical and social models of disability

- Appreciate the role of the professional in the construction of an enabling environment

- Have knowledge of assistive and enabling technologies.

7.1 Introduction

In this chapter we will be looking at the broad issue of equal access to ICT. John Perry Barlow, was, in its early days, a well-known promoter of the Internet and the World Wide Web; he wrote:

> We are creating a world that all may enter without privilege or prejudice accorded by race, economic power, military force, or station of birth.

The quotation was based on the belief of universal, and equal, access to the Internet, but in hindsight is perhaps somewhat naïve. The fact that the Internet is a global network means that in principle it can be accessible by anyone. However, as we shall see in this chapter, there are a number of obstacles that prevent the Utopian vision described by Barlow.

To begin with, we shall present the argument for the right to equal access for individuals, and the international drive for universal access, that is, to bring IT to less developed countries.

We will look at the obstacles to universal and equal access, and point to the impact these obstacles have on certain groups of people. We shall see that in some cases it is the design of the technology that provides the impediment, and will briefly discuss how this may be overcome. Finally, we assess the role of the professional in removing obstacles to access, and promoting equality as a right.

7.2 Principle of equal access

The principle of equal access to ICT is based on the claim that all people have a right to access this technology. How do we justify this claim – after all, we would not claim that everyone has a right to a video recorder or car! What is different about ICT?

The argument put forward is that in this 'information age' anyone that does not have access is disadvantaged in a number of ways. Jeremy Moss (2002) indicates that people without access are disadvantaged because:

- Their access to knowledge is significantly limited
- Their ability to fully participate in the political process and to receive important information is greatly diminished, and
- Their economic prospects are severely hindered.

In other words, in this day and age access to this technology is almost a fundamental prerequisite for fully participating in society. Consider the move to online banking. If the trend for online services continues, and high street facilities are reduced as a result, anyone who does not have online access will be restricted from banking. Similarly, there is currently a move to online voting – how can anyone place their vote if they do not have ICT access? The easy answer is to provide access in public places – such as libraries, or Internet cafes – but as we will see, accessibility is not just about providing the technical resources.

The argument for a right to equal access rests on the extent to which citizens in a given society need to have access to ICT to function in a society. For example, in the UK, people who do not have access to computer technology are thought to be at a disadvantage because there are certain services they are not able to get access to, and many jobs depend on computer skills. But what of countries where citizens have adequate access to education, political participation, and job opportunities in more traditional ways?

In these circumstances the citizens do not appear to be at a disadvantage, and we can question whether equal access should be thought of as a right. People who argue for the right to equal access would say that, in a global context, ICT is so influential that the right of access should be universal, that is, all people in the world should be able to have access to ICT. There has been a great deal of discussion to promote universal access, and various initiatives have been taken to get this technology into developing countries.

Although the question of universal access is a legitimate one, and should be of wider concern to the computer professional, it is beyond the scope of this book. The remainder of this chapter concentrates on aspects of equal access for individuals, and in particular examines the difficulties of access for people with disabilities.

7.3 Obstacles to access for individuals

We said earlier that accessibility is not just about providing the technical resources – although clearly this is the first step. Anyone who uses ICT needs to be physically and mentally competent, and if they want to connect from home must have the financial means to:

- Buy the equipment
- Pay for a connection.

The alternative is, for example to gain connectivity via workplace equipment or a public library. If they use either of these two options, they must be able to travel. Language is another major obstacle that receives little attention in the English-speaking world. Finally, they must also have the motivation – that is, they either want to use ICT, or they need to use it.

Following on from the above we can, in general terms, identify groups unlikely to have equal access (see Figure 7.1).

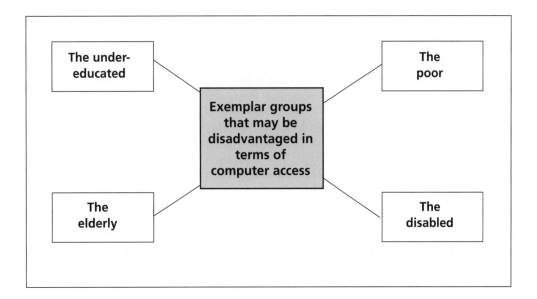

Figure 7.1: Exemplar groups which may be disadvantaged in terms of their ability to access ICT. See text for discussion.

The obstacles to access are not insurmountable and in many cases there are very simple measures that can be taken that would provide equal opportunity, and for some people this would make a tremendous difference to their lives. To illustrate this, we focus our discussion on the disabled, and show how this issue is one of social and professional responsibility rather than individual misfortune. We begin with a brief look at the recent legislation.

Activity 7.1

Obstacles to equal access

Imagine you have to write an essay and e-mail it to your tutor. Think about the skills you will need to employ and the equipment you will need use.

(a) List both key skills and necessary equipment.

However, anyone who does not have these skills, or equipment, would have difficult in accessing the Internet.

(b) Make a second list of the people who are unlikely to have access to the Internet because of a lack of skills, or equipment.

7.4 Legislation

In the preceding sections we have put forward the argument that equal access is a valid principle. This view is supported by legislation – in broad terms by the Human Rights Act, (1998) and, in relation to the disabled, by the Disability Discrimination Act, (2005).

The Human Rights Act, 1998 states that individuals should not be discriminated against on any ground such as '... sex, race, colour, language, religion, political or other opinion, national or social origin, association with a national minority, property, birth or other status'. In addition, individuals have a 'right not to be denied access to education'.

In the case of the disabled, the relevant words in the Act are 'other status'. The supporting legislation in the UK for people with disabilities is the Disability Discrimination Act, 2005 (DDA). This Act defines a disabled person as an individual with a:

> ... physical (including sensory) impairment or mental impairment which has a substantial and long term adverse effect on his/her ability to carry out normal day-to-day activities.

The Act protects disabled people in:

- Employment
- Access to goods, facilities and services
- The management, buying or renting of land or property
- Education.

Regarding employment, the DDA requires the employer to make 'reasonable adjustments' for a disabled person or employee if they are at a substantial disadvantage in relation to a non-disabled person. Specifically, it is 'unlawful for an employer to treat a disabled applicant or employee less favourably than others because of their disability'.

Part of the DDA made provision for the setting up of the Disability Rights Commission. The Disability Rights Commission (DRC) is an independent body established in April 2000 by Act of Parliament to stop discrimination and promote equality of opportunity for disabled people.

It sets out its vision as:

'A society where all disabled people can participate fully as equal citizens.'

source: **www.drc-gb.org**

Activity 7.2

Legislation

Go to a university or company homepage (for example, Middlesex University) and determine what the organisation does to comply with the Disability Discrimination Act, 2005.

Answer the following questions:

Is the information readily available and easy to find?

Does the organisation make 'reasonable adjustments' for students or employees with disabilities?

What specifically does the organisation offer for students or employees with disabilities?

7.5 Enabling the disabled

Changing perspectives

So far in this chapter we have used terms such as 'the disabled' and 'people with disabilities'. This has been a deliberate choice in that this is common terminology and descriptions that the majority of people use and understand. This terminology is, however, very contentious in that it places the focus on the person and implies that they are somehow responsible for their unequal status. The preferred terminology is 'people with impairments' – we explain why below.

The following explanation of the distinction between disability and impairment was given by Geoff Busby and Diane Whitehouse in a presentation given to the International Federation for Information Processing Working Group 9.2 on Computers and Social Accountability (June 2001). Dr Geoff Busby is the British Computer Society Advisor on Disability Issues.

The British Council of Disabled People (BCODP) has used the following definitions to distinguish between disability and impairments, and clarify who are disabled people.

Disability is the disadvantage or restriction of activity caused by a society which takes little or no account of people who have impairments, and thus excludes them from a mainstream activity. Therefore, disability, like racism or sexism, is discrimination and social oppression.

Impairment is functional limitation within an individual caused by a physical, mental or sensory condition.

Disabled people are therefore those people with impairments who are disabled by society. Busby [2001]

These two different perspectives on disability – the first that says people are 'disabled', and the second that says 'society is disabling' – are known respectively as the medical model of disability and the social model of disability. These two models are important in that the consequences of each view are very different, and have a tremendous impact on how we, as a society, confront the issue.

The medical model is the traditional and most common view of disability and, as we have pointed out, places the emphasis on the person. This has resulted in a general conception of the disabled person as a victim – someone who has some condition which we sympathise with (and are relieved that we do not have). To remove the problem these people face, we would need to remove the medical condition.

The alternative view – that of the social model – places the emphasis on the way society is physically constructed. So, to reiterate content in the above quotation, disabled people are: 'people with impairments who are disabled by society'. The solution to this problem is to design society in a different way.

In the words of Geoff Busby [2001]:

> These two models show how important preconceptions and definitions are, and how important it is for technologists to take note of the difference.

Enabling technology

The discussion above raises the issue of design, and its enabling or disabling effects. We only have to think how we use computer technology to see the physical and cognitive expertise we must utilise. Using a computer to write this chapter requires looking at a screen, reading the text, using the keyboard, and reading the printouts. To do this on standard equipment requires good eyesight and manual dexterity as the keys on the keyboard are set quite closely together. Someone with impaired vision and/or arthritis in the hands (a condition that severely limits movement) would find it extremely difficult, if not impossible, to perform these actions.

If we think of computers as input/output devices, we need to think about how input and output are produced and what this means to people who cannot use standard equipment. Technologists have been, and still are, addressing this issue. There are a variety of ways of inputting data and accessing output that go some way to meeting various needs. Examples are listed below:

Ways to input data

- Keyboard
- Braille keyboard (for the visually impaired)
- Mouse (various designs)
- Stylus pen
- Voice recognition software
- Touch screen
- Devices that respond to touch (so, for example, the head can be used to touch a device that instructs the computer to perform an action).

Ways of accessing output

- Reading the screen: text magnification, colour choice
- Text-to-voice software
- Braille printout.

The broader consequences of equal access

We can assume then that the broader consequences of equal access for the disabled are equal access to information and the opportunity of equal participation in communication.

Some people with disabilities have problems communicating; technology can help. For example, someone who has difficulty speaking can communicate via e-mail, and can give presentations using text-to-voice software.

Physical presence is not necessary to communicate. This has an impact in two ways:

- Preconceptions and prejudices are removed. Society has a tendency to treat people who they see as disabled in a different way. Physical anonymity enables equality in communication
- Modern communication technology, particularly the Internet, allows people to 'join in' from a distance. Some people find it easier to stay at home – either because travelling is difficult, or because they need access to special equipment/medication. Therefore, computer technology opens access to work and education.

To illustrate the effectiveness of the Internet as a means of communication for people with disabilities, we relate the story of Hero Joy Nightingale, a teenager who can only communicate with hand gestures, interpreted by her mother. Through the medium of the Internet she has been able to produce an online magazine, *From the Window* (**www.atschool.eduweb.co.uk/ hojoy/**). She says (Dixon (2002):

> From the Window … has restored my energy and optimism … taught me huge amounts about journalism and IT … I have passion not passivity, demand a right to participate, to grow into a contributing member of our global society, to be an artist.

Activity 7.3

Enabling the disabled

For this activity you are asked to do some research on technologies that are available to help the disabled to use computer technology. Using a search engine, type in the keywords 'assistive technology', and visit some websites of your choice. Identify four different technologies that are available to help people with disabilities to use a computer.

In the case of each technology that you have chosen, what particular impairment(s) is it designed to overcome and in what way(s) is it helpful?

7.6 Professional responsibility

Throughout this chapter we have emphasised the relevance of the equal access issues to computing professionals. Professionals, as experts in their field, have an obligation to consider the impact of their activities on those who are affected by their decisions. We might also say that they have a wider moral obligation to society to improve, where possible, the lives of others.

In the context of this discussion the professional has a responsibility to:

- Uphold the values of the society in which he/she operates
- Recognise and abide by the relevant legislation
- Promote the good for the public at large, and vulnerable groups in particular.

In the section on the public interest, The British Computer Society Code of Conduct takes into account the right to equal treatment as discussed in this chapter. The relevant clauses are:

- You shall have regard to the legitimate rights of third parties
- You shall ensure that within your professional field(s) you have knowledge and understanding of relevant legislation, regulations and standards, and that you comply with such requirements
- You shall conduct your professional activities without discrimination against clients or colleagues.

The above principles are very general, and are intended to be for guidance only. Of course, the specific field in which a computer professional works will dictate how the principles may be put into practice. For example, the web designer should take into account accessibility issues and consider users who have visual impairments, the programmer should make provision for alternative user interfaces, and the systems administrator should be aware of alternative assistive technologies. Professionals working in the field of smaller devices – mobile phones and PDAs for example – need to consider input functions (such as the small keys) and the reduced size of the display. As we have seen from the above discussion concerning enabling technologies, thinking in terms of access to input and output is quite a useful approach.

Making provision for disadvantaged groups and promoting equal access is not just about being a 'good' professional; in the case of providing for disabled people, it is a legal requirement.

7.7 An ethical dilemma

So far in this chapter we have not paid any particular attention to the impact of ICT on older people – people who have previously lived within a fairly stable environment. Today the momentum of change (in which computer-based technologies play a pivotal role) is ever-increasing. Consequently, older people are becoming ever more concerned and bewildered by the constant alterations that are occurring in practically every aspect of their daily lives. Stability is being replaced by instability. As younger people embrace e-mail, cellular phones, text messaging and the like, the older generations see their post offices closing, no longer is there any personal contact at the bank, and who knows for how much longer they will be able to use a chequebook?

- *How do you perceive the ramifications of computer-based technologies, and the current pace of change impacting on older people?*

- *To what extent are they becoming increasingly isolated?*

- *Is direct personal contact being gradually eroded?*

- *Perhaps discuss these issues with an older person that you know, such as a family member. Identify key issues.*

- *Have these people gained as a consequence of the proliferation of and reliance we place upon computer-based technologies and the pace of change that has ensued?*

7.8 Summary

In this chapter we have briefly discussed issues relating to equal access to computer technology. Essentially, this concerns the right of any individual to have an equal opportunity to the use of computer technology. Based on the premise that information and communication technology (ICT) forms the infrastructure of today's society, it has been argued that anyone who is denied access is at a disadvantage.

There are a number of groups who, in one way or another, find access difficult. These are often the poor, the illiterate (or computer-illiterate), people with disabilities, and those living in countries without the necessary technical infrastructure.

We have discussed the principle of equal access and reviewed the legislation that supports it. In addition, we have highlighted the particular case of disabled people, the obstacles to equality and we have briefly examined means to overcome those obstacles. The role of the professional is crucial in addressing the issue of accessibility, and throughout the chapter we have highlighted the areas where the professional can make a difference.

7.9 Review questions

 **Review question 7.1**

There is an argument that in this 'information age' anyone that does not have access is disadvantaged in a number of ways. Give three reasons why people without access are disadvantaged.

Review question 7.2

In your own words, explain the difference between the 'medical' and 'social' models of disability.

Review question 7.3

According to Geoff Busby [2001], 'Disabled people are those people with impairments who are disabled by society'. As a professional, you should try to make things better. In what ways could you make a difference?

7.10 Feedback on activities

Feedback on activity 7.1

Anyone who uses ICT needs to be physically and mentally competent, and if they want to connect from home must have the financial means to

a) buy the equipment and

b) pay for a connection – unless they use workplace equipment or a public library. If they use either of the latter two options, they must be able to travel. Language is another major obstacle that receives little attention in the English-speaking world. Finally, they must also have the motivation – that is, they either want to use it, or they need to use it.

Following from the above, we could say that generally the groups of people who are unlikely to have equal opportunity for access are:

- The disabled

- The uneducated

- The poor

- The elderly

- Women.

Some are disadvantaged mainly due to the lack of computer training; in the case of the elderly, possibly because of reduced physical or mental capabilities, and lack of motivation. Many elderly people cannot see the need and as a result are not interested in going 'online'; in the case of women, the technology is generally designed from a male perspective, and perhaps does not appeal to some women (Tavani, 2004).

Feedback on activity 7.2

If we use the example of Middlesex university:

Is the information readily available and easy to find? *Not really. A search has to be done. The url for information on students with disabilities is:* **www.mdx.ac.uk/disability/ index.htm**

Does the University make 'reasonable adjustments' for students with disabilities? *Physical environment: 80% of buildings are accessible to wheelchairs. The University recommends that prospective students with mobility difficulties visit the campus where they would be studying before confirming acceptance of a place. Trent Park has particular access difficulties (because of special planning constraints). Therefore it would seem that students with mobility difficulties would be restricted from studying the courses that are offered from Trent Park. However, there is a continuing programme of improving accessibility.*

What specifically does the University offer for students with disabilities? *A support service that can offer help with Disabled Students Allowances: they offer an educational support service, support for dyslexic students, and specialist equipment. They can assess student requirements and can provide specialist equipment where necessary. The University also runs courses for staff on a variety of topics relating to teaching students with special needs.*

Feedback on activity 7.3

For the purposes of this exercise the following devices were found:

Example 1:

Brand Name: HEADMOUSE FOR PORTABLES

Description: The HeadMouse for Portables is a head-controlled optical pointing device designed to act as a mouse emulator for individuals who have physical disabilities and have no or little control of their upper limbs but have good head control.

Designed to overcome: This device helps people with physical disabilities that cause them to have little control of arms/hands, but who have good head control.

What it does: The device is worn on the head and acts in the same way as a mouse – that is, the laser light can be pointed at a particular place on the screen.

How it is helpful: This overcomes the difficulties of input that the traditional mouse devices would create.

Example 2: BOOK PORT (MODEL 1-07440-00)

Description: Book Port, model 1-07440-00, is a voice output electronic book reader designed for use by individuals who are blind or have low vision. This portable device reads computer text, web content, and digital audio books. Electronic files are read with synthetic speech, and digital talking books are read with recorded human speech.

Designed to overcome: This device helps people that are blind or who have low vision.

What it does: It reads computer text, web content, and digital audio books.

How it is helpful: By translating the written word into voice output the visually impaired person can access the information by 'hearing', rather than 'seeing'.

References

Barlow, JP, *A declaration of the independence of cyberspace*, at **www.eff.org/~barlow/ Declaration-Final**)

Busby G& Whitehouse D (2001), *Computers and Social Accountability,* Presentation given to the International Federation for Information Processing Working Group 9.2, June

Busby, G (2006) 'The Economic Arguments for Inclusive Design', *Computer.* **www.bcs.org/ server.php?show=ConWebDoc.3050**

Dixon, R (2002), 'The Internet: A menace to society?' in *The Internet: Brave New World?*, Hodder & Stoughton, p.40.

Moss, Jeremy (2002), 'Power and the digital divide', *Ethics and information technology*, vol 4 (2), pp159-165.

Tavin, HT, (ed) (20005) *Ethics Computing and Genomics,* Jones & Bartlett Publishers

Further reading

Baase, S (2003), *A Gift of Fire: Social, Legal and Ethical Issues for Computers and the Internet*, (Chapter 9), Pearson.

Blundell, BG & Schwarz AJ (2006), *Creative 3-D display and interaction interfaces: a transdisciplinary approach*, John Wiley and Sons. (General reading on alternative interface paradigms)

Rosenberg, R (1997), *The Social Impact of Information Technology*, Academic Press.

CHAPTER 8

Empowering computers in the workplace

OVERVIEW

The impact of computers on the workplace has been a major source of debate – both in terms of their effects on the quantity and quality of work. In this chapter we look at the impact that computing technologies have had on the workplace and at some of the ethical and legal issues invoked by these processes. We begin by addressing two particular concerns: firstly, whether computers have been replacing people, leading to greater unemployment (while also creating new kinds of jobs) and secondly, whether computers have diminished the quality of working life, for example by 'deskilling' the workforce. We shall be looking at some of the psychological effects, and the health and safety hazards, that have resulted from the introduction of computer technology. In companies with modern internal computer networks, management has a greater ability to monitor its employees than in the past. We address the issue of computerised monitoring in the workplace, and weigh the opposing arguments of managers and employees. Technological changes have transformed the very idea of an office from a spatial to a temporal concept, and in the final section of this chapter we look at some of the advantages and drawbacks of telecommuting (i.e. working remotely).

Learning outcomes By the end of this chapter you should be able to:

- Discuss the changes brought by computers in the working environment and on work practices

- Understand the environmental and health and safety issues involved in the computerised office

- Present arguments for and against computerised monitoring and surveillance in the workplace

- Appreciate the benefits and drawbacks of telecommuting.

8.1 Introduction

We begin this chapter by looking at some of the debates concerning the effects of computerisation on levels of employment/unemployment and on the quality of people's working lives. We shall be addressing two concerns in particular: firstly, whether computers have been replacing people, leading to greater unemployment, but also creating news kinds of jobs in the process; and secondly, whether computers have affected the quality of working life (by 'de-skilling', psychological effects and health and safety hazards). We then address the issues of computerised monitoring and surveillance in the workplace, outlining arguments for and against such practices. Finally, we look at the advantages and drawbacks of telecommuting (working from home).

8.2 Computers and employment

The impact of new technologies in the workplace has long been a source of controversy. As computer technologies became increasingly accessible, dire predictions were made about the impact of this latest new technology on employment levels in the manufacturing industry and commerce. However, according to Forester and Morrison (1994) the impact was not as great as first envisaged – for three main reasons

- The introduction of computers into the workplace was slower than expected (due to financial, technical, human and organisational problems – including oversell by the computer industry)
- The alarming rate of unemployment (that existed at that time) was not seen to increase dramatically
- Particularly in the US and Europe, the baby boom generation's entry into the workforce was largely complete by the end of the eighties, and the arrival of the baby bust generation in the 1990s saw some shortages of labour developing.

Despite the above comments, there is little doubt that the computerisation of factories and offices has led to the steady erosion of employment opportunities, particularly in the case of less skilled manual and clerical workers. Job losses have been particularly severe in traditional manufacturing industries, where competition from newly industrialised countries and the process of de-industrialisation have made matters much worse. According to a BBC report in 2002, jobs in the manufacturing industry had more than halved over the previous 25 years (**news.bbc.co.uk**, 17 September 2002).

The introduction of computerisation in the manufacturing sector has had an impact on jobs in those industries. A new industry has emerged – the IT industry, which incorporates hardware, software, development, web design, technical and administrative support, and computer services. The software industry now accounts for around 3 per cent of the UK's gross domestic product, around 130,000 companies are behind the software and computer services market in the UK, and over one million people are employed in ICT (information and communication technology). (**www.dti.gov.uk/industries/software/**)

Although employment in jobs relating to high technology grew by 46 per cent in 1995, this accounted for no more than 6 per cent of all new jobs created in the US economy. One trend that has further reduced job generation in the high-tech sector is the growing tendency of European countries and the US to export routine data-processing jobs to cheap labour countries (a process supported by the use of satellite and telecommunication technologies). US corporations are sending data across the Atlantic for processing in Ireland, where thousands of programming and data entry clerk jobs have been created. US companies also extensively use Indian programmers, and India has invested in a high-quality satellite link to boost this transnational trade in offshore programming.

Activity 8.1

Statistics on computers and employment

Using an appropriate search engine, find some statistics that support the following two trends in any country of your choice:

Employment fields where computers have replaced people (leading to unemployment)

Employment fields where computers have created new jobs.

8.3 Computers and the quality of work

Some argue that computers provide an opportunity to increase worker skills, and introduce variety into otherwise mundane jobs. Many reports suggest that workers engage with the technology, are pleased to develop IT skills, and see potential for promotion as a result of increased technical abilities.

However, another, more cynical, point of view arises from the idea that skilled workers are a threat to management because they can set their own pace and control the work process. Therefore, by introducing new technologies, management can maintain control of the workforce and exploit them. This argument – of 'automating the office' – is supported by the following quotation which describes a less empowering environment for the office worker:

> Our principal point is that the lessons of the factory are the guiding principles of office automation. In large offices, clerical work has already been transformed into factory-like production systems. The latest technology – office automation – is simply being used to consolidate and further a well-established trend. For most clerical workers, this spells an intensification of factory discipline. For many professionals and managers, it signals a gradual loss of autonomy, task fragmentation and closer supervision – courtesy of computerized monitoring. Communication and interaction will increasingly be mediated by computer. Work will become more abstract … and opportunities for direct social interaction will diminish.   (Mowshowitz in Kling (ed. 1986).

In the manufacturing industry, this transfer of skills to machines reduces the jobs available for skilled workers, and increases employment for less-skilled 'machine minders'. Also, despite the promise that new technology can improve the quality of working life, many of the new jobs being created in futuristic factories are every bit as tedious, fast paced, and stressful as the old-style assembly line jobs.

However, it can be argued that new technologies require different skills, and the unreliability of IT systems actually increases the dependence of managers on their skilled workforce and not vice versa. The new technologies introduce new modes of machine failure, new flaws in the control systems themselves, and new challenges to the design of jobs. In such settings, workers must control the controls. Far from deskilling the workforce, computer technology demands that employers need to constantly improve staff quality through learning and retraining. This lack of stability can lead to stress and staff disillusionment.

One argument for the introduction of new technologies is the need to compete in the marketplace, and 'move with the times'. This implies that the pace at which new technologies are introduced has gathered its own momentum – it is outside the control of any individual or company.

Psychological effects

There are indications that the introduction of computerisation in offices has resulted in increased levels of stress for workers.

> Automation is often seen as the solution to a messy office problem. But automating a mess only creates automated mess. Many workers are inadequately trained for new technology and they need help in coping with the stress arising out of change. Stress in the modern office leads to loss of job satisfaction, low morale, absenteeism and poor management labour relations. (Cox [1986])

From an ethical perspective, it has been suggested that interaction with computers – instead of people – leads to a reduced sense of personal responsibility.

> Interactions with computers tend to depersonalise both the user community and the application itself. The resulting sense of anonymity can inspire a lack of respect for the system and its resources, and a diminished sense of ethics, values, and morals on the part of the affected people. The depersonalisation can increase the temptations to commit misdeeds, diminish human initiative, and cause the abdication of decision-making responsibility. The sense of ethical behaviour seems much more diffuse, even though in principle it should be no different from ethical behaviour in general. (Neumann [1988])

Health and safety hazards

There are indications that prolonged use of video displays can have a detrimental impact on health. In the 1980s there were concerns regarding harmful radiation from CRT-based displays. In 1985, a Japanese study of 13,000 workers reportedly found a high level of miscarriages, premature births and stillbirths among computer operators. In 1987 a study of 1,600 women clerical workers who had become pregnant since 1984 found that expectant mothers who had spent more than 20 hours per week at terminals were more than twice as likely to suffer a miscarriage as other clerical employees. However, a Swedish study of 10,000 programmers concluded that there were no statistically significant differences between the pregnancies of women who had experienced low, medium or high levels of exposure to computer displays.

Other research has highlighted effects from monitors resulting in eyestrain, double vision, neck and shoulder problems, and depression.

Excessive use of computer keyboards, and other hand-held input devices (e.g. mouse) can lead to injuries to the arm, hand and fingers. This type of physical stress is commonly known as repetitive strain injury (RSI). In the UK:

> The Trades Union Congress (TUC) estimate that 1 in 50 workers nationwide are suffering from Repetitive Strain Injury (RSI) – a condition with numbness and pain in the upper limbs, extending as far as the neck. There is also a reported increase in incidence of headaches, eyestrain, neck and back problems, complaints mostly associated with computer use. As the workforce becomes increasingly desk and computer-bound and education and leisure time for young and old centres more and more around the use of IT, employers and employees ignore the issue of computer-related injury at their peril. In

what may be considered a vision of the future, a new law in New Zealand threatens jail (at the very least, prosecution) for an employer found failing to apply health and safety regulations. This is intended to include protection against RSI and related symptoms.

www.egrindstone.co.uk/computer_related_illness.htm

Activity 8.2

Computers and the quality of work

It has been argued that the introduction of computers into the workplace has degraded the quality of working life. Discuss three ways in which this may happen, giving specific examples.

8.4 Computerised monitoring in the workplace

A more recent issue that has caused considerable controversy is that of computerised monitoring and surveillance of employees. In the past, employees were monitored directly by progress chasers, foremen and supervisors. But these days, monitoring can be done surreptitiously by computer technologies. Computerised monitoring is constant, cheap and reliable. Supervisors are no longer limited by what they can observe with their own eyes. A complete record of employee performance can be recorded. Consider the following case (from Forester and Morrison, 1994):

> At Pacific South West Airlines' offices in San Diego and Reno, the main computer records exactly how long each of their 400 reservation clerks spends on every call and how much time passes before they pick up the next one. Workers earn negative points for such infractions as repeatedly spending more than the average 109 seconds handling a call and taking more than 12 minutes in bathroom trips beyond the total one hour allocation they have for lunch and coffee breaks. If employees accrue more than 37 points in any single year, they can lose their jobs.

Computerised monitoring in call centres is now a routine practice. What is more recent, however, is the monitoring of employees' computer and Internet use in workplaces. This trend has emerged in response to the growing problem of employee misuse of company computers. This includes abuse of company time by browsing the Internet, downloading illegal software and 'inappropriate' content such as pornography, exchanging that content with work colleagues, sending abusive e-mails, and conducting private or personal work during company time.

To protect themselves, and to monitor their employees, companies are increasingly installing employee Internet management (EIM) software. EIM is a new class of software which is able to detect, among other things, the presence of particular file types on a network (such as music or video files); changes in hardware or software; particular content or text strings stored on a computer network (for example, pornographic material or abusive e-mails); excessive use of certain applications; browsing on unauthorised websites; and monitoring bandwidth consumption (for example, the downloading of large files).

Activity 8.3

Workplace monitoring software

Visit the following website: **www.netintelligence.com**

What features are included in the Internet management software available from this company?

In defence of monitoring in the workplace

The Internet Misuse Survey 2002 was conducted among 544 human resources (HR) managers and officers from some of Britain's largest corporations, employing an average of 2,500 people. Among its key findings were:

- 72% of UK firms have had to deal with Internet misuse in the workplace
- As many as a quarter of the UK companies surveyed have dismissed employees for Internet misconduct
- 69% of all dismissals were associated with online pornography.

After pornography, web chat rooms (26 per cent) and personal e-mail browsing (23 per cent) were the second and third most frequent complaints brought to the attention of the HR department.

Such activities can have serious implications for companies which have to be careful of falling foul of the law and/or offending other employees. Organisations have ethical and legal obligations to protect themselves against illegal activities in the workplace, particularly from allegations of libel (involving, for example, defamation of other companies or individuals) and the existence of illegal software or obscene material on a company's computer network. For example, it is understood that the mobile phone company Orange dismissed 45 staff in 2000 from its offices in Darlington, Hertford and Peterlee, for downloading 'inappropriate material'. Files such as MP3 and video not only take up space on a network, consuming valuable resources, but also expose a company to liability for copyright infringement. E-mails can also be a source of embarrassment for companies.

As well as protecting themselves against illegal activities, organisations also use monitoring to improve productivity and competitive performance. Computer monitoring provides clear, accurate performance measures and, in principle, enhances the ability of managers to motivate employees.

Many companies have also suffered from industrial espionage and employee thefts. Because of the growing sophistication of manufacturing processes and office information systems, mistakes are more costly and computer systems are more prone to employee sabotage.

As part of this general defence, supporters of computer monitoring argue that it is also used to provide incentives for employees and effectively rewards individuals for true merit and reward. They also point out that what is being measured is factual, and that workers tend to favour such systems – they have seen too many cases of the wrong people being promoted for the wrong reasons. Armed with the facts that the computer gathers, diligent workers can legitimately argue a case for better pay and conditions and, in theory, this case does not rely upon personal opinions and personalities.

Furthermore, these systems can help eliminate rampant waste: for example, employees telephoning long distance for private uses, a team carrying the load for an unproductive team member, identifying the theft of materials by matching the stock used with the amount processed by line workers and discovering discrepancies. Monitoring on a computer network can assist in troubleshooting and fine-tuning of a system, as well as streamlining job design and fairly apportioning workloads.

Management argue that monitoring is an important tool for keeping records of transactions, maintaining quality of service and ensuring that employees are dealing with customers in the correct manner, particularly in call centres. By having a record of conversations to refer back to in the event of customer complaints or abusive calls, employees can be protected. Monitoring also allows companies to identify the training needs of individual employees.

Activity 8.4

Monitoring illegal activities

Employers may justify monitoring their staff's online activities on legal grounds. Discuss two illegal activities that staff may be engaged in, and how these could be prevented.

Arguments against monitoring in the workplace

Critics suggest that computerised employee monitoring undermines trust, encourages competitiveness among co-workers and is more concerned with measuring *quantity* rather than *quality*. For example, although reservation clerks may be given an incentive to process more calls when they are being monitored, it may also eliminate any human spontaneity or friendliness in their communications with clients. It is argued that the practice of monitoring in itself causes stress and is ultimately counterproductive because employee morale declines and with it productivity. By reducing employees' autonomy, there is a danger of turning workers into 'battery hens', denying them job satisfaction and eliminating the human element from their work. Most fundamentally, computerised employee monitoring represents an intolerable invasion of privacy and disregards the human rights of workers. Moreover, it is often seen as 'the thin end of the wedge' – that is, as a precedent for other invasive practices.

Ethical and legal issues

One of the principal ethical issues in the case of computerised monitoring in workplaces has been how to balance the rights and expectations of employees with the obligations and objectives of employers. Forester and Morrison (1994) state that profits are clearly important to the continued functioning of capitalist societies, and profit itself is dependent upon competitiveness. However, just how far we are willing to proceed in the pursuit of competitiveness and profitability is a matter of judgement. For example, the use of cheap child labour was once regarded as a sensible business strategy, but now our ethical sense and labour protection laws prohibit this practice. It remains to be seen in which direction our ethical institutions will take us in determining the nature of future employment: whether we can all be monitored in the interest of profit and accountability, or whether we shall see a renewed interest in designing jobs for people.

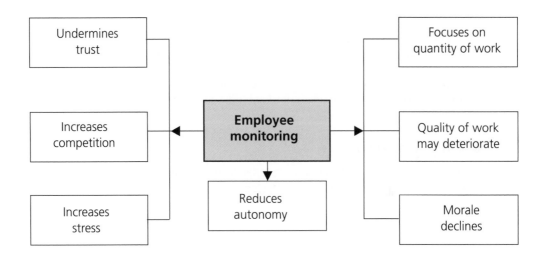

Figure 8.1: Some possible negative consequences of employee monitoring

In addition, we need to ask what kind of precedent computer-based monitoring of employees will set for other invasive practices. For example, similar arguments can be marshalled for the compulsory drug testing of key personnel such as pilots, train drivers, and power plant operators. If these people have the potential to kill thousands by accident, then do we not have the right to ensure that they are in a fit state to work? On the other hand, why not also monitor the alcohol purchases of convicted drunk drivers? This highlights the most contentious aspect of any form of computer-based monitoring; it is not so much the harm it may currently be causing, but what it represents.

One answer is to establish a 'code of ethics' on workplace monitoring. A five-point code of ethics to control the use of computerised monitoring and to safeguard privacy is proposed in Forester and Morrison (1994):

- Applying to monitoring the same protection that applies to pre-employment background checks, that is, permit only information to be collected which is directly relevant to the job
- Requiring employers to provide employees with advance notice of the introduction of monitoring as well as appropriate mechanisms for appeal
- Requiring people to verify machine-produced information before using it to evaluate employees
- Providing workers with access to the information themselves and providing mechanisms for monetary redress for employees whose rights are violated or who are victims of erroneous information generated by monitoring systems
- Applying a 'statute of limitations' on data from monitoring. The older the data, the less potential relevance and the greater the difficulty employees have in challenging it.

Activity 8.5

Arguments against monitoring

A large catalogue sales company has introduced new software at its order processing and customer service centre. This software monitors and records all aspects of employee work – for example, phone calls and computer use. Suppose that you are a trade union official representing 100 workers who handle customer service calls and online orders. Make a list of the arguments and concerns you would like to present to the management of the company.

8.5 Telecommuting

Telecommuting or teleworking are synonyms for the use of telecommunications and Internet technologies to work outside the traditional office or workplace, usually at home or in a mobile situation. In the United States, the International Telework Association & Council (ITAC) estimated that, in 2004, there were 44 million US teleworkers, and furthermore that a teleworker with broadband in the home can save their employer up to $5,000 a year. (**www.workingfromanywhere.org**)

Technologies that have enabled telecommuting include faxes, laptops, modems, PCs, mobile phones, e-mail, video conferencing, high-bandwidth computer networks, and satellite and telecommunication technology. With the arrival of the Internet and the Web as a kind of standard for groupware, a number of organisations developed as virtual organisations, whose members work almost entirely through telecommunications, with occasional face-to-face meetings. These technologies have enabled people in organisations to work across large distances, and across different time zones.

Technological changes in the office have transformed the very idea of an office from a spatial to a temporal concept. Companies like AT&T pioneered the introduction of the virtual office. Employees were provided with a mobile office, complete with laptop, fax, and mobile phone, and literally sent home. Russell Thomas, a telecommuting specialist at AT&T stated that::

> Before we adopted telecommuting we had situations that people would drive one and a half hours to the office, stay for a few hours, drive an hour to visit a client, come back to the office, then leave for the day. Obviously there was a big loss in productivity going on.

Factors that will continue to affect the future of telecommuting include the availability of bandwidth and infrastructure in a given country; social methodologies for balancing work control and work freedom; the perceived values and economies in telecommuting; and the opportunities and need for working collaboratively across large distances, including globally.

The benefits of telecommuting

One of the most obvious benefits of telecommuting is the associated reduction of office space required for employees. For example, it is understood that IBM took away the desks of more than 5,000 of its employees and told them to work at home, in their car, or at their clients' offices. By doing so, IBM expected to save between 15 and 20 per cent in space requirements.

Other benefits, described by Quinn (2004), include:

- **Increased productivity** (studies indicate that teleworkers show increased productivity)
- **Reduction in absenteeism** (less likely to take time off work)

- **Improved morale** (e.g. more freedom to schedule their work)
- **Improved recruitment** (employees can work from a wider geographic area)
- **Benefits to the environment** (less commuter traffic – reduced carbon emissions)
- **Lower costs for the worker** (e.g. child care expenses, 'office' clothes, travelling).

There are also significant health benefits to telecommuting. These include:

- **Reduced spread of communicable diseases.** People, who can stay at home and work rather than bringing a cold, or the flu, for example, into the office, are preventing illness from spreading to other co-workers (and their co-workers' families). Conversely, by staying home, they are not becoming infected by communicable diseases from co-workers, who bring them into the office
- **Reduction in stress-related illnesses.** Commuting itself, is enough to cause stress-related illnesses for many people and sometimes just the distance and time involved in commuting to and from work can cause unnecessary physical and mental discomfort
- **Reduced production of pollutants that lead to increased health problems.** Because they are not producing as much pollution by commuting every day back and forth to the office, telecommuters are improving not only the quality of the air they breathe, but the air that everyone breathes
- **Improved access to individual health needs for persons with existing health problems or disabilities.** Many people do not have the access they need to their medications during commutes or during the time they spend on their job sites. Many people also require or desire special equipment and facilities in order to address a variety of health conditions or physical limitations. Telecommuting accommodates the needs of people who would prefer to be closer to their homes, where they can better access their own familiar facilities and living environment.

The drawbacks of telecommuting

Although some employees welcome the new freedom that comes with less supervision, others say they miss the camaraderie and social interaction that comes with face-to-face office work.

> Field-based employees typically complain of their "isolation" from a central office which 'never understands' the conditions of their work – that lack of empathy or interest represents a fundamental negativism toward office absence. Those not working in a central office may be regarded as quasi-employees, similar to contract, part-time, or temporary employees within the organization … Overall, both physical and social distance, independent of all other considerations, attenuates organizational legitimization and managerial trust. (Perin in Kling (1996))

Video conferencing can help ease the psychological trauma that comes with spatial disengagement, allowing groups to converse and work together in an electronic version of face-to-face communication.

Some employees have highlighted the intrusion of the workplace in the home setting. The office at home is a constant reminder of work. In addition, there is the real problem of defining concrete working hours when the distraction of home life is a constant presence. This may result in the boundaries between working hours and social or home time becoming blurred, and a tendency to work longer hours (perhaps accounting for the increase in productivity noted in the previous section).

Other noted aspects are given below – these are adapted from Quinn [2004]:

- The threat to management control of worker autonomy
- Lack of face-to-face interaction with customers at the workplace
- Security issues (particularly sensitive information)
- Difficulty of scheduling team meetings
- Lack of visibility with management (and the potential for being 'overlooked' for promotion)
- Lack of support for the office worker from the 'remote' worker (the office worker is unlikely to contact the remote worker for help)
- The teleworker feels the need to be 'always available' to prove they are working
- Isolation – not just socially, but for the stimulation of ideas, peer support, technical support
- Tendency to work longer hours.

Activity 8.6

Impact of telecommuting

Computer technology has made it possible for many people to work from home instead of the traditional office.

What impact might this new way of working have in relation to:

a) home life?

b) the office experience?

Support your answers with references from the press, journal articles and/or textbooks.

8.6 An ethical dilemma

In this chapter we have discussed the use of computers to monitor the performance and activities of employees. As we have seen, this sort of monitoring process can be carried out for a number of reasons, not the least of which is to increase productivity by enhancing the quantity of work carried out by employees. Naturally, by and large the raison d'etre for increasing the quantity of work is to increase profits.

In Chapter 1 we briefly discussed the negative impact that the disposal of computer-based equipment can have on the environment, and here we highlight a simple situation in which computer technologies can be used to ameliorate negative environmental impact – specifically in relation to carbon emissions – atmospheric pollution. At the same time we illustrate frequent reluctance on the part of management to adapt their working procedures to embrace these technologies. Our simple example is as follows.

Consider Alice, who is a staff member in a computer science department in New Zealand. She applies for a job at a university in the UK and is invited to travel to the UK for a three-hour interview. Thus, Alice will have to fly some ten thousand miles each way in order to be present for three hours at the interview. Let us suppose that you are heading the interview committee in the UK, and are therefore Alice's primary point of contact. Alice sends you an e-mail asking whether it would be possible for her to be interviewed using videoconferencing facilities. She points out that this will not only save her a huge amount of flying time (at least 20 hours each way), but also will alleviate stress, and furthermore – as she mentions – avoiding long-haul journeys that are not absolutely necessary has a positive impact on the environment. In this respect she points out the significant amount of fuel that will be burnt in transporting her from New Zealand to the UK and on her return journey. She has access to high-quality videoconferencing facilities, and so does your university in the UK.

You bring this situation to the attention of other members of the interview committee – your head of department, and the like – but find that nobody is particularly willing to make use of videoconferencing facilities. This surprises you, especially as after all you are working in a computer science/IT department and therefore had supposed that staff would have been quite willing to embrace new technologies. You mention that costs will be saved in not having to pay Alice's airfare, and also stress that this is an opportunity to make use of computer technologies to avoid negative impact on the environment (in actual fact it is surprising how much fuel is consumed in supporting Alice's round-the-world trip).

What are your views on this situation? Do you feel that this highlights (even in a small way) the opportunity to reduce environmental damage by using technologies to support communication and therefore avoid unnecessary travel?

Do you believe that people should be willing to adapt to the use of such videoconferencing technologies – is this an ethical issue? Given a willingness to adapt, is it possible that the interview process can be carried out in such a way as to overcome the possible deficiencies of the technology – so that the candidate is not disadvantaged by not being physically present, and also provide the interview committee with the opportunity to gain a clear impression of Alice?

Finally, in the chapter we have briefly discussed the imposition of computer-based technologies to monitor the activities of members of a workforce. Do you feel that if members of a workforce are expected to adapt to the deployment of such technologies, then members of a management team should be willing to do likewise (in the above discussion, we have demonstrated an example of the unwillingness of a management team to employ even videoconferencing facilities)? To what extent to you think senior management is generally willing to accept the introduction of computer-based technologies to monitor their own activities during the working day?

8.7 Summary

In this chapter we have briefly considered the impact of computing technologies on the workplace, and at some of the ethical and legal issues invoked by these processes. We began by addressing two concerns: firstly, whether computers have been replacing people, leading to greater unemployment (while also creating new kinds of jobs); and, secondly, whether computers have diminished the quality of working life (by, for example, 'de-skilling' the workforce). We have looked at some of the psychological effects, and the health and safety hazards, that have resulted from the introduction of computer technology into the workplace. This chapter has also addressed the issue of computerised monitoring in the workplace, outlining the opposing arguments of managers and employees. Finally, we have briefly considered advantages and drawbacks associated with telecommuting.

8.8 Review questions

Review question 8.1

In the 1980s and 1990s, dire predictions were made about the impact of computer technology on employment levels across manufacturing industry and commerce. Why did these predictions not come true?

Review question 8.2

What are the arguments supporting the notion that computers deskill workers?

Review question 8.3

What are some of the potential psychological side effects of prolonged working with computers?

Review question 8.4

Describe two principal health and safety hazards possible in a computerised office.

Review question 8.5

What are the arguments for computer monitoring of employees in the workplace?

Review question 8.6

Discuss some of the main health and social benefits to employees of telecommuting.

8.9 Feedback on activities

Feedback on activity 8.1

We have chosen to focus on the US job market to demonstrate how to approach these questions. The following statistics are taken from Sara Baase (2003):

Employment fields where computers have replaced people

The number of bank tellers dropped by about 37% between 1983 and 1993. A study by Deloitte and Touche predicted that another 450,000 bank jobs would be lost because of automation and electronic banking services.

The number of telephone switchboard operators dropped from 421,000 in 1970 to 164,000 in 1996.

The jobs of 35,000 electric meter readers were expected to disappear as utility companies installed electronic devices that broadcast meter readings to company computers.

A bank holding company receives 1.5 million customer enquiries by telephone each month; 80% are handled by computer. The company reduced the number of customer service employees by 40%.

Railways computerized their dispatch operations and eliminated hundreds of employees.

The New York Stock Exchange eliminated the last 150 of its floor couriers who carried messages between brokers – this process is now performed electronically.

Travel agencies closed as more consumers made aeroplane reservations online. As the prices of digital cameras decline, more film processors will go out of business.

During the early 1990s, newspapers were full of headlines about layoffs and corporate 'downsizing'. IBM, General Motors, Sears, and other large companies laid off tens of thousands of workers.

Employment fields where computers have created new jobs:

In 1995, an estimated 36,000 new Internet-related jobs were created; in 1996, about 100,000 more. By 1997, more than 109,000 people worked in the cellular communications industry in the United States.

In 1998, the Semiconductor Industry Association reported that chip makers employed 242,000 workers directly in the US and 1.3 million workers indirectly. The chip industry, which did not exist before the microprocessor was invented in the 1970s, ranked fourth among US industries by annual revenue.

According to the Department of Commerce, in 1996, there were 506,000 computer scientists and engineers, 427,000 computer systems analysts, and 568,000 computer programmers. The Department expected these figures to grow to 1,026,000, 912,000, and 697,000 respectively by 2006.

New technology has also created jobs for support staff, such as receptionists, janitors, and stock clerks.

There are countless new products that use computer technology: VCRs and DVD players, computer games, fax machines, cell phones, medical devices, etc. These new products have created new jobs in design, marketing, manufacture, sales, customer service, repair, and maintenance.

In 1998, 7.4 million people worked in information technology jobs in the United States.

Feedback on activity 8.2

- Deskilling the workforce by reducing control, responsibility and job satisfaction. For example, the automation of assembly plants in manufacturing industries; the creation of routine, data-entry jobs for low-skilled computer operators; the creation of call centres with routine 'customer service' jobs; the growth of the service industries, with large numbers of low-paid jobs for check-out clerks

- Increasing stress, depersonalisation, fatigue and boredom.

  People spending longer hours at work, or longer periods of their working day, sitting in front of computer terminals

- Creating health and safety hazards. Problems associated with prolonged use of computer displays and working for long hours in modern office buildings – for example, eyestrain, headaches, back problems and repetitive strain injury.

Feedback on activity 8.3

NetIntelligence's Internet management software includes the following features:

- **Web-blocking:** If an employee is attempting to reach a site which has been found and classified within the NetIntelligence database, they will be denied access

- **End-point device control:** Records all changes to hardware and software and by default updates the database every 10 minutes. This enables an alert to be sent if unauthorised changes are detected

- **Porn detection:** Identifies and removes inappropriate materials and ensures the enterprise remains protected. The content database contains in excess of 30 million digital fingerprints. These fingerprints are generated from an assessment process that identifies threatening or inappropriate material, with pornography having the largest volume and the highest priority

- **Removable devices:** Monitors, detects, actions and reports upon all activities on both the local and the extended network. Records the use of removable drives in addition to detailing which files were accessed or copied

- **Malware detection:** Detects categories of malicious software, including:-

  Spyware (adware, snoopware, sneakware)   Hacking utilities and tools

  Password crackers and utilities   Keystroke loggers

  Browser hijackers & plugins   Virus generators

  Network Management Tools & Sniffers

- **IPR copyright theft**

  Reports on presence of movie & music files Download activity

  Specific file locations and access reports   Application usage

  Application presence, e.g. media players   Streaming activity

  Internet activity

- **Reports on instant messaging and peer-to-peer activity**

- **Application monitoring**

Detailing productivity across the enterprise

Productivity peaks and troughs

Highlighting areas of risk and potential liability

Analysing work patterns and practices

Detecting unlicensed or non-approved software

Enforcement of company policies

Determining which applications are used and which are not.

Feedback on activity 8.4

Activities could include: illegal downloading –for example of software, pornography, copyrighted music or films; or illegal use of e-mail, for example libel, defamation or slander.

Prevention could include monitoring/audit software, filtering software, checking e-mails and company policy notices.

Feedback on activity 8.5

- What kind of monitoring does the company plan to introduce – for example, Internet use, e-mails and phone conversations?

- Legal issues – is monitoring legally justified under the Human Rights Act?

- What data will be collected from monitoring procedures, where will this data be stored, who will have access to it, and for how long will it be kept?

- Contractual issues – whether monitoring and surveillance is to be written into the terms of employment/company policy

- Arguments for a code of ethics to be established on the limits, scope and policies of monitoring

- Arguments that any personal data that is collected through monitoring should comply with the principles of the Data Protection Act

- Concerns about invasion of privacy (see the Human Rights Act)

- Concerns about the impact on employee morale, absenteeism and work atmosphere.

Feedback on activity 8.6

Home life

- Benefits: flexible working hours, more involvement with family/children, less travel time and cost

- Possible disadvantages: longer working hours, intrusion of family in work hours, intrusion of work in family time, finding appropriate space to work, cost of office provision (computer equipment etc), defining office hours, non-work-related distractions.

Office experience

- Benefits: No commuting or travel costs, fewer communicable diseases

- Possible drawbacks: Less social interaction, loss of camaraderie, weakening loyalties and bonds.

References

Baase, S (2003), *A Gift of Fire: Social, Legal and Ethical Issues for Computers and the Internet*, (Chapter 8), Pearson.

Cox, S (1986), *Change and Stress in the Modern Office*, Further Education Unit, Department of Education and Science, London.

Forester, T & Morrison, P (1994), *Computer Ethics: Cautionary Tales and Ethical Dilemmas in Computing*, MIT Press.

Mowshowitz, in Kling, R (ed) (1996), *Computerization and Controversy: Value Conflicts and Social Choices*, 2nd Ed, p285, Morgan Kaufmann.

Neumann, PG (1988), 'Are risks in Computer Systems different from those in other technologies?' *Software Engineering Notes*, Vol 13 (No 2) April pp.2-4.

Perin in Kling, R (ed) (1996), *Computerization and Controversy: Value Conflicts and Social Choices*, 2nd Ed, p289, Morgan Kaufmann.

Quinn, Michael (2004), *Ethics for the Information Age*, Addison Wesley.

Further reading

Ayres, R (1999) *The Essence of Professional issues in Computing*, (Chapter 4), Prentice-Hall.

Blundell BG (November 2003), 'E-learning: Adapting to the Future', *Times Higher Educational Supplement*.

Blundell, BG (May 2007), 'Empowering Technology: An Uncertain Voyage', *IT Now* (OUP).

Lyon, D (1994), *The Electronic Eye : The Rise of Surveillance Society*, University of Minnesota Press.

CHAPTER 9

The use of artificial intelligence and expert systems

OVERVIEW

The aim of this chapter is to outline some of the social, ethical, legal and professional issues associated with the use of 'intelligent' systems. Naturally the idea of machines being 'intelligent' and performing human-like functions inspires both excitement and fear. Over the years this has catalysed human imagination – demonstrated, for example, in writing by Isaac Asimov or L Frank Baum, and via the media in films such as *AI*. Research into artificial intelligence (AI) has not lived up to many of the early visions of producing human-like robots, but the underlying concepts have generated hot debate about the nature of intelligence, and whether we should be creating machine intelligence at all.

Developments in technology have progressed and we are now familiar with so called 'smart' and 'intelligent' devices. The premise behind these devices is that they act independently and, in effect, have decision-making capabilities. In short, human judgement and control has been passed to a computer chip. In some cases this may not be a problem, but there may be some areas where this delegation of control is of great concern.

The theme of this chapter is to ask what decisions are being made and on what information. What are the benefits and risks when 'intelligent' devices are deployed? If a piece of software is making decisions on our behalf, and gets it wrong, who (or what) is responsible? What should we, as computer professionals, take into consideration when designing, implementing, or managing intelligent systems?

Learning outcomes

By the end of this chapter you should be able to:

- Demonstrate knowledge of the history of AI and expert systems

- Discuss concepts and applications of artificial intelligence

- Understand and articulate the implications of agent-based decision making

- Appreciate the social, legal and professional aspects of intelligent systems

- Appreciate aspects of professional responsibility in the development and application of future technologies.

9.1 Introduction

This chapter opens with a summary of the background to the development of computer intelligence and explains the differences between AI and expert systems. This short history is intended to show how the grand ideas of intelligent machines have developed into devices that simply exhibit intelligent behaviour, and that claims of intelligence in respect to computing are overplayed. To illustrate this point we present the main arguments for and against intelligent computing summarised by the Turing Test, and the Chinese Room Scenario.

We then give some contemporary examples of intelligent devices and their uses, and move on to discuss how these devices are designed to either benefit the user, or inhibit certain activities. From this discussion, we will see that intelligent systems act on choices made on behalf of the user. We ask what programming rules advise the choices, on what information the choices are made, and the wider implications of many agents operating over the Internet. It follows that certain issues should be taken into consideration during the design of the application.

Subsequently, we discuss various social implications, which are summarised in the story of Joseph Weizenbaum. We consider whether there are some applications of intelligent systems that should not be developed. Secondly, the legal aspects are considered, together with the difficult issues of agent responsibility, responsibilities of the designer, the programmer, the provider and the user.

Finally, we look at issues relevant to the computing professional in the areas of design, implementation and management and, as with other chapters, outline an 'ethical dilemma'.

9.2 Origins of AI and expert systems

Interest in artificial intelligence (AI) can be said to have begun when it was realised that computers could perform problem-solving activities and, moreover, that they could perform certain functions in a faster, more reliable, way than humans. In other words, they could be used to replace some human mental operations.

Two areas of research emerged, one trying to achieve some replication of human intelligence (i.e. artificial intelligence), and the other trying to use human intelligence (in the form of expert knowledge) combined with computation to provide fast and reliable information (expert systems).

Intelligent machines

Academics working in the field of AI could see similarities between the computational aspects of the human mind and the way these machines worked. From that point it was just a short step for visionary thinkers to conceive the idea of 'intelligent machines'. The reasoning behind the idea of intelligent computers runs something like this:

- **Step 1**
  1. Logic and rationality are properties of human thought
  AND
  2. Logical arguments are properties of computation
  THEREFORE
  3. Human 'thinking' can be replicated by computational methods.

- **Step 2**

   4. Human thinking is equated with 'intelligence'

   AND

   5. Computers can replicate human thinking

   THEREFORE

   6. Computers can be 'intelligent'.

Expert systems

So far we have been discussing only one aspect of machine intelligence – that is, where computers are used to replicate aspects of intelligent behaviour. A second approach is to 'put' intelligence into computers. Rather than trying to get computers to exhibit intelligence (a task fraught with tremendous difficulties), developers concentrated on creating knowledge-based systems. The idea is simple – obtain expert knowledge from, for example, a doctor or lawyer, and put that knowledge into a database. The best properties of computation (speed, search, pattern matching) can then be utilised to maximum advantage. So, for example, a medical diagnosis can be generated from a database of signs, symptoms and example cases – but who gets the blame when mistakes are made?

9.3 The debate on computer intelligence

Naturally, if computer scientists are to try to replicate intelligence they need to have some idea of what would be considered 'intelligent'. Two opposing points of view are given below: the first is a test of computer intelligence, and the second denies that computers can be intelligent at all.

One of the most influential tests of computer intelligence came from Alan Turing, a British mathematician. Put simply, he suggested that if a person could be fooled into thinking they were having a conversation with another person, when in fact they were conversing with a machine, then the machine could be said to exhibit intelligence. His idea took shape in what later became known as the Turing Test. This particular idea influenced research and debate for many years.

One program that was written to interact with a human operator and simulate conversation was called ELIZA, created by Joseph Weizenbaum. With this program, a person could sit at a computer terminal and engage in a fairly realistic conversation with the machine. The design of the program meant that the type of interaction it allowed was similar to the interaction between a psychologist or therapist and a client.

Further research went into producing computers that could play chess, based on the assumption that 'clever people can play chess, therefore if a computer can beat a world-class chess player, then the computer must be intelligent'.

The philosopher John Searle argued against these ideas of computer intelligence – he claimed that computers are simply 'symbol manipulators' and cannot be said to exhibit intelligence at all. He explained his position by using an example, now commonly known as the 'Chinese Room Scenario'. (Searle, (1994).)

An explanation of Searle's Chinese Room Scenario

Suppose that a man is inside a room, which has a gap under the door; through this gap, he receives sheets of paper from someone outside. No other form of communication is possible. The sheets of paper have Chinese symbols written on them and the task before this individual is to translate these symbols into some other language, such as English. To do this, he simply looks up a table on the wall and writes down the equivalent of the Chinese symbol in the required language. He then passes these under the door to the person waiting outside.

Searle's claim is that, although the man in the room has manipulated symbols so that Chinese language has been 'translated' into English words, in no sense could the man be said to understand Chinese. He has simply followed rules in order to change one particular input format into a desired output format, and this is essentially what digital computers do. Hence, any claim that rule-governed symbol manipulation can allow a computer to understand language or, more broadly, exhibit intelligence, is totally without foundation. Humans may manipulate symbols, but in communicating or demonstrating intelligence in other ways they must be doing additional things as well.

Thinking about what defines intelligence continues to baffle philosophers. The essential abilities for intelligence as indicated by Hofstadter (1979) are summarised in Figure 9.1.

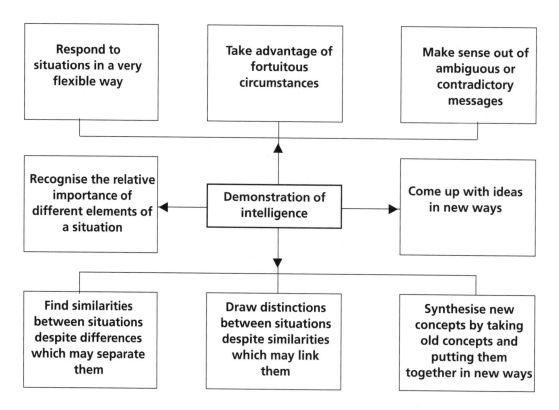

Figure 9.1: A summary of essential abilities for intelligence as indicated by Hofstadter (1979)

Activity 9.1

Background of AI and expert systems

Using library facilities or the Internet, research the "Turing Test"

What was the aim of the Turing Test?

What is another name for the Turing Test?

Explain how the Turing Test is carried out.

Do experts believe it's a good test?

9.4 Applying intelligence

In the above sections, we have looked at the development of AI and expert systems, from attempts to replicate intelligence to the more practical aspects of capturing knowledge in expert systems. These different approaches give rise to differing concepts of AI. In the first instance, AI is concerned with producing applications that developers may claim 'do' intelligent things (for example, gather information, make judgements, respond flexibly to the environment). In the second instance, AI is concerned with producing programs that deliver information based on prior knowledge gained from experts. In simplistic terms we could say that the concept behind AI is that systems respond to changing external circumstances, and the concept behind expert systems is the delivery of output based on internally stored information. As we shall discuss later in the chapter, these different approaches raise substantially different ethical questions.

Applications

We only have to look at media reports, advertisements and current news items to see that the quest for machine intelligence has not diminished, and has resulted in a proliferation of 'intelligent' and 'smart' devices. The results of search engines alone show their application, not just in the list of results to a query, but also in the lists of associated 'useful' websites (for example, 'if you're interested in … then you're likely to be interested in ….'). The commercial advantages of cheap and fast information processing leading to information delivery has resulted in a trend for 'intelligent' computing.

When intelligent devices are designed to act independently, they are called agents. An agent may operate singly, or in conjunction with other agents. Clearly, since the advent of the Internet and the World Wide Web, the context for the application of intelligent programs has changed from individual systems to globally connected systems. Wireless networks and blue-tooth technologies have also extended the range of application – 'intelligence' has moved into the environmental, domestic and personal sphere. This convergence of technology, and intelligent applications, has resulted in the term 'ambient intelligence', which may be defined thus:

> ....ambient intelligence: people living easily in digital environments in which the electronics are sensitive to people's needs, personalized to their requirements, anticipatory of their behaviour and responsive to their presence.

www.research.philips.com/technologies/digsoc/index.html#ambintel

Applications in the environment

One of the early aims of applying artificial intelligence was in the field of robotics, and in particular to use robots to carry out work that is either dangerous or inaccessible to humans. This aim was realised when robots were used from 11 September to 2 October 2001 in the rescue operation at the site of the collapse of the World Trade Center. They were used to pass through areas where there was no breathable air, and went into spaces too small for humans to pass through.

On a more everyday level, most people are familiar with in-car navigation systems which have been in use for some time – offering suggestions on the most efficient route a driver can take to get from 'A' to 'B'. Intelligent in-car systems that are not yet in the public domain, but are predicted to be in use before too long, are devices that control the speed of the car in relation to the speed limit in effect on particular sections of the road. Intelligent speed adaptation (ISA) technology and its adoption is seen as 'virtually inevitable in the car industry ... either through increased legislation or voluntary use'. (*IEE Review*, February 2004) ETC...Trials using ISA systems in specially adapted cars have begun in the UK.

> 'The MIRA-designed ISA system uses a GPS receiver to continuously identify the position of the vehicle and match its location with a digital map of permitted speeds. The speed limit is displayed inside the car and also sent to the throttle. When the driver reaches the speed limit, the ISA system will intervene so that however hard the driver presses on the accelerator pedal, the engine produces no further power.' (*IEE Review*, February 2004)

'Smart' homes

Bringing intelligent devices into the home is the vision of the future, and research into 'smart' homes is the latest trend. A number of projects are under way using technologies that learn user preferences, and that can respond to changing circumstances. One of these projects – 'The Aware Home' – uses technology to support elderly people living in their own homes. The following is an example of how the technology can be applied, and is part of a project called 'The Aware Home Research Initiative' (AHRI) at the Georgia Institute of Technology:

- Software which automatically constructs family albums from video pictures collected in the house
- An intercom system which uses voice recognition to allow people to speak to one another by saying their name
- Software that telephones a person when their photograph is spoken to
- Electronic tagging of easily mislaid items such as keys
- Reminders about appointments.

www.cc.gatech.edu/fce/ahri/ (accessed 23/4/07)

Activity 9.2

Concepts and applications

Explain the purpose of an application.

Is it intended to respond to external circumstances or internally stored knowledge?

Would you describe it as an example of artificial intelligence or as an expert system?

What is it about the system that leads you to think of it as either artificially intelligent, or an expert system?

9.5 Implications on agent-based decision making

Programs are designed to respond to rules and to perform certain functions. This principle applies whatever the program and whether it exhibits intelligent behaviour or otherwise. However, when programs are designed to be intelligent agents, that is, to act on their own or someone else's behalf, the consequences of their actions need to be considered. Relevant questions that should be considered are summarised in Figure 9.2.

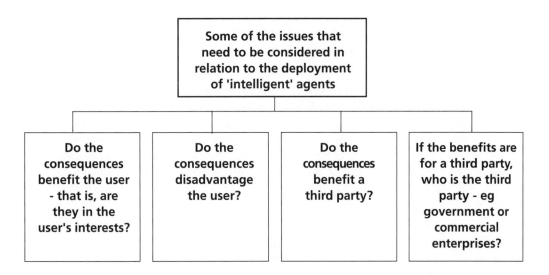

Figure 9.2: Considerations relating to the deployment of so-called intelligent agents

Two examples are given below of intelligent software that have very different outcomes for the user.

The first example, given in the following extract, describes a software agent that was developed at the University of Southampton to act on behalf of a user.

> Funded by consumer electronic companies such as Nokia, Sony, and Vodafone ... the software agent would monitor the activities of cell phone users until it is able to determine certain preferences ... for example, the software agent would be able to determine a pattern of behaviour such as going to the movies every Friday, and would then seek information online in an effort to buy movie tickets for the user. What is more, by entering a trip in the cell phone schedule, the agent would go online to check the availability of flights and hotels in an effort to reserve a room and buy a ticket for the user. (Graham- Rowe, 2003)

Not all programs are designed to act on behalf of the user – sometimes they are designed to inhibit user preferences. For the second example, we refer to the intelligent speed adaptation (ISA) device described in the previous section. This device is designed specifically not to respond to the users' preferences. If the car driver (the user) wants to go faster and presses the accelerator pedal, the ISA will prevent an increase in speed. Here we see intelligent devices utilised to prevent citizens from acting outside the law.

Any decision to take action is based on making a choice based on information held. In the first example, the device has information on user preferences and patterns of behaviour; it then makes a choice of looking for films on a Friday to book tickets, presumably for a film based on user preferences. In the second example the decision to inhibit the speed is made based on a more formal rule – that of not exceeding the speed limit. The information in this case is the speed limit that applies in the location of the car.

Choices and decisions are not only based on information, but also influenced by underlying assumptions. One assumption from the film-booking example is that the user wishes to continue seeing films on a Friday, and therefore has no other commitments that day. It may be, however, that the user would prefer to see a film on another night if it was cheaper to do that, or the user would still like to see a film on a Friday, but is more concerned with the price than the content of the film. Problems abound – the technology cannot embrace all possible circumstances and changes in human preferences.

These examples relate to very simple situations – one device, one user. However, in a networked world such as provided by the Internet, where a number of agents are operating over a network, there may need to be a process of negotiation and compromise. Again, taking the film-booking example, the intelligent agent may have to make a decision between a preferred film and a preferred price, or there may be a compromise in location – a cheaper film in a location not quite so convenient to the user. We can see that in an ideal situation there are many factors to be taken into consideration, and different users are likely to make different choices.

There are programs that exhibit characteristics of negotiation. A good example of a negotiating program is one designed by the World Wide Web consortium (W3C) known as the Platform for Privacy Preferences Project (P3P). It has been developed to protect online users' privacy rights, and at the same time take account of the law. The idea is that the user sets their privacy preferences using P3P and, when they visit a website, their privacy preferences are compared to the privacy policy of that website. If the user preferences match the policy of the website, the interaction is allowed; if they do not match, then the user is alerted to the possible privacy violation. This interaction – the checking of one set of requirements against another – is a form of negotiation. It should be noted, however, that websites could get around this system. The World Wide Web consortium does warn that there is no guarantee that a website will actually stand by the privacy policy it may be displaying.

In all of these examples, the rules for decision making and negotiation are first determined by the designer of the device – we will be discussing this in the next section.

Activity 9.3

Implications of agent-based decision making

Design a questionnaire to find out the preferences of a 'user' for booking a hotel to attend a conference. Your aim is to find out their priorities – for example, is location more important than cost?

Some aspects you might want to include, in the case of the hotel, are cost, location, quality and services provided.

Ask a few of your friends or family to complete the questionnaire – you may be surprised by the results.

9.6 Social, legal and professional issues

In this section we look more closely at the social, legal and professional issues associated with the use of intelligent systems.

Social issues

Some of the social issues raised by artificial intelligence have been documented by Whitby [1996] as:

- Loss of employment due to replacement of jobs
- Dangers in safety-critical applications
- Centralisation of power
- Dehumanising effects of AI
- Unrealistic expectations due to sensationalising the capabilities of AI.

Many of these aspects are encapsulated in the following story told by Joseph Weizenbaum.

In the early days of artificial intelligence, when the prospect of being able to simulate human intelligence was considered by some to be viable, the computer scientist Joseph Weizenbaum became very concerned about how AI would be applied. As we described earlier, Weizenbaum had developed a program (ELIZA) that could emulate conversation – the test for intelligence that Turing had suggested. Using the ELIZA program, a person could sit at a computer terminal and engage in a fairly realistic conversation with the machine. The design of the program meant that the type of interaction it allowed was similar to the interaction between a psychologist or therapist and a client. Weizenbaum was horrified by the suggestion that a program such as this could be used instead of using human counsellors, and this inspired him to write the book *Computer Power and Human Reason*. He wrote:

> ... there are some human functions for which computers ought not to be substituted. It has nothing to do with what computers can or cannot be made to do. Respect, understanding and love are not technical problems.

He gives three specific areas where computers should not be applied:

- Applications 'whose very contemplation ought to give rise to feelings of disgust in every civilized person'. This comment refers to the connection of animals to computers, specifically in areas of visual and brain research
- 'All projects that propose to substitute a computer system for a human function that involves interpersonal respect, understanding and love in the same category.' This is in reference to the substitution of therapists by a 'conversing' machine as mentioned above
- Anything which 'can be seen to have irreversible and not entirely foreseeable side effects', especially when there is 'no pressing human need for such a thing'. This refers to the research being conducted in speech recognition devices.

Interestingly, and with amazing foresight, he refers specifically to voice recognition devices: '... such listening machines, could they be made, will make monitoring of voice communication very much easier than it now is ... '

And,

> Perhaps the only reason that there is very little government surveillance of telephone conversations in many countries of the world is that such surveillance takes so much manpower … speech-recognizing machines could delete all 'uninteresting' conversations and present transcripts of only the remaining ones to their masters.

We only have to read the news, or look at organisations protecting privacy rights (such as the Electronic Frontier Foundation – **www.eff.org**) to realise the visionary nature of Weizenbaum's observations, which date back to 1976.

Legal issues

There are two issues that we will consider here – one concerns the use of agents to implement and enforce the law, and the second is the issue of responsibility. In Section 9.4 we briefly outlined a system used to implement the law: the MIRA Intelligent Speed Adaptation system.

The issue of responsibility raises many complexities. If the program or device goes wrong, or acts illegally, who should be held responsible? For example:

- The person or organisation that commissioned the system
- The requirements or specification designer
- The programmer
- The provider
- The user – whether an individual or an organisation.

For example, consider the MIRA system. A child runs out into the road in front of a car. Despite the speed control enforcement, there is insufficient space for the car to stop. The only course that the driver can take is to swerve and accelerate. The car swerves, but the speed control system prevents a brief period of acceleration. An accident ensues. Who is to be blamed?

A wider issue, and one that has been discussed a number of times in this book, is that of national versus international law, together with the problems of enforcing such laws in a global context.

As we have already seen, there are many different areas of application for AI and expert systems – in the home, in dangerous environments, and in safety-critical situations. Another major area of development, now and in the future, is eCommerce. The following extract describes how intelligent systems (also called software agents) can be used on the Internet:

> The long term vision is of legally compliant agent mediated electronic commerce over public global networks, perhaps on the semantic web, involving multi-agent systems or societies. Agents will represent different participants and services and interact to create legally binding agreements, enforceable both on and offline. Negotiation and compliance processes will relate to all legal aspects of a commercial relationship (privacy, intellectual property, contract, consumer protection, tax, etc.), with various agents providing the appropriate processes and taking on functions of privacy protector, consumer protection monitor, contracting assistants, security protocol management (e.g. digital signature mechanism) trust, auditing and recording. (Subirana & Bain, 2004)

In other words, what these authors foresee are intelligent agents communicating between themselves over a global network such as the Internet. These agents will negotiate with each other to reach agreements on contracts, and to make sure legal requirements are met.

For example, if personal information is required in a contract the agent should make sure that the information given, and the way it will be used, complies with any data protection legislation. Another agent could be looking after intellectual property interests. So, for example, if someone tried to sell you illegal software your agent would refuse it.

According to Subirana & Bain, particular areas of difficulty when using intelligent agents in this context are:

- The allocation of responsibility (where agents are used in a contract situation)
- Compliance with consumer protection regulations (notifications, confirmations, contracting procedures)
- Privacy risks (for example, notifying users of privacy risks, and gaining consent for personal data processing)
- Creating legally valid agent-based digital signatures.

Other difficulties of complying with the law, especially in a global context such as that provided by the Internet, are where intelligent agents are used to access content such as video clips, music and written reports. In this instance, compliance with intellectual property rights will be another issue. Where agents are acting on our behalf, as for example gaining access to music, or negotiating our privacy requirements, it is important that they act within the law. For those involved in developing, managing, or using intelligent agents, key questions are 'does your agent obey the law?', and if so, 'whose law is it obeying?'.

Professional issues

In the previous sections we have given examples of applications for intelligent devices and have summarised a number of key implications. As we have indicated, these devices can be designed to be of benefit to the user, or can inhibit what the user does. We could of course say the same about any computer application. However, we have also seen from the previous discussions that intelligent devices may be required to make decisions, interact with other intelligent applications, and obey the law. Computer professionals have a responsibility not only to consider the usability of the device, but also to consider the wider effects of its decision-making capabilities, and the extent of the interaction with other devices.

Where intelligent devices are used in a social context (as in the examples given earlier) the issues to be considered are:

- Reliability
- Trustworthiness – both in the functioning, and the limits of decision making
- Privacy issues – where data is stored, such as user preferences, this information should meet privacy requirements
- Security issues – information should be secure, and so to should the ownership of the device.
- Burden on the user – is there a burden on the user in respect of managing the device?
- Identity verification – can anyone else impersonate the user?
- Decision-making procedures – can they, or should they, be controlled by the user?
- Is it legal?

Professional responsibility extends to the design, implementation and management of intelligent agents.

Social, legal and professional issues

In this section we have summarised three instances in which, according to Joseph Weizenbaum [1976], computers should not be applied.

Identify and describe three similar, contemporary examples.

9.7 An ethical dilemma

A couple of years ago Patricia returned to the UK to take up an academic position at a British university. She had been out of the UK for over twenty years working at universities in a number of countries, and had a good professional employment record. She decided to open a bank account with one of the large banks that had a branch on the campus.

She met the bank manager, was given the necessary forms, and duly completed them. A few days later she returned to the bank to open her account. Much to her surprise, she was told that she could only have a cash account, i.e. she would not be given any bank cards, cheque book, or the like, nor could she have any overdraft facility.

Patricia again met with the bank manager as she naturally felt there must have been some misunderstanding. Key points here are that she already had a bank account in the UK since her student days (although this had been largely unused during her years away), she owed no money on credit cards or the like, was a UK citizen, and had a good track record with banks overseas. In addition, her salary from the university was to be paid into her account each month.

Despite her explaining these points, the bank manager was adamant that she could only have a cash account. When asked to explain this decision, the bank manager indicated that it was not in fact her decision, but a decision made by an expert system. The bank always used this computer technology when making decisions about opening accounts for new clients, and in fact the bank manager could not overrule the restrictions that the expert system imposed. In short, the expert system was empowered in the decision-making process to such an extent that it actually replaced the human decision-making process. The bank manager went on to explain that the problem was that the expert system had not previously encountered a person with Patricia's particular background, and the key point to the computer was the extensive years of residency outside the UK.

To what extent do you think it is appropriate to replace the human decision-making process with computer technologies such as expert systems?

During the conversation Patricia asked the bank manager whether she felt that it was appropriate for the expert system to be empowered in this way. The response she obtained was that it was a great idea because computers do not make mistakes. What do you think about this comment? Do computers make mistakes? Is any computerised system free from mistakes? Should we be educating people to believe that computers are infallible – are computers infallible? What do you think are the ultimate ramifications of believing in infallible computerised systems?

9.8 **Summary**

In this chapter we have outlined various ethical, social, legal and professional issues associated with the use of intelligent systems. We began with a summary of the background to the development of computer intelligence and explained the differences between AI and expert systems. We summarised arguments for and against intelligent computing as represented by the Turing Test, and the Chinese Room Scenario.

We have provided various contemporary examples of intelligent devices, have outlined their uses and have discussed how these devices can be designed to either benefit the user, or inhibit freedoms.

9.9 **Review questions**

 **Review question 9.1**

Using the list of abilities for intelligence as described by Hofstadter, give examples of how each of these can be applied to student lectures.

Review question 9.2

One of the examples of an intelligent application given in this section was a project to support the elderly in their homes. What are the benefits and disadvantages of this project to a) the user and b) the wider community?

Review question 9.3

The context of the extract quoted below is a 'ballroom scenario' – that is, a social situation where people arrive wishing to dance with others: they can choose their dance partners, choose a particular dance, or choose to go to the bar.

Read the extract and make a list of the underlying assumptions of this social situation. Against each point you make, write down any other choices that may have been possible. When you have finished, you may like to make a guess at the gender, age and nationality of the designer.

> The authors demonstrate the application of the program by setting it in the context of a 'ballroom scenario' thereby enabling elements of negotiation, choice and action. Their agents are able to distinguish between male and female partners, negotiate with prospective partners for dance engagements, and make choices between alternative dances and activities. By attributing the concepts of belief, desire and intention to the agents, the authors can encompass 'key behavioural features of agents: autonomy, adaptability and responsibility'. This scenario describes a familiar context and incorporates social norms, such as male and female dance partners, the male approaching the female to request a dance, and with the alternative to dancing given as going to the bar! So, with a given set of social norms in a familiar, and fairly restricted context, negotiations can be pursued. Ethical considerations in this case could concern the application of social conventions – what happens for users who do not conform? (Duquenoy, 2004)

? Review question 9.4

Assess the issues that arise from one of the following examples (which have been discussed in this chapter):

1. The car speed device (MIRA Intelligent Speed Adaptation)

2. The 'smart home'

3. The 'smart' cell phone.

9.10 Feedback on activities

Feedback on activity 9.1

The aim of the Turing Test was to assess whether computers could exhibit intelligent behaviour by imitating human interaction via conversation. Another name for the Turing Test is the 'Imitation game'.

A computer terminal would be in one room and the human 'player' would be in another room. The human would attempt a conversation via a keyboard (using question and answers). They would not be told whether they were interacting with a computer or another human being. If they thought they were conversing with a human being (via the keyboard), then it could be said that the computer had 'fooled' them, and was convincing in replicating human intelligence.

This idea generated a great deal of debate, but on the whole most experts do not think this is a good test of intelligence – merely symbol manipulating (see John Searle's argument).

Feedback on activity 9.2

For the purposes of this exercise we have researched ambient intelligence via the Philips research site which was one of the returns from the search engine in response to the keywords 'ambient intelligence'. Philips is a leading research establishment and has an active involvement in projects on the theme of ambient intelligence. The following was selected from their list of current projects.

The project is described as follows:

PHENOM is a long-term company research project, which aims at creating an environment that is aware of the identity, location and intention of its users, and that eventually is capable of butler-like behaviour.

An intelligent 'Memory Browser' system has been designed as carrier application. A first prototype has been built and evaluated. The system recognizes multiple users, devices and objects, and learns from their behaviour. Interaction with the system is very natural: users can, e.g., select photos using souvenirs. The project generates concepts and builds capabilities, particularly in system integration.

Source: **www.research.philips.com/InformationCenter/Global/ FArticleDetail.asp?lArticleId=2213&lNodeId=684&channel=684&channelId=N684A2213**

What does this application do?

The application is essentially a searching device that learns from user behaviour and can recognise multiple users.

Is it intended to respond to external circumstances or internally stored knowledge?

It has internally stored prior information, but primarily is designed to respond to external circumstances (different users, and user preferences).

Would you describe it as an example of artificial intelligence or as an expert system?

I would describe it as an example of artificial intelligence.

What is it about the system that leads you to think of it as either artificially intelligent, or an expert system?

Although it has stored information (a property of an expert system), the stored knowledge is not expert in nature. Its characteristics of responding to externally given information (different users, and learning user preferences) would make us categorise it as artificial intelligence.

Feedback on activity 9.3

A number of considerations need to be taken into account when making a booking on someone else's behalf. The aim of this exercise is to demonstrate that different users may have different priorities, and would change their decisions depending on circumstances. For example, if booking a train ticket they may wish to travel at a certain time of day, and take the fastest train available. But, the question might be asked: 'At what cost?' If the price for this ticket is more than they could afford, they may choose to compromise, and travel at a different time, or take a slower train. Below is an example of a simple questionnaire for finding out user preferences in booking a train ticket, taking the various options into account. For guidance we use an example of booking a train ticket.

Train booking questionnaire

Departure station:

Destination station:

Direct service*: yes/no (* Note: an indirect service may result in a slower journey)

Single / return:

Day of departure:

Day of return:

Time of departure:

Time of return:

Food provision: yes/no

Restaurant service: yes/no

Buffet trolley service: yes/no

Please indicate your priority choices:

	High priority	Low priority
Travel day		
Travel time		
Journey time		
Fastest (direct service)		
Cost:		
Economy		
Standard		
Business class		
Restaurant service		
Buffet trolley service		

Feedback on activity 9.4

Below are given the three instances described by Weizenbaum [1976], and contemporary examples are included below each point. The examples we have used are not necessarily the only ones that could have been chosen.

- Applications 'whose very contemplation ought to give rise to feelings of disgust in every civilized person'.

  Current example: experiments have been carried out in the area of computer implants, and computer chips are now widely inserted into animals. Further research is likely to investigate the potential of implanted technology in humans for medical assessments, monitoring and ID verification.

- 'All projects that propose to substitute a computer system for a human function that involves interpersonal respect, understanding and love in the same category.'

  Current example: simulation techniques are the backdrop for virtual reality (VR) – a technological representation of the physical world which includes human representation. Representations in a virtual world could have an impact on personal identity (impersonation and misrepresentation), or on human dignity (violence or degrading behaviour) (Whitby, 1996). Will we be replacing 'interpersonal respect, understanding and love' by simulated, virtual technology?

- Anything which 'can be seen to have irreversible and not entirely foreseeable side effects', especially when there is 'no pressing human need for such a thing'.

  Current example: voice recognition, and now text recognition, has led to extensive monitoring capabilities which according to privacy groups are in danger of violating basic human rights.

References

Duquenoy, P (2004), *Intelligent Ethics*, Topical sessions, IFIP World Computer Congress 2004, Toulouse, France, Kluwer.

Graham-Rowe, D (2003), Smart cellphone would spend your money, *New Scientist, 6 November 2003*

Hofstadter, D (1979), *Gödel, Escher, Bach: An eternal golden braid*. Basic Books Inc.

Searle, J (1994), *The Rediscovery of the Mind*, London: MIT Press.

Subirana, B & Bain, M (2004) *Legal Programming: designing legally compliant RFID and software agent architectures for retail processes and beyond*, Springer.

Weizenbaum, J (1976), *Computer Power and Human Reason*, W H Freeman and Company.

Whitby, B (1996), *Reflections on artificial intelligence*, Intellect (UK).

Further reading

Belavkin, R., Blundell BG, Cairns, P, Huyck, C, Mitchell, I & Stockman, T (2005), *Management Support Systems*. Middlesex University Press.

Negnevitsky, M (2004), *Artificial intelligence: a guide to intelligent systems*. (2nd edn), Addison-Wesley.

Orwell, G, (2004), 1984, *Nineteen Eighty-Four*. Penguin Books Ltd.

Russell, SJ &Norviq, P, (2002), *Artificial intelligence: a modern approach*. (2nd edn), Prentice-Hall.

Talbott, S, (1995), *The Future does not compute*. O'Reilly and Associates. (Also available online at: **http://natureinstitute.org/txt/st/details/fdnc.htm**).

CHAPTER 10

The failure of IT projects

OVERVIEW

Complex IT systems play an important role in the operation of modern society. However, IT project failures are commonplace and there are few indications that we are getting better at implementing ever more complex systems. So as to remedy this situation, it is crucial that we examine the reasons for such failures. In this chapter we outline the problems associated with the production of reliable systems. Professional bodies such as the BCS and the IET are attempting to address the problem of IT failure by advocating best practice in the IT industry. We will briefly discuss the efforts that are being made by these professional institutions.

Often, a 'post mortem' analysis of failed IT projects reveals that legal and professional problems arising due to the actions of stakeholders (individuals in the customer and supplier organisations) have a negative impact on projects and reduce the chance of a successful outcome. We will review the ramifications of such problems.

Learning outcomes On completion of this chapter you should be able to:

- Define failed IT projects

- Outline the problems of producing successful IT projects

- Briefly describe how the profession is addressing problems

- Explain the relationship between professional codes of conduct and IT projects

- List the most relevant elements of national legislation governing project failure.

10.1 Introduction

Complex IT systems play an indispensable role in many diverse areas. For example:

- Air traffic control
- Hospitals
- Nuclear power stations
- Toxic chemical plants
- Spacecraft
- Missiles
- Ships
- Defence.

IT systems are also deployed to maintain government services, financial systems, stock markets, and communication systems. On the basis of reports relating to IT systems, it is readily apparent that reliability is often poor; in the case of some systems, this can have life-threatening ramifications. In a study on the state of IT project management, Sauer and Cuthbertson (2003) report that only 16% of IT projects were considered to be successful.

The report of a working group from the Royal Academy of Engineering and the British Computer Society (2004) (hereinafter referred to as RAE/BCS) presents a review, which estimates 'a phenomenal US$150 billion per annum was attributable to wastage arising from IT project failures in the United States, with a further US$140 billion in the European Union'.

Besides the financial costs involved with failed IT projects there is a high human cost which relates to the increasing reliance and complexity of software in safety-critical, business-critical and medical systems.

Definitions of failed IT projects

The RAE/BCS report uses the term 'failure' generically for projects which 'fail to deliver all the key features and benefits to time, target cost and specification'.

In conducting a survey of the literature relating to IT projects, Lyytinen and Hirschheim (1987) identified four major theoretical categories of project failure:

- **Correspondence failure** (failure to deliver in accordance with the specification)
- **Process failure** (failure to deliver within specified time and cost)
- **Interaction failure** (failure to deliver any key benefits, which implies that the system is hardly used)
- **Expectation failure** (failure to deliver any key features and benefits to time, cost and specification).

Although the Lyytinen and Hirschheim publication is somewhat dated, these categories remain valid and suggest that any project that fails to deliver an IT solution in accordance with the specification and within time and cost constraints should be deemed a failed IT project.

Below we provide several examples of failed projects:

- **The Strategic Defence Initiative:** This 'Star Wars' project dates back to the 1980s and perhaps denotes the most colossal computer-centred project to have failed to date. The then US president Ronald Regan was determined to protect the US from nuclear attack and perhaps on the basis of his extensive lack of knowledge of computer technologies believed that these 'infallible' machines could solve any problem. The defence system represented a formidable undertaking – computer systems being empowered to make decisions of a potentially cataclysmic nature. Often human input or mediation would not be possible – decisions would have to be made rapidly – there simply would not be time to include humans in the decision-making process. How could such a system be tested – perhaps this key aspect should have been considered from the outset! The project was a total failure – although it was partially revived by President Bush in 2001.

- **Rural Payments Agency's failed IT project:** *Computer World* (2007) reports: 'The UK government has responded to a devastating report by MPs on the failure of an IT project to implement a new payments plan for farmers by saying it is "confident" a new management team can deliver.' The article goes on to say: 'The Rural Payments Agency's failed IT project to implement the Single Payments Scheme – which consolidates 11 separate EU subsidies – left farmers out of pocket by a total of up to £22.5 million (US$44 million), while the cost to Defra [the Department for Farming and Rural Affairs] is estimated at up to £500 million. The MPs called for former environment secretary Margaret Beckett – now foreign secretary – and Sir Brian Bender, the former permanent secretary at Defra who now occupies the equivalent post at the Department for Trade and Industry, to be held accountable for the debacle.'

- **The Generic Clearing System (GCS) Project:** Andy McCue (2006) writes: 'Clearing house LCH.Clearnet has written off €47.8m after scrapping a failed three-year project to build an integrated clearing IT platform for the company.' He goes on to add: 'A review of the GCS programme last year had already written off €20.1m on part of the investment after it failed to deliver any of the benefits originally promised and LCH.Clearnet said a further review last month has now concluded any further development of the GCS system is "not economically or technically viable".'

- **The Iraq War:** Matt Rogers (2007) suggests that some of the strategies that have been employed in Iraq reflect a failure in IT planning and a gulf between expectations and reality. He writes: '…if we sidestep the political arguments for a minute and look at the systems underpinning the war, there is plenty of evidence of what retired US Army Colonel Andrew Bacevich calls "the assumption among forward thinkers that technology – above all, information technology – has rendered obsolete the conventions traditionally governing the preparation and conduct of war". Bacevich's comments appear in *Fiasco*, the account of the Iraq War's strategic shortcomings written by two-time Pulitzer Prize-winning journalist Thomas E Ricks. Ricks chronicles several mistakes made by the US and its allies in Iraq, but many of the most dire ones are a direct outgrowth of new military efficiencies driven (supposedly, at least) by IT. For example, the US Defense Department's belief that the war could be fought with a relatively small number of troops can, at least in part, be attributed to a misplaced confidence in IT-related advances in warfare, such as better battlefield communications, more precise global positioning, and superior command and control capabilities.'

- **The NHS Computer Initiative:** In a *Sunday Times* article, Simon Jenkins (2005) writes: 'As long ago as 1997 *Computer Weekly* estimated that some £5 billion had been lost by Whitehall on botched computer projects. Consultants had found selling computers to ministers was like giving sweets to children. Labour claimed it would stop all this, but it did the opposite. Ministers traded up from candy to cocaine and are now hooked.

The money being wasted subsidising the computer industry far outstrips what used to be wasted on nationalised cars, steel, coal and shipbuilding. Government computers are the new lame ducks.' He goes on to say: 'The NHS computer was supposed to list everyone in the country with their various ailments so any doctor or hospital could treat them "on screen". Nobody ever asked for this machine, which was supposed to start in 2004. It was a pure top-down sales pitch. The medical establishment pleaded naively that the cost not be met from other health spending. The price soared within a year to £2.3 billion and is now £6.2 billion, with no known delivery date.' Although this system was finally delivered, failure is implied by the massive cost overrun and non-conformance to the delivery date. Jenkins writes: 'These computer fiascos come on top of similar ones with the Child Support Agency, the Criminal Records Bureau, the Passport Agency, the benefits card, traffic control, the e-university and countless others. All suggest a government in thrall to fee-driven consultants and computer subcontractors.'

The ethical issues involved

The issue of project failure and its potentially disastrous consequences raises a number of questions, which have ethical, legal and professional aspects:

- Why can't we build computer systems with the same inherent reliability that we find in other designed artefacts such as bridges and buildings?
- Why is software not guaranteed in the same way that other purchased goods are?
- Why does so much poor-quality software exist and how can so much of it appear in important systems?
- Should we entrust responsibility for the conduct of military warfare, the control of massive energy sources and even (inter) national economies to computer systems that are less than totally reliable?

Since the late 1960s, issues relating to our inability to produce high quality software within an agreed time frame and at an acceptable price have been the subject of intensive research and debate and led to the establishment of the software engineering discipline. The RAE/BCS stress that difficulties encountered in IT projects often arise due to individuals in both the customer and supplier organisations failing to follow good practice. This is viewed as a 'general absence of collective professionalism in the IT industry'.

The chances of a successful completion of a project are improved if all individuals, on both the customer and supplier sides, implement good practice. Many professional bodies, including the BCS and IEJ, advocate the importance of good practice in the development and deployment of IT systems.

Activity 10.1

A real-world example of a failed IT project

Using your library or Internet resources, find an example of a failed IT project.

Write a brief description outlining reasons as to why the project failed. Now identify which of the four major theoretical categories of project failure as suggested by Lyytinen and Hirschheim [1987] best describes the failure in the example you have found.

10.2 The problems of producing successful IT projects

The problems associated with undertaking successful IT projects can be categorised as those that are specific to IT (essentially technical) and those which are generally common to all large-scale projects. We now briefly consider these two aspects.

Problems specific to IT

The Parliamentary Office of Science and Technology [2003] suggests that there are problems specific to IT, which make IT projects 'prone to longer over-runs in time and cost and less likely to meet user requirements'. These are summarised in Figure 10.1 and then briefly outlined:

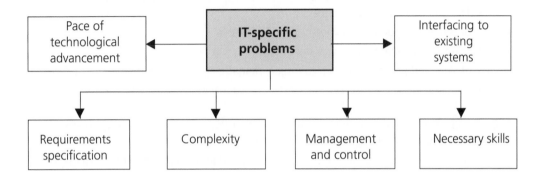

Figure 10.1: Some of the IT-related problems that (unless properly handled) are likely to negatively impact on an IT-centred project

- **Rapidly advancing technology:** IT differs from other projects in that the technology used is developing rapidly. Three important implications to note are:
  1. A supplier may oversell a technology to a customer by taking advantage of the lack of knowledge and experience the customer may have of the latest IT developments.
  2. Due to rapid technological advances, a project may become obsolete before its deployment.
  3. There is often a tendency, both on the customer and the supplier sides, to desire cutting-edge solutions. Such solutions will carry a greater risk when compared to the alternative of using tested commercial 'off the shelf' products.
- **Defining requirements:** explicitly stated, fixed and understandable user requirements increase the chances of success. Any changes to user requirements, however simple, may require a fundamental redesign of the system. This might have significant time and cost implications
- **Complexity:** large-scale IT projects can be extremely complex and may necessitate the production of millions of lines of software code. To predict all possible states, including error states, that such a system might take is infeasible
- **Oversight:** it is difficult for management (especially non-technical managers) to judge the quality and completeness of software as it is being developed. Providing oversight in the years between project initiation and implementation can be very difficult

- **Interoperability:** more often than not, an IT project may include interfacing to other systems. This can be very challenging
- **Limited skills:** the BCS suggests that a better-regulated computing profession may improve the competence and quality of those involved in the development of IT systems. Currently, many software developers do not have formal qualifications in the subject nor the necessary experience to be involved in IT development.

Common causes of project failures

A study, conducted by the National Audit Office and Office of Government Commerce, identified the eight most common causes of IT project failure as follows:

- Lack of a clear link between the project and the organisation's key strategic priorities, including agreed measures of success
- Lack of senior management ownership and leadership
- Lack of effective engagement with stakeholders
- Lack of skills and proven approach to project management and risk management
- Lack of understanding of, and contact with, the supply industry at senior levels in the organisation
- Evaluation of proposals driven by initial price rather than long-term value for money (especially securing delivery of business benefits)
- Too little attention paid to breaking development and implementation into manageable steps
- Inadequate resources and skills to deliver the total portfolio.

(Better Projects Directorate, December 2004,
Office of Government Commerce (OGC) **www.ogc.gov.uk**)

10.3 How the profession is addressing the problem of IT failure

Improving the chances of IT project success can be viewed at both the micro and macro levels. At the microlevel, RAE/BCS suggest some measures that individual companies and project teams can take. At the macro level they advocate recommendations aimed at advancing key facets of the national IT project management capability.

Measures that individual companies and project teams can take

Individual companies and project teams can improve their chances of delivering a successful IT project by considering the following factors:

- **Client/supplier relationship:** it is advisable that both money and time are invested in the supplier selection process. A supplier's capability must be assessed alongside cost
- **Contractual arrangements:** the terms of a contract between customer and supplier must reflect the uncertainty associated with development and deployment of IT systems and also apportion the risks appropriately
- **Evolutionary project management:** the consensus among IT practitioners is that projects should be managed by rapid learning cycles as opposed to sequential methods of project management

- **Requirements management:** both functional and performance requirements need to be explicitly stated. The requirements definition is one of the most critical and challenging phases of the project
- **Change management:** changes often occur in large-scale IT projects, and an appropriate contingency plan must be in place from the outset, which will define what will be done if alterations to the scope of the project are involved
- **Measuring progress:** a clear plan must exist at the outset of the project which defines objectively measurable milestones related to the overall project deliverables
- **Risk management:** it is vital that in successful project management, risks are identified and managed accordingly. Crucial elements of risk management include:
    - learning lessons from past projects and problems
    - taking account of organisational culture
    - limiting the degree of novelty to be introduced into a project
    - anticipating software upgrades
    - comprehensively planning testing activities
- **Technical issues:** the main technical issues that should be taken into consideration are:
    - requirements capture
    - systems architecture
    - integration
    - reuse
    - verification and validation.

Concerted action at the national level

The RAE/BCS also highlight a number of key findings that should be addressed at the national level so as to ensure that there is an improvement in the IT industry and a strengthening of the national infrastructure supporting IT project delivery. Their conclusions and respective recommendations are summarised below:

1. In comparison to other branches of engineering, the levels of professionalism found in software engineering were relatively low, although exceptions were noted.
    - Customers should ensure that all senior IT practitioners involved on an IT project have attained chartered status and maintain their technical know-how through the continuing professional development (CPD) offered by professional bodies
    - The Office of Government Commerce, alongside professional bodies such as the BCS and IET, should enforce registration of senior practitioners working on 'high consequence' projects and monitor their professional competence via the CPD
    - Professional bodies should work in conjunction with the Confederation of British Industry (CBI) and the Institute of Directors to promote awareness of the benefits of employing chartered IT practitioners.
2. Educational institutions in the UK (universities and management schools) were not producing IT practitioners with the required IT application and project skills.
    - Professional bodies such as the BCS and IET should assess and accredit undergraduate courses, so as to encourage a greater engineering emphasis
    - Intellect (the Trade Association for the Information Technology, Telecommunications and Electronics Industries in the UK) should take the lead in forming links with companies, government departments and universities to promote greater applications focus on undergraduate courses.

3. The importance of the role played by project management within the IT project development life cycle was not generally recognised, and senior management were viewed as being ill-qualified to handle the issues involved in complex IT projects.
   - management schools must develop courses specifically addressing IT project management. This can be achieved with close collaboration with computer science and engineering departments and the relevant professional bodies
   - project management and IT must be compulsory modules on any MBA course delivered in management schools.
4. The failure to apply effectively (in the case of IT and software) risk management, which was viewed as critical to the success of complex IT projects.
   - the Royal Academy of Engineering should produce guidance to addressing risks of IT projects.
5. The role of the systems architect was underappreciated in major IT projects. Also there was a shortage of appropriately skilled individuals.
   - professional bodies working closely with the Engineering and Physical Sciences Research Council (EPSRC) and the Department for Education and Skills should investigate ways of identifying and developing skills of people with the potential to become systems architects.
6. The urgent need to adopt best practice among both customers and suppliers was vital to ensure a successful IT project.
   - with government leading the way, with the collaboration of industry, establish a UK Software Engineering Institute for the purposes of research, advice, and training to promote best practice in software engineering and IT project management.
7. Basic research into the complexity and associated issues raised by IT projects was advocated to enable the effective development of complex, globally distributed systems.
   - the government and EPSRC should establish a UK research programme to address the development, deployment and evolution of complex distributed systems.

Chartered IT professionals

The BCS defines what it means to be a chartered professional, as follows:

- They will take personal responsibility for their actions, which will be bound by the Code of Conduct
- They will normally be educated to a four-year degree (or equivalent level), where the course of study should be accredited by a professional body
- They will then be required to demonstrate their technical and managerial competences over four to five years, which must be peer-approved
- They are also required to maintain their professional competence throughout their active professional careers, for example via the CPD programme.

To increase the likelihood of a successful IT implementation, IT professionals are required to be competent in a number of areas including:

- Project / programme management
- Systems design, development and operation
- Relationship management
- Security and safety
- Change management

- Software engineering
- Systems maintenance
- Quality assurance and control.

Many of the computer-related professional bodies of other nations also provide certification programs which involve members in continual education and skills development.

10.4 The relationship between professional codes of conduct and IT projects

A **professional code** is a set of rules that states principal duties that all professionals should endeavour to discharge in pursuing their professional lives. **Codes of conduct** will be discussed in more detail in the next chapter.

The British Computer Society (BCS) Code of Conduct

The BCS Code of Conduct defines professional standards (governing a member's personal conduct) required by the Society as a condition of membership. In essence, it is concerned with issues such as honesty, confidentiality and impartiality.

The professional responsibilities are grouped around four sections:

1. **The public interest.**
2. **Duty to relevant authority** (the person or organisation which has authority over the IT practitioner, i.e. an employer or client. In the case of a student this will an academic institution.).
3. **Duty to the profession.**
4. **Professional competence and integrity.**

A copy of the Code of Conduct is available via the BCS website at
www.bcs.org/server.php?show=nav.6030

The BCS Code of Good Practice

The BCS Code of Good Practice describes standards of practice relating to the present-day complex demands found in information technology (IT). Four key areas covered by the code are:

1. **Practices common to all disciplines:** they include among others the maintenance of technical competence; using appropriate methods and tools; managing workload efficiently; and respecting the interests of customers.
2. **Key IT practices:** they include program/project management, relationship management, security, safety engineering, change management and quality management.
3. **Practices specific to education and research.**
4. **Practices specific to business functions:** they include requirements analysis and specification, software development, system installation, training, system operations and support and maintenance.

The BCS Code of Good Practice is available via the BCS website at
www.bcs.org/server.php?show=nav.6029

The Association for Computing Machinery (ACM) Code of Ethics and Professional Conduct

The Association for Computing Machinery (ACM) is a professional US body for both computing professionals and students. Professional conduct is expected of every member of the Association. The professional responsibilities are spelt out in the ACM Code of Ethics and Professional Conduct. The Code consists of 24 rules (imperatives), which are categorised into the four sections listed below:

- Section 1: outlines the rules that are essential ethical considerations
- Section 2: outlines the rules that address specific considerations of professional conduct
- Section 3: outlines the rules that apply to those in leadership roles in the workplace
- Section 4: outlines the principles involved in compliance with the Code.

You may find it helpful to download a copy of the ACM Code of Ethics and Professional Conduct, which can be found at: **www.acm.org/about/code-of-ethics**

Activity 10.2

Professional duties

Download and consult the BCS Code of Conduct from the BSC website at **www.bcs.org/server.php?show=nav.6030**

As an aid to understanding the rules in the Code, they have been grouped into principal duties which all members should endeavour to discharge in pursuing their professional lives. What are the principal duties a professional has towards the relevant authority (i.e. the customer)?

A Code of Best Practice

Intellect (the Trade Association for the Information Technology, Telecommunications and Electronics Industries in the UK), in association with the Office of Government Commerce, the BCS and IET have advocated a Code of Best Practice. The Code aims to facilitate 'a more mature IT acquisition and delivery environment' and comprises of 10 commitments, which range from understanding the requirements through to commitments to individual skills and professionalism.

The Intellect Code of Best Practice can be found at:
www.intellectuk.org/markets/groups/public_sector_council/guidelines.asp

A library of codes from around the world

A library of codes of conduct, codes of practice, or codes of ethics from around the world have been collected, as part of an International Federation for Information Processing study. This initial study resulted in a useful publication by Berleur and Brunnstein (1996).

Access to the library is available at:
http://courses.cs.vt.edu/~cs3604/lib/WorldCodes/WorldCodes.html

Best practice and professionalism

The RAE/BCS argue that there is a critical need for software engineers to adhere to best practice. Failure to adhere to codes of practice, poor definition and inability to learn from past experiences all contribute to the failure of IT projects.

In the case of the failed London Ambulance Service Computer Aided Despatch (LASCAD) system project, Beynon-Davies [1995] interpreted the failure in terms of professionalism. In his conclusion he wrote that a clear implication of the LASCAD project failure was that the builders of the LAS system were seen as having neglected a number of duties defined by professional ethics which contributed towards the failure of the system. This was one instance of a case, among many reported, where a neglect of professional ethics had led to the failure of a computer systems project. Such case histories were particularly useful in allowing for a more realistic view of project failure, replacing naïve, simplistic textbook analysis with hard-reality case facts.

Software engineering is also a relatively young profession, compared with other branches of engineering; it dates back to the late 1960s. Software engineering has no tradition of professional accreditation. Although chartered engineer status is available, there has been little response to gaining accreditation among the IT community. Software engineers can enter the profession via a variety of different routes, including those that do not require a formal university education. To address this issue, the British Computer Society has established a chartered IT engineer status comparable to the chartered engineer.

In summary

The builders of systems often neglect a number of duties defined by professional codes of ethics and this contributes towards project failure. To address this problem, professional computing bodies such as the BCS, IET and ACM have produced codes of conduct. A professional code is a set of rules that states the principal duties that all professionals should endeavour to discharge in pursuing their professional careers. Adherence to these professional duties is required as a condition for membership of these societies. Increasing professionalism is a key to improving project success rates.

10.5 An overview of national legislation

Contractual arrangements between customer and supplier can vary in nature, from fixed price with well-defined user requirements and explicitly stated timescales and budget through to 'cost plus', with requirements, timescales and budgets being ill defined. When things go wrong in the development and deployment of the IT project, a number of legal issues can be raised. These are outlined below.

In addition, further legal issues must be considered when a customer either purchases or signs a licence agreement for software and/or hardware from a supplier. These are also looked at in greater detail in this section.

Contract law

Many contracts for the purchase and use of computer hardware and software are not sale contracts as such but licence agreements (particularly so with the respect to computer software). Generally, contracts for hardware and software are governed by different legal rules:

- Computer hardware, if it is sold, will be subject to the Sale of Goods Act 1979
- An agreement for bespoke software will be within the scope of the Supply of Goods and Services Act 1982.

Limited liability and unfair contract terms

Legally speaking, the following points must be considered when assessing whether it is reasonable for a supplier to exclude liability:

- The relative bargaining powers of the parties involved
- Opportunities to contract with others who do not use the same exclusionary terms
- Whether the customer knew or ought reasonably to have known, of the existence and extent of the term
- Whether the goods were manufactured, processed or adapted to the special order of the customer.

The law governed by the Unfair Contract Terms Act 1977 briefly provides that the liability for death or personal injury can never be excluded. Liability for other forms of damage can be excluded, but only in so far as it is reasonable to do so.

Misrepresentation

If you are negotiating with a salesperson with the view to acquiring computer software, they may make statements regarding the software and its performance.

There are three forms of misrepresentation:

- **Fraudulent**
- **Negligent**
- **Innocent.**

If the representation has been made fraudulently or recklessly (i.e. not caring whether it is true) then at common law the remedy of rescission is available. This sets the contract aside as if it had never been made at all and gives the right to recover any money paid. In terms of representation made by salespersons, the approach is to insist that an express term be inserted into the contract to the effect of the representation made.

Law of negligence

Negligence is a part of law known as tort. It imposes legal liabilities on a person who has acted carelessly, failing to exercise a duty of care. Salient points of the legislation are:

- A claim in negligence does not depend on the presence of a contract, so if the individual injured is someone else other than the buyer, that individual can still sue
- The buyer should also be able to sue if the software and / or hardware is defective and fails to comply with the implied terms such as those concerning quality and fitness for purpose
- The fact that an action can be considered negligent, regardless of any contract, is important both for computer programmers and manufacturers of computer hardware:
  - if a publisher licenses a program, the program author could be liable in negligence, even though they were not a party to the licence agreement
  - in the case of computer hardware, an individual suffering loss or injury as a result of the negligence of the manufacturer will have a claim in negligence against the manufacturer, regardless of the fact that the hardware was bought from a dealer
- A computer programmer or a computer equipment manufacturer will not necessarily be potentially liable to the world at large in negligence; they will be liable, however, to those whom they could contemplate being adversely affected by any negligent act or omissions of theirs.

Product Liability Law (Consumer Protection Act, 1987)

Related to negligence are the product liability provisions contained in the Consumer Protection Act, 1987. Important points of the legislation that apply are:

- Under the Act, a customer can claim against the producer of a defective product, regardless of the lack of a contractual relationship between them
- A computer comes within the definition of 'product' but computer software might be outside the scope of this part of the Act
- The producer of a defective product is liable for damage resulting from the defect.

Activity 10.3

Legal and professional issues raised by 'misrepresentation'

Read the case facts of the London Ambulance Service Computer Aided Despatch System (LASCAD) project failure and the accompanying Public Inquiry Report, which presented the findings of the investigation into the LASCAD project failure. Highlight what you think are the important professional and legal issues involved.

Apply the BCS Code of Conduct and the BCS Code of Good Practice to these professional issues. Did any stakeholders (customer, supplier or third party) act unprofessionally?

The case facts for the London Ambulance Service Computer Aided Despatch System (LASCAD) project failure can be found at:
www.scit.wlv.ac.uk/~cm1995/cbr/cases/case12/12.HTM

The Public Inquiry Report, which presented the findings of the investigation into the LASCAD project failure, can be found at:
www.scit.wlv.ac.uk/~cm1995/cbr/cases/case12/121.HTM

10.6 Summary

This chapter has introduced some of the key concepts and issues raised by failed IT projects. Statistics show that failed IT projects are commonplace and that, besides the financial cost, there are considerable human costs, especially when we consider society's reliance on safety-critical systems. An IT project failure can be summarised as one which 'fails to deliver all the key features and benefits to time, target cost and specification'. There are a number of problems associated with producing reliable systems. These can be defined in one of two broad categories: those that are specific to IT and those that are common causes of project failure in general. These problems have been summarised in this chapter.

In response to society's increasing reliance and overseas competition in this area, RAE/BCS argue that the failure to improve the 'collective professionalism of the IT industry and strengthen the national infrastructure supporting project delivery' will have serious economic impact for the UK. They outline measures that individual companies and project teams can take and advocate recommendations aimed at adding to key elements in the national IT project management capability.

A professional code is a set of rules that states principal duties that all professionals should endeavour to discharge in pursuing their professional lives. In this chapter, the BCS Codes of Conduct and of Good Practice have been highlighted as sources that defined professionalism and good practice. In addition to these professional issues, a number of legal issues are raised when things go wrong in an IT project. These include contractual issues (contract law), negligence (law of negligence) and liability (product liability law, Consumer Protection Act, 1987).

10.7 Review questions

Review question 10.1

What are the three forms of misrepresentation recognised by common law?

Review question 10.2

IT projects differ from other projects in that the technology used is developing rapidly.

List three important implications of this difference.

Review question 10.3

Explain how interoperability is a problem specific to IT projects.

Review question 10.4

What is meant by the term 'correspondence failure'?

Review question 10.5

What are the technical issues that must be taken into consideration for an IT project to be successfully implemented?

Review question 10.6

List the characteristics, according to the BCS, that go to define what it means to be a chartered professional.

Review question 10.7

The BCS Code of Conduct defines professional standards (governing a member's personal conduct) required by the Society as a condition of membership. The professional responsibilities are grouped around what four sections?

Review question 10.8

Generally, contracts for hardware and software are governed by different legal rules. What law is hardware subject to?

Review question 10.9

Generally, contracts for hardware and software are governed by different legal rules.

What law is software subject to?

10.8 Feedback on activities

Feedback on activity 10.1

Some examples of real-life failed IT projects from the United Kingdom include:

- Department of the Environment (Northern Ireland) v Systems Designers, EDS

- International Stock Exchange: TAURUS Project

- Wessex Regional Health Authority

- The Performing Rights Society

- London Ambulance Service Computer Aided Despatch

- St. Albans City & District Council v International Computers Ltd.

- LIBRA (IT system for magistrates' court)

- The Department for Work and Pensions (DWP), Child Support Agency (CSA) system

- Swanwick Air Traffic Control IT project.

What is important for this activity is that, for the example chosen, the failure is defined by answering the following questions:

- Did the IT system fail to fulfil user requirements? (Correspondence failure)

- Did the IT project overrun in terms of budget and time? (Process failure)

- Does the delivered IT system have unsatisfactory performance? (Process failure)

- Is the delivered IT system hardly used? (Interaction failure)

- Is the answer 'yes' to all the above questions for the delivered IT system? (Expectation failure)

Feedback on activity 10.2

The principal duties a professional has to the relevant authority (i.e. the customer) according to the BCS Code of Conduct are (BCS Code paragraph numbers in brackets):

- (6) You shall carry out work or study with due care and diligence in accordance with the relevant authority's requirements, and the interests of system users. If your professional judgement is overruled, you shall indicate the likely risks and consequences.

- (7) You shall avoid any situation that may give rise to a conflict of interest between you and your relevant authority. You shall make full and immediate disclosure to them if any conflict is likely to occur or be seen by a third party as likely to occur.

- (8) You shall not disclose or authorise to be disclosed, or use for personal gain or to benefit a third party, confidential information except with the permission of your relevant authority, or at the direction of a court of law.

- (9) You shall not misrepresent or withhold information on the performance of products, systems or services, or take advantage of the lack of relevant knowledge or inexperience of others.

Feedback on activity 10.3

Salient professional and legal issues involved include:

Systems Options is reported as having had no previous experience of building despatch systems for ambulance services. Coupled with the very tight deadline, delivery would have been seen as almost impossible. As professionals, Systems Options should not have offered to do work or provide a service which was not within their professional competence.

Systems Options failed to use the PRINCE project management method as prescribed for public sector projects. The Inquiry Report findings state that there was no real project management experience on the team. In addition, the LAS management should have ensured adequate project management experience and application of the prescribed PRINCE method.

Systems Options had a duty to inform the client of their concerns over the proposed timetable. If they accepted the tight deadline for delivery of the CAD system, then as professionals they were obliged to complete work undertaken on time.

Systems Options should have conformed to recognised good practice in systems development and implementation which includes testing and quality assurance.

Systems Options and LAS management should have considered training – in particular, crew training and central ambulance control staff training – as part of the systems development life cycle.

LAS management clearly underestimated the difficulties involved in changing the deeply ingrained culture of London Ambulance Service and misjudged the industrial relations climate so that staff were alienated to the changes rather than brought on board.

References

- Berleur, J & Brunnstein, K (eds) (1996), *Ethics of computing: codes, spaces for discussion and law*. A handbook prepared by the IFIP Ethics Task Group, London: Chapman & Hall.
- *Better Projects Directorate* (December 2004), Office of Government Commerce (OGC) (**www.ogc.gov.uk**).
- Beynon-Davies, P (1995), *Information systems failure and risk assessment : the case of the London Ambulance Service Computer Aided Despatch System*. European Conference on Information Systems, Athens.
- Jenkins, S (2005), in *The Sunday Times*, 26 June 2005.

- Lyytinen, K & Hirschheim, R (1987), 'Information system failures: a survey and classification of empirical literature'. *Oxford Surveys in Information Technology*, 4, pp.257-309.
- McCue, A (2006), *Failed IT project costs clearing house €47m*. (Available from: **www.silicon.com/financialservices/0,3800010322,39160768,00.htm**).
- Parliamentary Office of Science and Technology (POST) (2003), *Government IT Projects*.
- Rogers, M (2007), *Iraq – another failed IT project?* computerworld.com (Available from: **www.computerworld.com.au/index.php/id;1195102115;fp;;fpid;;pf;1**).
- Royal Academy of Engineering and the British Computer Society (April 2004), *The challenges of complex IT projects*. The report of a working group from the Royal Academy of Engineering and the British Computer Society. The Royal Academy of Engineering, London.
- Sauer, C & Cuthbertson, C (2003), *The state of IT project management in the UK 2002-2003*, Templeton College, Oxford.   (Available from: **www.cw360ms.com/ pmsurveyresults/surveyresults.pdf**).

Further reading

- Baase, S (2003), *A Gift of Fire: social, legal and ethical issues for computers and the Internet* (Chapter 10), Pearson.
- Pressman, R (2004), *Software Engineering: A practitioner's approach* (6th edn), McGraw-Hill.

CHAPTER 11

Codes of conduct

OVERVIEW

The purpose of this chapter is to introduce professional codes of conduct in defining duties and prescribing minimum standards of practice that should be observed by computing professionals. In this chapter we endeavour to provide a clear understanding of such codes, and use the British Computer Society and its code of conduct to exemplify the issues.

Learning outcomes	By the end of this chapter you should be able to:

- Appreciate the rationale behind professional bodies

- Understand the role of codes of conduct in a profession

- Articulate key aspects of the BCS Code of Conduct

- Have knowledge of a national code of conduct for computer professionals.

11.1 Introduction

The purpose of this chapter is to introduce the role of professional codes of conduct in defining duties and prescribing minimum standards of practice that should be observed by computing professionals. The chapter uses the British Computer Society and its code of conduct to exemplify the issues. Firstly, the role of professional bodies is introduced and the nature of their services discussed. The general role of codes of conduct are introduced and key aspects of the BCS Code of Conduct are described.

11.2 Professional bodies and the British Computer Society

The British Computer Society (BCS) introduces itself as 'the leading professional body for those working in IT. We have over 58,000 members in more than 100 countries and are the qualifying body for Chartered IT Professionals (CITP).' Whereas this claim is undoubtedly true in the United Kingdom, it would certainly be disputed in some other countries, particularly in the US by, for example, the Association of Computing Machinery (ACM). Many countries have their own professional bodies in IT or in computing and there is an international professional society, the International Federation for Information Processing (IFIP).

The 'vision' and long-term goal of the BCS 'is to see the IT profession recognised as being a profession of the highest integrity and competence'. The mission statement of the BCS, which it claims encapsulates its 'core purpose', states that:

> The BCS will lead the development and implementation of standards for the IT profession through innovative and valued products and services and by being the respected voice informing and influencing individuals, organisations and society as a whole.

> The BCS will lead the change in the standing of the IT profession by creating an understanding of what is required to implement successful IT projects and programmes, and to advise, inform and persuade industry and government on what is required to produce successful IT enabled projects.

Of course, any professional society must make some similar set of claims and there is a need to ensure that the BCS is proactive in meeting these well-intended objectives.

There are many tens of thousands of professional societies around the world; some are small, informal groupings of people, but some are very large and, like the BCS, have a legal status. In the case of the BCS it is a 'chartered' organisation, which simply means that it has a charter – a document, that is recognised in UK law. The BCS's Royal Charter was approved in 1984 by Her Majesty Queen Elizabeth II on the advice of her Privy Council. The Privy Council is the highest organisation in the UK, sitting between the monarch and the Houses of Parliament. Obviously, arrangements in other countries are different, but there is a critical difference between a legally recognised professional society and other groups who claim to represent some profession.

One obvious difficulty is what is meant by 'a profession'. A naïve distinction is between professionals and amateurs. Professionals are paid for their work and amateurs are not. The definition of a profession, however, needs more than this. It must be recognised that there is a discipline, a body of knowledge, skills and activities that are pursued by some group of people. Although not logically necessary, such recognition should be by people who are not members of the profession. The BCS has itself struggled for years to identify what profession it represents. Its use of 'computer' in its title is a historical legacy, and a more modern preference would be for 'computing', which would recognise the activity, rather than the thing – the computer itself.

After all, the BCS does not represent computers but the people who work with them. These days, the BCS prefers to use 'IT' to describe its members' profession, but whether this is clearer, or even whether there is a universally acceptable definition of information technology (IT), is doubtful. The title 'information systems' (IS) is also frequently used as, increasingly, is 'information communication technology' (ICT).

Even when a professional society is recognised in law, there is a further consideration – whether a person must belong to the professional society to practise the profession. The case of mainstream medicine in the UK is fairly straightforward since it is illegal to interfere physically with other people's bodies. Even here, however, there are limits, particularly if the person receiving some treatment, that is the patient, is willing to receive it. Thus, for example, it is not illegal in the UK for someone to stick needles in other people, to create tattoos or for acupuncture. The situation becomes even more complicated with professions such as accountancy. In the UK there are legal requirements on a variety of types of company to have their accounts approved and reported and this work must be done by a chartered accountant, that is, by someone who is a member of one of the legally recognised chartered accountancy professional societies. The problem for the BCS is that there are no such legal requirements for anyone to practise in the IT profession. Legally, no one has to be a member of the BCS to work on any aspect of IT. Furthermore, it is still far from common in the UK for those who pay IT professionals to require them to be members of the BCS. Whether BCS membership would significantly reduce the number of failed software and IT projects (see Chapter 10) is unknown, but it could not make the situation worse! However, a recent report (March 2007) by a BCS Management and Qualification Working Group found that:

> Almost 90 per cent of organisations stated that it was the experience of their IT managers that was important to them, compared with 41 per cent who claimed that their IT qualifications were important.

www.bcs.org/upload/pdf/surveymgt.pdf.

As with all professional societies, the BCS is in the business of service. There are four types of service identifiable by who, or what, is being served. These are indicated in Figure 11.1.

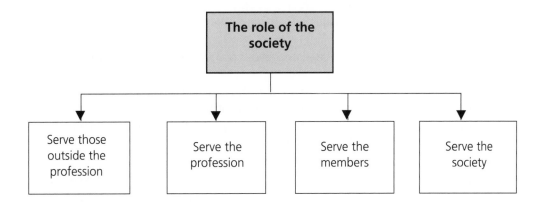

Figure 11.1: The society 'serves' in a number of ways

From an ethical perspective, service to those outside the profession is the most important. People and organisations have to trust the expert advice and the quality of the work of the IT professionals they employ. Often, they have to trust almost 'blindly' because no one disputes that IT systems are extremely complicated, and their potential consequences even more so. Furthermore, because computers are a relatively new invention, and because they often do things that have never been done before, it is difficult for the lay person, who has little or no knowledge of IT, to even recognise that advice or work is of poor quality.

So as to support those outside the profession, it is essential to also serve the profession. This is because IT is a rapidly changing field. All fields of expertise undergo change, but IT is somewhat unusual in that it does not have many firm foundations which can be built upon over time. Thus, previous good practice may rapidly become dated. Therefore, the profession itself must continually change and those working in it must continually develop their skills.

In practice, the main work of a professional society such as the BCS is focused on serving its members and this is undoubtedly the simplest form of activity. The needs and requirements of members can be readily identified. In contrast it is much more difficult to define and address the needs of those who work outside the profession – it is even difficult to accurately identify the types of people who should be targeted for support. However, the membership of the society is clearly defined and their requirements can be readily determined via, for example, questionnaires. The BCS serves its members in a number of ways. In this context, the BCS indicates:

> The essential requirement for professional competence coupled with appropriate professional standards lies at the heart of almost all BCS activity and the services that it provides. BCS enables individuals, organizations and society to realise the potential of and maximise the benefits from IT by:
>
> - Setting and maintaining the highest professional standards for IT professionals including
>   - accrediting individual professional competence and integrity through the award of BCS professional qualifications and those of the Engineering Council and of the Science Council; and by inspection and accreditation of university courses and company training schemes
>   - defining standards for professional conduct through the BCS Code of Conduct and Code of Good Practice
> - Initiating and informing debate on IT strategic issues with Government, Industry, and Academia
> - Advising the UK Government and its agencies on IT-related matters regarding proposed legislation
> - Representing the profession on issues of importance and liaising with other professional bodies, including other engineering institutions and overseas societies
> - Examining and initiating debate on topical IT issues, most recently through the BCS programme of Thought Leadership debates
> - Supporting individuals in their career development.
>
> source: **www.bcs.org**

In reality, for the IT professional who is a member of the BCS, the services they receive tend to be quite specific. While the BCS does undoubtedly contribute to all of the above aspirations, its coverage is variable. For example, its 'cutting-edge products and services' are far from exhaustive and there are many areas of computing currently being researched which are not part of central BCS operations. Similarly, the debates on IT strategic issues tend to be relatively short-term. In addition, as we have noted, the IT field is rapidly evolving and advancing.

Consequently, an organisation such as the BCS must also be highly dynamic and adaptable. This is certainly not always the case.

At the core of the BCS are its specialist groups. With more than approximately 40 Branches throughout the UK, a number of International Sections and over 50 Specialist Groups, ELITE, ASSIST, Disability and YPG, BCS provides both members and the public with an unrivalled opportunity to keep abreast of current developments in numerous areas of interest.

The BCS also has a number of affiliated groups, and member groups (as mentioned above) such as the Young Professionals Group (YPG) – dedicated to the needs of younger members; the ELITE Group – a leading UK forum for IT Directors and Senior Managers; ASSIST – for people working in and for informatics in healthcare and social care; and the Disability Group which focuses on the role of IT in giving disabled people a better quality of life.

Unfortunately, not all specialist groups are particularly active (some are distinctly dormant/ inert), and efforts to establish new groups can be frustrating at the least.

A relatively small cadre of paid and volunteer workers carries out the central operations of the BCS. The Society's annual budget is several million pounds per year and the 's main source of income is its annual subscription fee: it is therefore essential that it maintains its membership and, not surprisingly, the Society is always trying to recruit new members. To this end, the Society has a major role as the supplier of professional qualifications, and accredits undergraduate and postgraduate degree programmes in universities and colleges.

Activity 11.1

BCS services

Visit the British Computer Society (BCS) website: **www.bcs.org**

Identify four different services provided by the BCS that primarily serve one of the four areas indicated in Figure 11.1. Briefly describe (1 sentence will suffice) each service and note if each example might support more than one type of service.

Figure 11.2: The complexity of IT?

11.3 The role of codes of conduct

As discussed in previous chapters, the BCS provides a code of conduct that is intended to support the professional obligations of those working within the area of computing and IT in general. In this context, the BCS states:

> This Code sets out the professional standards required by the Society as a condition of membership. It applies to members of all grades, including students, and affiliates, and also non-members who offer their expertise as part of the Society's Professional Advice Register.

The BCS Code of Conduct is specifically targeted at individual members and their professional work:

> The Code governs your personal conduct as an individual member of the BCS and not the nature of business or ethics of the relevant authority. It will, therefore, be a matter of your exercising your personal judgement in meeting the Code's requirements.

The specificity of the BCS Code of Conduct appears extreme in the quotation above, in that it appears only to apply to the professional work done with IT systems, and the consequences of the use of the work must be judged by each member. What is probably missing is an extension to the general definition above of the 'relevant authority' so that it should include national and international legal requirements, as it does explicitly in the Code itself. Thus, for example, a member should not knowingly engage in work for criminal or terrorist organisations. On the other hand, some people will choose not to work on military projects, whereas others will do so – working in what they might prefer to call the 'defence industries'.

Finally, BCS members are supposed to monitor their own conduct and that of other members:

> Any breach of the Code of Conduct brought to the attention of the Society will be considered under the Society's disciplinary procedures. You should also ensure that you notify the Society of any significant violation of this Code by another BCS member.

Informing on other members is sometimes termed 'whistle-blowing'. Here, there are well-recognised problems. If it is not done anonymously, then the innocent whistle-blower might be penalised. Anonymity is sometimes difficult to maintain, even if it were guaranteed – for example, when working with a small number of people. Vexatious whistle-blowing – reporting other members unreasonably – is itself a breach of the BCS Code of Conduct. The use of the word 'significant' in 'significant violation' in the above quotation, is not a particularly helpful modifier. The BCS Code of Conduct is supposed to be interpreted flexibly; it provides guidelines rather than being rigidly prescriptive. Thus it seems hardly worth having two thresholds: 'any breaches' (which members apply to themselves) and only 'significant' ones, that apply to other members.

Activity 11.2

Non-members' conduct

The BCS Code of Conduct requires BCS members to monitor their own behaviour and that of other members. However, what would you do if you observed a non-BCS member, with whom you are working on an IT project, flagrantly breaching the BCS Code of Conduct?

11.4 Key aspects of the BCS Code of Conduct

The BCS Code of Conduct has 17 elements, separated into four sections. The sections (with the Code's element numbers given in brackets) are:

- **The public interest** (1-5)
- **Duty to relevant authority** (6-9)
- **Duty to the profession** (10-13)
- **Professional competence and integrity** (14-17).

Activity 11.3

The public interest

Make a list of the types of people, groups or organisations that a BCS member should consider 'in the public interest' when working on an IT project.

Hint: To be systematic it is best to try to produce categories before listing example types.

Activity 11.4

Classifying the Code of Conduct

For this activity, you need the BCS Code of Conduct.

Each item in the Code applies to BCS members, but different terms refer to other types of people or organisations. Use the following four-part classification to go through each of the items 2-17 in the BCS Code of Conduct and identify the applicability of the various terms that appear. So as to help you get started, item (6) in the code is considered below.

Classification:

R Relevant authority   **O** Other people

L Law   **B** BCS, other members, peers and colleagues

For example, item 6 of the Code might be classified in the following way:

*6. You shall carry out work or study with due care and diligence in accordance with the relevant authority's (**R**) requirements, and the interests of system users (**O, B**). If your professional judgement is overruled, you shall indicate the likely risks and consequences.*

- The crux of the issue here, familiar to all professionals in whatever field, is the potential conflict between full and committed compliance with the relevant authority's (**R**) wishes, and the independent and considered exercise of your judgement.

- If your judgement is overruled, you are encouraged to seek advice and guidance from a peer or colleague (**B**) on how best to respond.

11.5 An ethical dilemma

Approximately one year ago an editor of this book carried out an informal survey among his academic colleagues who were members of the BCS. He approached each and asked if they could state two points contained within the BCS Code of Conduct. Two of these people responded by indicating that they did not know that the BCS had a professional code of conduct. Two indicated that while they knew the code of conduct existed, they had never looked at it. The remaining two – who indicated their awareness of the code of conduct and recalled having looked at it – stated that they could not recall its contents.

These were clearly dismal results, particularly as the question was asked of people who had been members for some time.

In this book we have discussed the BCS Code of Conduct in some detail – to what extent do you believe this code of conduct is important and/or relevant? Why would YOU join the BCS? If you are a student in a university department studying Computer Science or IT, have you been offered a BCS membership application form? Are you aware of the opportunities for networking, and for joining special interest groups? These are certainly good reasons to join the BCS – but on the other hand, during your professional career, do you believe that the framework defined within the BCS Code of Conduct is likely to be relevant and/or useful?

11.6 Summary

Professional societies such as the BCS need to serve many people, groups, organisations and society itself. Agreement to abide by the BCS Code of Conduct is a requirement placed on all of the Society's members and everyone working on behalf of the Society. Codes of conduct are not easy to prepare and, given the wide range of work carried out by IT professionals, it is essential that the BCS Code is written in such a manner that it can be interpreted in a flexible and appropriate manner. The current version of the BCS Code is organised into four sections and, in total, contains 17 items.

11.7 Review questions

Review question 11.1

Many countries have their own IT professional body.

Is there a need for a single, international one?

What would be the difficulties and disadvantages of setting up such a global professional body?

Review question 11.2

Currently the BCS Code of Conduct relies on its members policing compliance, that is, it is the duty of members to take action when they perceive that the Code has been breached. Is there a need for other mechanisms? What might they be?

Review question 11.3

Could the number of items in the BCS Code of Conduct be reduced? If so, what would you suggest?

Review question 11.4

BCS members are required to comply with the Code of Conduct. How likely is it that most members really know what it contains? What needs to be done?

11.8 Feedback on activities

Feedback on activity 11.1:

The 'Site Map' on the BCS website provides a wide range of services listed under a number of topics. Identify particular instances (not general ones) as done below. The 4 Ss:

- Serve those outside the profession; e.g. accessibility for the disabled

- Serve the profession; e.g. training, conferences

- Serve the members; e.g. specialist groups

- Serve the Society. e.g. membership recruitment.

Feedback on activity 11.2

The BCS member is required to take some form of action – otherwise the member is colluding with the Code, breaching non-member. The obvious first thing would be to discuss it with the non-member. If this provides no resolution, then the member might discuss the situation with 'a peer or colleague'. The member may subsequently alert the 'relevant authority', that is, the IT project owner. Finally, if there is no resolution the member should contact the BCS.

Feedback on activity 11.3

The purpose of this activity is to encourage you to think about who and what is 'the public interest'. A good answer should include the following examples, but these are not exhaustive. Other categories from the three suggested might be used.

1. Individuals

- Indirect end users – people who do not use the IT system but are directly affected by it, for example a government IT records system which might contain erroneous information about the individual

- Family and dependants of indirect end users who may suffer consequences of an IT systems failure

- People who receive a service that requires an IT system, for example air traffic control

- Family and dependants of the above people.

2. Groups

- Any small, private organisation, for example a local sports club

- Organisations that buy off-the-shelf computer technology.

3. Society

- Legal organisations, for example courts or solicitors

- Government, local and national; the armed forces, police, prisons, education, health and social services etc

- The media, for example newspapers, radio and television.

Feedback on activity 11.4

The Public Interest

1. In your professional role you shall have regard for the public health, safety and environment (O, B).

   - This is a general responsibility, which may be governed by legislation, convention or protocol (L).

   - If in doubt over the appropriate course of action to take in particular circumstances you should seek the counsel of a peer or colleague (B).

2. You shall have regard to the legitimate rights of third parties (O, B). The term 'third Party' includes professional colleagues, or possibly competitors (O, B) , or members of 'the public' (O) who might be affected by an IS project without their being directly aware of its existence.

3. You shall ensure that within your professional field/s you have knowledge and understanding of relevant legislation, regulations and standards (L), and that you comply with such requirements.

   - As examples, relevant legislation could, in the UK, include The UK Public Disclosure Act, Data Protection or Privacy legislation, Computer Misuse law, legislation concerned with the export or import of technology, possibly for national security reasons, or law relating to intellectual property. This list is not exhaustive, and you should ensure that you are aware of any legislation relevant to your professional responsibilities.

- In the international context, you should be aware of, and understand, the requirements of law specific to the jurisdiction within which you are working, and, where relevant, to supranational legislation such as EU law and regulation. You should seek specialist advice when necessary.

4. You shall conduct your professional activities without discrimination against clients or colleagues (R, O, B)

- Grounds of discrimination include race, colour, ethnic origin, sexual orientation

- All colleagues have a right to be treated with dignity and respect.

- You should adhere to relevant law (L) within the jurisdiction where you are working and, if appropriate, the European Convention on Human Rights (L).

    – You are encouraged to promote equal access to the benefits of IS by all groups in society (R, O, B), and to avoid and reduce 'social exclusion' from IS wherever opportunities arise.

5. You shall reject any offer of bribery or inducement (R, O, L, B).

Duty to Relevant Authority
7. You shall avoid any situation that may give rise to a conflict of interest between you and your relevant authority (R). You shall make full and immediate disclosure to them if any conflict is likely to occur or be seen by a third party (O, B) as likely to occur.

8. You shall not disclose or authorise to be disclosed, or use for personal gain or to benefit a third party (O, B), confidential information except with the permission of your relevant authority, or at the direction of a court of law (L).

9. You shall not misrepresent or withhold information on the performance of products, systems or services, or take advantage of the lack of relevant knowledge or inexperience of others (R, O, B).

Duty to the Profession
10. You shall uphold the reputation and good standing of the BCS (B) in particular, and the profession in general (R, O, B) , and shall seek to improve professional standards through participation in their development, use and enforcement.

- As a Member of the BCS you also have a wider responsibility to promote public (O) understanding of IS – its benefits and pitfalls – and, whenever practical, to counter misinformation that brings or could bring the profession into disrepute.

- You should encourage and support fellow members (B) in their professional development and, where possible, provide opportunities for the professional development of new members, particularly student members (O) . Enlightened mutual assistance between IS professionals (O, B) furthers the reputation of the profession, and assists individual members (B).

11. You shall act with integrity in your relationships with all members of the BCS (B) and

with members of other professions (R, O) with whom you work in a professional capacity.

12. You shall have due regard for the possible consequences of your statements on others (R, O, B) . You shall not make any public statement in your professional capacity unless you are properly qualified and, where appropriate, authorised to do so. You shall not purport to represent the BCS unless authorised to do so.

- The offering of an opinion in public (O) , holding oneself out to be an expert in the subject in question, is a major personal responsibility and should not be undertaken lightly.

- To give an opinion that subsequently proves ill founded is a disservice to the profession, and to the BCS.

13. You shall notify the Society (B) if convicted of a criminal offence or upon becoming bankrupt or disqualified as Company Director (L).

Professional Competence and Integrity
14. You shall seek to upgrade your professional knowledge and skill, and shall maintain awareness of technological developments, procedures and standards which are relevant to your field, and encourage your subordinates (O, B) to do likewise.

15. You shall not claim any level of competence that you do not possess (R, O, B). You shall only offer to do work or provide a service (R) that is within your professional competence.

You can self-assess your professional competence for undertaking a particular job or role by asking, for example,

i. am I familiar with the technology involved, or have I worked with similar technology before?

ii. have I successfully completed similar assignments or roles in the past?

iii. can I demonstrate adequate knowledge of the specific business application and requirements successfully to undertake the work?

16. You shall observe the relevant BCS Codes of Practice (B) and all other standards which, in your judgement, are relevant, and you shall encourage your colleagues (R, O, B) to do likewise.

17. You shall accept professional responsibility for your work (R) and for the work of colleagues who are defined in a given context as working under your supervision (O, B).

Further reading

- Ayres, R (1999), *The Essence of Professional Issues in Computing*, (Chapter 12), Prentice-Hall.
- Baase, S (2003), *A Gift of Fire: Social, Legal and Ethical Issues for Computers and the Internet*, (Chapter 10, and Appendix A), Pearson.
- British Computer Society website: **www.bcs.org**

Towards the future: some ethical and social issues

OVERVIEW

The fields of IT and computer-related disciplines are rapidly advancing. Changes are not only being introduced at a rapid pace as far as digital technologies are concerned but also in terms of their deployment. At the present time, there are a number of areas which are attracting considerable attention, and which have strong ethical, social, and legal ramifications. These include the gathering of biometric data, the intention to introduce compulsory ID cards (coupled with the National Identity Register), and a general trend in the UK which seems to be inexorably leading to a so-called 'database society'. In this chapter, we highlight various issues in relation to these ongoing developments, and pay particular attention to ethical and social considerations. In addition, we also briefly refer to aspects of another 'hot topic' – digital rights management, and the Content Protection and Copyright Management proposal.

Learning outcomes By the end of this chapter you should be able to:

- Discuss key aspects of the so-called 'database society'

- Develop a personal standpoint in relation to the ethical and social consequences associated with the 'database society' and the increasing use that is being made of biometric data

- Understand key issues arising from the various 'ethical dilemmas' introduced in previous chapters of this book

- Appreciate the ramifications associated with the pace at which IT-related systems are developing and are being deployed.

12.1 Introduction

In this final chapter, we particularly focus on ethical and social issues relating to ways in which we are currently using and deploying computer-based technologies. We begin by considering the present thrust within the UK to establish what is commonly referred to as the 'database society'. This embraces the development of systems that in principle enable data that has traditionally been stored on separate databases to be accessed in a seamless manner and, when coupled with the introduction of compulsory ID cards and the use of biometric information, has ramifications for personal liberty and human privacy. Within this section we also delineate the information that is provisionally to be stored within the ID card/ National Identity Register (NIR) framework. Certainly, when viewed in a critical light, this project has Orwellian overtones. On the other hand, as we saw in Chapter 10, large-scale IT projects – especially those which are government initiated – often fail and therefore this project may go the same way as many of its predecessors, but only after a great deal of money has been spent! In this section we also refer to the 'Children's Information Sharing Index' – a proposed national database for all children (although it appears that 'celebrity' children will not be included because of the potential security breaches that could occur, which are thought acceptable for more 'ordinary' children).

In Section 12.3, we turn our attention to highlighting advantages and disadvantages associated with the introduction of digital systems; we consider aspects of digital rights management (DRM) – specifically the Content Protection and Copy Management (CPCM) proposal as applied to the transmission and playback of video content. Subsequently, in Section 12.4 we review several of the 'ethical dilemmas' introduced in previous chapters and particularly focus on various ethical and social issues that they raise.

Finally, in Section 12.5 we briefly consider issues that arise as a consequence of the pace of change of computer, and computer-related, technologies. Here we refer to the increasing reliance that is being placed on biometrics – including the use of fingerprinting in schools (with children as young as three years of age being required to provide fingerprints) and the deployment and use of similar technology in English pubs.

12.2 The database society

During the last thirty years or so, tremendous advances have taken place in relation to computer technologies. These not only relate to advances in computational performance, but also to the ability of computers to support the storage and rapid retrieval of almost unlimited amounts of data. In addition, the high-speed interconnection of computers allow vast amounts of data to be transferred seamlessly and with little delay. With the advent of the Internet and World Wide Web, the geographical location at which data is stored no longer has any great significance. From a computer located in an office or home, we can now rapidly access data held on servers that are physically located in practically every part of the globe.

Over the years, governments, organisations, institutions, and companies have placed ever-greater reliance upon computer technologies. As a result, ever-larger amounts of data relating to the individual have accumulated. However, these databases have generally operated independently and therefore have, in essence, represented isolated entities. At the present time (within, for example, the UK) there is a move towards integrating these databases in such a way that they will soon no longer operate in isolation. A fundamental key to this development takes the form of the identity card and National Identity Register (NIR) which it now seems will inevitably be introduced in the near future – initially on a voluntary and then on a compulsory basis.

Below we indicate the data that is likely to be encompassed by identity cards linked to the National Identity Register (NIR):

Personal information

- full name
- other names by which person is or has been known
- date of birth
- place of birth
- gender
- address of principal place of residence in the United Kingdom
- the address of every other place in the United Kingdom or elsewhere where person has a place of residence.

Identifying information

- a photograph of head and shoulders
- signature
- fingerprints
- other biometric information.

Residential status

- nationality
- entitlement to remain in the United Kingdom where that entitlement derives from a grant of leave to enter or remain in the United Kingdom, the terms and conditions of that leave.

Personal reference numbers

- National Identity registration number
- the number of any ID card issued
- allocated National Insurance number
- the number of any relevant immigration document
- the number of their United Kingdom passport
- the number of any passport issued to the individual by or on behalf of the authorities of a country or territory outside the United Kingdom or by or on behalf of an international organisation

- the number of any document that can be used by them (in some or all circumstances) instead of a passport
- the number of any identity card issued to him/her by the authorities of a country or territory outside the United Kingdom
- any reference number allocated to him/her by the Secretary of State in connection with an application made by him/her for permission to enter or to remain in the United Kingdom
- the number of any work permit relating to him/her
- any driver number given to him/her by a driving licence
- the number of any designated document which is held by him/her and is a document, the number of which does not fall within any of the preceding sub-paragraphs
- the date of expiry or period of validity of a document, the number of which is recorded by virtue of this paragraph.

Record history

- information falling within the preceding paragraphs that has previously been recorded about him/her in the Register
- particulars of changes affecting that information and of changes made to his/her entry in the Register
- date of death.

Registration and ID card history

- the date of every application for registration made by him/her
- the date of every application by him/her for a modification of the contents of his/her entry
- the date of every application by him/her confirming the contents of his/her entry (with or without changes)

- the reason for any omission from the information recorded in his/her entry

- particulars (in addition to its number) of every ID card issued to him/her

- whether each such card is in force and, if not, why not

- particulars of every person who has countersigned an application by him/her for an ID card or a designated document, so far as those particulars were included on the application

- particulars of every notification given about lost, stolen and damaged ID cards

- particulars of every requirement by the Secretary of State for the individual to surrender an ID card issued to him/her.

Validation information

- the information provided in connection with every application to be entered in the Register, for a modification of the contents of his/her entry or for the issue of an ID card

- the information provided in connection with every application confirming entry in the Register (with or without changes)

- particulars of the steps taken, in connection with an application mentioned in paragraph (a) or (b) or otherwise, for identifying the applicant or for verifying the information provided in connection with the application

- particulars of any other steps taken or information obtained for ensuring that there is a complete, up-to-date and accurate entry about that individual in the Register

- particulars of every notification given by that individual for changing details in the register.

Security information

- a personal identification number to be used for facilitating the making of applications for information recorded in his/her entry, and for facilitating the provision of the information

- a password or other code to be used for that purpose or particulars of a method of generating such a password or code

- questions and answers to be used for identifying a person seeking to make such an application or to apply for or to make a modification of that entry.

Records of provision of information

- particulars of every occasion on which information contained in the individual's entry has been provided to a person

- particulars of every person to whom such information has been provided on such an occasion

- other particulars, in relation to each such occasion, of the provision of the information.

(source: BBC News: **http://news.bbc.co.uk/1/hi/uk_politics/4630045.stm**)

The use of biometric data will facilitate the establishment of a direct link between the card and the individual. Ultimately it is likely that data held on the card (coupled with other data stored by computer systems) will provide the key via which the individual is linked with a vast amount of personal data.

As indicated above, three key ingredients that are making this 'advance' possible are:

- the processing capabilities of the computer
- support for the storage and rapid retrieval of almost unlimited amounts of data
- high bandwidth interconnects between computer systems.

In addition the system is based on the use of microchip technology (incorporated on the ID card) and support for the capture and recording of biometric data.

In principle, and for example, data stored on the DVLA computers (vehicle and driver data), on law enforcement computers, on NHS computers, etc, may be brought together within one unified framework. In addition, there is the possibility that this could be supplemented with personal data held by banks and credit card organisations, through to the computers storing data concerning our personal shopping habits (which is often made available via 'loyalty cards'), etc. In short, the potential ramifications of introducing the identity card system, coupled with unified access support to personal data stored on different computer systems and computer networks, has great social and ethical implications. Here, it is important to realise that within the terms of modern society it is very difficult (if not impossible) to opt out of such an infrastructure, and this has serious consequences for personal privacy.

ID cards were last deployed in the UK during WWII – although these were extremely primitive when compared to the cards which are now to be introduced. However, in 1952 their use was terminated:

> During the WWII the ID card was seen as a way of protecting the nation from Nazi spies. But in 1952, Winston Churchill's government scrapped the cards. The feeling was that in peacetime they simply were not needed. In fact they were thought to be hindering the work of the police, because so many people resented being asked to produce a card to prove their identity.

> (Source: BBC News: **http://news.bbc.co.uk/2/hi/uk_news/politics/3127696.stm**)

Of course, it can be argued that if the individual has nothing to hide, then the individual need have no concern regarding the ramifications of a 'database society'. However, from an ethical perspective, the individual has a fundamental right to privacy, and in fact perhaps there should be the opportunity for the individual to hide minor infractions and personal information from the state. In this latter respect, let us take a simple example. Suppose that you were fortunate enough to own a top end of the range BMW coupe, Ferrari, or the like. It is early morning and in front of you is a long, straight road – you are in the middle of nowhere (perhaps a desert region) – there is no other traffic around, and for a brief time you succumb to your natural instincts – the desire to see just how fast this car will actually go. For the next ten minutes you put it through its paces, and subsequently once more return to being a law-abiding citizen travelling always within the speed limits. Within that ten minutes you certainly broke the law as far as speeding is concerned. However, in a futuristic society, we can imagine that the ten minutes of pleasure could have been recorded by the car's onboard computer, and consequently when the car is next inspected by a garage (perhaps for its MOT or the like), one's brief stint as a racing driver will go on record. Perhaps you will be given an on-the-spot fine, perhaps points will be deducted from your driving licence.

This simple example is intended to highlight the fact that there are occasions when many law-abiding citizens will in fact do something which is outside the law. This is generally a facet of human nature. On the other hand, computer systems can be deployed in such a way as to absolutely restrict our ability to do something which, although strictly speaking is outside the law, causes no harm to anybody.

Having succumbed to those minutes of human exuberance mentioned above, it is most unlikely that we would turn ourselves in at the next police station. Equally, we would be most sorry to have to pay for this experience at some future date as a consequence of the car's on-board computer revealing our actions. Clearly, our minor infringement provides an example of something that we would prefer to hide – an incident that we would not like to have recorded on a government database. On perhaps a more serious note, there may be other matters that we feel uncomfortable about revealing, and which we may feel could count against (or disadvantage) us in some way.

In relation to ID cards, there is an assurance (at least for the present time) that certain information will not be stored. For example:

> The government has sought to allay some fears about ID cards by saying they will not store details about someone's race, religion, sexuality, health, criminal record or political beliefs.

> (Source: BBC News: **http://news.bbc.co.uk/2/hi/uk_news/politics/3127696.stm**)

Consider the issue of an individual's religion. History and current events provide us with an insight into the possible ramifications of ones personal religion. Certainly, it is evident that to reveal one's religion as Jewish in Nazi Germany, or in Nazi-occupied countries before and during WWII had fatal consequences. For some years in Ireland, to reveal one's religion as Catholic could cause problems in terms of gaining employment. At the time of writing, there are suggestions that the US will introduce visa requirements perhaps for all UK citizens, or alternatively only for UK citizens with certain backgrounds (ethical or religious). On the basis of history, we can conclude that one's religion is not always interpreted in a neutral manner. On the other hand, it is important to note that the introduction of a 'database society' (as discussed above) provides no assurance that such information is not readily available. For example, although the identity card and NIR are not in themselves intended to record religion, this information can be obtained (or inferred) from alternative sources, such as place of marriage, applications for tax relief in relation to donations made to a church or choice of school for children.

In conclusion, although many people have nothing that they deliberately wish to hide (in terms of serious wrong-doing), there may well be minor infringements that they do not wish to reveal, or alternatively information that they are uncomfortable about revealing – as summarised in Figure 12.1. As one looks into the short-term future, it is evident that it will become increasingly difficult to hide or simply not reveal practically every aspect of one's background and everyday life.

Activity 12.1

Inferring personal information

Consider the quotation provided on page 210, in which we are reassured that the ID card system will not include various categories of information. Outline how two categories of your choice (other than religion which we have already discussed) can be inferred (or directly determined) from database records.

Finally, we should consider one other important aspect of the so-called 'database society'. Although over the years it has been possible for governments, organisations, institutions, and the like to obtain ever-increasing amounts of information in relation to the individual, this data has often been of relatively little value. In short, the sheer volume of data that could be gained has provided protection. After all, how could anybody have the time or inclination to work through vast amounts of data – neither time nor human resources could be made available for such a feat. Here it is worth mentioning the remarkable book written by George Orwell (*Nineteen Eighty-Four*) in which 'telescreens' in homes, offices, and the like, continually observe the behaviour of party members. This scenario would have necessitated a vast number of observers. Today, the situation is somewhat different. Tireless software ('intelligent agents') can be used to search databases in an extremely flexible manner. Whereas Orwell suggested the use of human observers, spies and the like, modern technology provides the opportunity for an alternative approach in which humans need have little input. This provides the opportunity for tremendous efficiency – despite the vast amount of personal data that is held on computer systems.

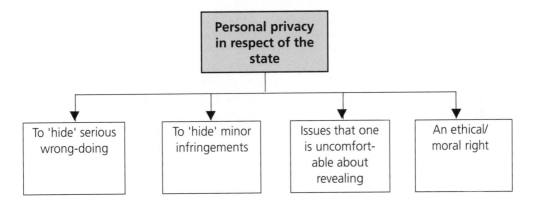

Figure 12.1: A desire for personal privacy can be based upon various factors/views. An individual may wish to 'hide' behaviour in respect of the law or may, for example, wish to do so because of a fundamental belief that privacy is an ethical/moral right.

Automated searches may not simply be intended to reveal past wrong-doing but may be used to indicate possible future behaviour. For example, in relation to the 'Children's Information Sharing Index' (CISI), a proposed national database of all children, ARCH (Action on Rights for Children writes:

Although government guidance says that further information known to individual practitioners (beyond what is required to build the IS Index) should not normally be exchanged without consent, this is a very grey area. For example, the Youth Justice Board believes that consent is not necessary when practitioners are trying to identify a child who may become an offender. Many practitioners believe that information can be shared under wide legal powers such as 'preventing crime' or 'improving the local area'.

Naturally, using personal data to predict the likelihood of an individual's future actions has strong ethical and social ramifications which become increasingly important when we look towards the more powerful IT systems which will become available in the future. Interestingly, in relation to the CISI project in general, ARCH writes:

> Government IT projects have an appalling record of failure and breakdown. If practitioners are dependent on a database to alert them to signs of neglect or abuse, a breakdown could place vulnerable children at even greater risk. Similarly, families who need services are likely to experience serious delays in getting what they need.

And as far as the cost of this project is concerned:

> The government says that it will cost £224m to set up the IS Index, and another £41m per year to run it. This is a major database project and, so far, all of the government's major IT projects have cost far more than was predicted. The £41m running costs appear very optimistic: this amounts to £270,000 per local authority. Bearing in mind the extra staff that will be needed, the training costs whenever a new practitioner is given access, the system maintenance and upgrade costs, it is difficult to see how it will only cost £41m per year. Will the additional costs have to be borne by local councils?

The Foundation for Information Policy Research (FIPR) has undertaken research in 'identifying the growth in children's databases and assessing the data protection and privacy implications'. This has led to an extensive and comprehensive report written in March 2006. Below we briefly quote from this document:

> One concern is what we might call 'e-discrimination'. In the past, it has been well documented that children who were black, or from poor neighbourhoods or travelling families, suffered disproportionate police attention because of the expectation that they would be more likely to offend. The expectation could easily turn into a self-fulfilling prophecy. A system that attempts to predict which children will become delinquent, by totting up negative indicators from health, school and other records, runs the serious risk of recreating the same problems – especially as the information, analysis and professional opinions it contains will be made available to many of the public-sector workers who come into contact with the child. A perfectly law-abiding youngster from a difficult home background, who has perhaps struggled to overcome learning and health difficulties, may find at every turn that teachers expect less, and that police attention is more likely. As the causes of this discrimination are online, the youngster cannot mitigate them simply by dressing neatly and being polite. The data and algorithms used as a basis for discrimination might not be accessible to the victim (whether practically or at all) and thus a victim of unjustified discrimination might end up with no recourse. This raises serious data protection concerns relating to the appropriateness of collecting, processing and retaining the data.

> ...Our third bundle of problems concern a rather cavalier interpretation of data protection law and privacy law by a number of the agencies involved in building the network of children's databases. For example, the Gillick precedent (confirmed recently in the Axon case) establishes that a child's parents should normally be involved in matters of consent, but that, exceptionally, the child may exercise the consent function to the exclusion of the parent if he or she insists on it and has the maturity to understand the consequences. This has been routinely turned into a principle that anyone over 13 can consent to sharing sensitive personal information without the involvement of their parents. In some circumstances the consent is obtained coercively, with implied threats of loss of access to services. This is unlawful. Another example is the proposed

collection of information on sexual activity of 16-18-year-olds, in the name of child protection, even though such persons are over the age of legal consent. This breaches human rights law. A third example we found was police sharing data on a 9-month-old baby without the parents' consent using the excuse of 'crime prevention'. To be fair, many of these abuses stem more from ignorance than from malice...

Our fourth bundle concerns the actual harm that sharing can do. Government documentation and guidance is mostly unbalanced in that it ignores the dark side; it pays little heed to family values, therapeutic effectiveness, trust and privacy. By failing to respect the users of the social-care system, it risks deepening rather than ameliorating social exclusion. There is specific harm: in a disturbing recent case, a nine-year-old was wrongly taken into care after social workers misunderstood medical information. Increasing the amount of poor-quality data available will lead to more errors, and out-of context information can easily cause risk-averse staff to panic, with serious consequences. There are also institutional and professional risks. US information-sharing pilots have in many cases shown negative outcomes, because of the diffusion of responsibility; and recently, professional disquiet in the UK has led to the *Social Work Manifesto*, whose authors object to having to 'collude with youth justice policies which demonize young people'. Even if one does not share this radical view, there are certainly growing problems of recruitment and retention within the profession.

Report published 22nd November 2006: **www.cl.cam.ac.uk/~rja14/Papers/kids.pdf**

To what extent the ID card and biometric technologies will be successfully introduced is questionable. Perhaps individual security and privacy will simply depend upon whether the various IT projects are successful – or fail. Certainly, at the present time there are no foreseeable limits as to our abilities to empower computers. The key question is to what extent we wish to have these machines monitor, impinge upon and even control our everyday lives.

Activity 12.2

Databases specifically for child-related data

Access the report produced by FIPR – the url for which is given above. Spend a little time reading through the report and identify what you consider to be the main ethical issues relating to the storage of child-related information. Also consider the ramifications of attempting to use computer technologies to predict delinquent behaviour. Discuss your thoughts with other students.

12.3 Restricting choice: digital rights management

Digital rights management (DRM) is one of today's 'hot topics' and is raising a number of important issues. By way of example, consider the transmission of films and the like via traditional broadcasting techniques or via satellite/cable links. At the present time we can record such content and play it back freely for our own private use. Undoubtedly, the move from conventional analogue broadcasting to digital transmission offers to open up many exciting opportunities for the end user. However, digital transmission also makes it much easier for providers to impose restrictions and define the technologies that must be used in order to view content.

In March 2007 the Electronic Frontier Foundation (which focuses on defending consumer rights, freedom of expression, etc) produced an interesting report entitled *Who Controls Your Television?* (EFF, 2007). They open by stating:

> Today, consumers can digitally record their favourite television shows, move recordings to portable video players, excerpt a small clip to include in a home video, and much more. The digital television transition promises innovation and competition in even more gadgets that will give consumers unparalleled control over their media.

> But an inter-industry organization that creates television and video specifications used in Europe, Australia and much of Africa and Asia is laying the foundation for a far different future – one in which major content providers get a veto over innovation and consumers face draconian digit rights management (DRM) restrictions on the use of TV content. At the behest of American movie and television studios, the Digital Video Broadcasting (DVB) project is devising standards to ensure that digital television devices obey content providers' commands rather than consumers' desires. These restrictions will take away consumers' rights and abilities to use lawfully acquired content, so that each use can be sold back to them piecemeal.

In the document they describe an elaborate digital rights management scheme called *Content Protection and Copy Management* (CPCM) which various content providers are attempting to impose. They provide several key examples demonstrating the possible ramifications of the CPCM scheme, for example:

> CPCM will allow content providers to apply copy restriction labels to broadcast streams. For example, a program could be marked as 'copy never'. In turn, your DVRs and other devices receiving the signal will have to obey and forbid copying even for home use. A content provider could opt to allow recording but still enforce a multitude of restrictions on copying to other devices.

The EFF goes on to indicate that content copyright holders will, in principle, be able to define the systems that can be used for recording and displaying content. In brief, they indicate a general scheme via which such goals can be obtained.

> Meanwhile, free over-the-air TV is currently broadcast unencrypted, but DVB is designing a way for it to be encrypted by devices at the point of reception. Broadcasts will include a DRM 'flag' – a set of data that rides alongside the broadcast video and can signal whether content should be CPCM-encrypted with a set of standard restrictions. The default will be to turn certain CPCM restrictions 'on'.

At the time of writing, it is not possible to determine the extent to which those promoting the CPCM scheme will succeed. However, this provides us with an interesting example of how on one hand the move to digital and computer-based technologies offers unprecedented opportunities for the end user, but on the other hand can also be used to readily impose Draconian restrictions. In this sense, the possibility exists that the move to digital transmissions will, in effect, represent giving with one hand and taking away with the other. Whether or not the overall effect is a net win or a net loss for the end user remains to be seen.

Certainly, the proposed CPCM scheme appears to be being introduced in a Draconian manner, and this raises various ethical issues and has important social consequences.

Figure 12.2: An ethical use of computers?

12.4 Review of the ethical dilemmas

In this section, we briefly review issues that arise in connection with several of the 'ethical dilemmas' that have been introduced in previous chapters. These are not discussed in chronological order, but rather in a way that is intended to more readily accommodate issues that they raise.

Computer fallibility and the use of expert systems

Recall in Chapter 9 that we introduced an ethical dilemma in which a bank employed expert systems to determine the type of account that could be offered to a new customer. In addition, we indicated that the bank manager was very happy (and confident) with this approach. This was demonstrated by her view that 'computers do not make mistakes'.

The hardware and software systems that comprise a computer are designed and implemented by humans. Computer systems are operated by humans. Humans are fallible and therefore the machines which we create and the way in which we operate such machines are also fallible. Consequently, it is entirely incorrect to consider that computers (and computer-related technologies) are able to provide infallible solutions.

We only have to take a brief look at history to gain a clear insight into the fallibility of human technical creativity, and also of our fallibility in the operation of our creative endeavours. During its construction, the *Titanic* was said to be an unsinkable ship – at its time it represented the pinnacle of human engineering achievement. On its maiden voyage, it sank.

In the 1930s, the *Hindenburg* represented the pinnacle of German achievement in the design and production of enormous and luxurious airships – the safest possible means of travel. On landing at Lakehurst in the US, this amazing feat of human creativity descended in a ball of fire. The British R101 airship represented a similar peak of engineering prowess but on its maiden voyage to India made the journey no further than Northern France before crashing in a storm. Of course these examples are quite dated, and perhaps our abilities have considerably advanced since those times?

However, when we look at some of the complex technologies that we have developed during the last forty years, we again see the fallibility of our efforts. Concorde in many ways represented an engineering feat that considerably outstripped the complexity of both today's supersonic fighter aircraft, and the manned rockets that travelled to the Moon. It took a small and inconsequential piece of debris lying on a runway to destroy one of these aircraft.

Here we note that the primary problem did not lie in the design of the aircraft itself, but rather in its operation. The space shuttle, which again represents a tremendous achievement, has catastrophically failed on two occasions. Rocket payloads sent to Mars have quite frequently completely failed during their descent onto the planet. On a more mundane level, even new models of car are occasionally recalled due to flaws in their design, and domestic appliances fail – even within their period of warranty.

We conclude that the vehicles, products, and systems that we engineer are fallible – computer systems are no exception. Computers can fail catastrophically (for example, in terms of hardware failure) or alternatively they may fail simply by generating erroneous results (due, for example, to operator or software error).

Surprisingly, there is quite a widely held opinion that computers are in some way infallible – the result that appears on the screen is often considered to be completely trustworthy. As discussed above, this is an entirely erroneous view, and leads to a further question concerning why we are willing to impart decision-making capabilities to a machine that is fallible. Let us return to the example given in Chapter 9 concerning the bank's use of, and faith in, expert systems. Certainly if the bank manager is told to act upon the decisions made by the computer, and does so, then the bank manager cannot be held accountable for mistakes made. In this sense, empowering the computer is alleviating the operator of responsibility.

Indeed, humans frequently make mistakes and it is likely that the world would be impoverished if we did not do so. We all know that parents frequently try to prevent their children from making the same mistakes that they have made. All too often their advice is ignored – we learn best from our own mistakes, and it is by learning from our mistakes that we gradually gain experience and wisdom. Once we remove the human element from the decision-making process then we are taking away human responsibility as far as decisions are concerned. In turn, this means that the people who would usually be making decisions are no longer gaining experience (on the basis of their own ability to make correct and incorrect decisions) – they are simply following the instructions of a machine.

In this ethical dilemma there is a further point that should be considered. When a human makes a decision, the decision is commonly based on a broad range of factors not all of which can be quantified and in some way encapsulated so as to be used by digital technologies. Therefore traditionally, for example, a bank manager may have made a decision not only on the basis of a client's previous track record and background, but also on the basis of other factors that arise through human communication – putting this in its simplest terms: gaining an overall impression of the person. This is not something a machine can do, but rather something that a person can accomplish and is often based upon years of experience. In the same way, an experienced doctor may not entirely focus upon a particular medical condition that a patient describes, or which is the result of their examination, but may rather take a more holistic view and consider the patient's overall health as a primary indicator. Again, this type of holistic impression is something based on years of experience, and cannot be imparted to a machine.

In the context of computer system fallibility and medical care, it is worth briefly alluding to the recently introduced NHS IT system (which has so far cost around £12bn). In the *Daily Mail* (8th May 2007) Jenny Hope wrote:

> The controversial new NHS computer program is churning out hundreds of inaccurate patient records due to a fault in the system. The problem affects patients in Greater Manchester who have hospital appointments booked via the online system.

> NHS Connecting for Health, the agency overseeing the £12.4 billion overhaul of the patient records system, stressed the fault would have no impact on patient care.

But a report in *Computer Weekly* magazine reveals there have been 200 'major incidents' over a four-month period in hospitals where the system has 'gone live'.

The latest problem arose after a computer software upgrade installed last month started to produce 400 incorrect duplicates of patient records every day. The fault means the computer automatically creates a new blank patient record without checking to see if one already exists. As a result, doctors could see patients with the wrong information and a team has been set up to ensure that important patient data is not lost...

Of course, a key problem is that such systems are (when viewed from a software perspective) extremely complex; software testing (however extensive) cannot hope to identify all faults (proof of correctness is impossible). In addition, when so much public money is spent, failures of any sort attract considerable media attention. This can ultimately lead to an undesirable situation in which the developers do not want to admit ongoing problems to the client – and the client tries to avoid revealing to the press issues relating to unreliability (and the like). In short a siege-like mentality develops. This places tremendous pressures on those involved in the project and can impact on staff moral. In particularly difficult cases, this may result in an increased turnover of staff and a consequent lack of continuity. Naturally, this inflames the situation.

Internet policing

Recall that in Chapter 5 we introduced an ethical dilemma in which an employee of a company is asked to develop a website that is intended to attract people interested in extreme forms of violence. This is to be used by law enforcement agencies to obtain information concerning individuals who are 'interested' in such matters. As we indicated in the ethical dilemma, the company's boss is particularly insistent that a certain employee undertakes the work.

This is a real-world dilemma, and the following is a possible outcome.

> On leaving work that day, the employee finds himself to be increasingly disturbed about the project. His initial reaction is that Internet policing flies in the face of the freedoms that the Internet is supposed to offer. Fortunately, it is Friday so the employee has the weekend to think about his position. Certainly he has no sympathies whatsoever with people who are interested in any form of violence – extreme or otherwise. On the other hand, his primary concern as an IT professional is that freedoms offered by the Internet should be maintained. He does not believe that covert policing operations should be carried out. During the course of the weekend he discusses this matter at length with several close friends (who do not work in the computing or IT sectors). The view of the IT professional is not shared by anybody – the overall opinion is that there can be no place for the promotion of violence and therefore law enforcement agencies should do whatever it takes to stamp out this activity. The concept of freedoms offered by the Internet is an abstract one that must be put to one side.
>
> The IT professional sends an e-mail to a professional computing organisation (of which he is a member) so as to obtain advice. A few days later, he informs his boss that on ethical grounds, he does not want to be involved in this project. His boss is far from pleased.
>
> Our IT professional is put onto other work and another employee of the company develops the website, is eventually promoted, and gains a significant salary increase. Therefore by following his conscience, the IT professional has been disadvantaged in terms of his career with the company – and naturally this impacts upon his family.
>
> One month later, he receives an e-mail response from the professional computing organisation that he had contacted, indicating that his query will be dealt with in due course...

In conclusion, involvement in IT projects offers many exciting personal opportunities. On the other hand, while it is easy to say that when becoming involved we should follow our conscience (perhaps supported by a code of conduct), the ramifications of doing so are not always positive (especially when viewed from a career or financial perspective). Furthermore, although professional computing organisations have codes of conduct and an infrastructure that should support those working within the computing community, they may not do so in 'real time'.

Ultimately, it is to be hoped that our own ethical position will determine our actions and our involvement in projects – but this is certainly not always an easy course to take. To what extent quoting a code of conduct to one's boss will actually be beneficial, is open to debate…

Computer pollution

Recall the ethical dilemma described in Chapter 1, in which a staff member at a university questioned the disposal of a large number of computers – which were to be sent to the local landfill/refuse dump. As we mentioned, she approached the university's Health and Safety Department who indicated that there was no problem in consigning this computer equipment to the landfill as at that time there was no legislation in place to prevent this practice. She went on to discuss the matter with the head of her computer science department – but to no avail.

It would be nice to know that this account had a satisfactory ending, but unfortunately this was not the case. This very large consignment of computer equipment did get sent to the landfill – a legacy from the early twenty-first century for future generations.

Many so-called first world countries have recently, or are in the process of, creating legislation intended to prevent the dumping of computers and other electronic products. While this is quite promising, it does not necessarily cure the problem. There are many reported cases of legislation creating a secondary problem – specifically, the exportation of defunct computers and the like to poorer (generally third world) countries. These countries are naturally keen to earn revenue and there is often no legislation in place (or means of enforcing legislation) that ensures proper disposal of the equipment. The result can be that significant parts of computer systems end up simply being burnt, and the remainder again ends up in landfill – not first world landfill, but rather those in the third world. The burning of the plastics, etc, releases toxins into the environment and can impact on the health not only of those involved in the activity, but also of local inhabitants. Furthermore, the shipping of computer scrap necessitates the use of fuel, which again negatively impacts on the environment.

It is interesting to note that the pollution caused by digital technologies is not entirely limited to the physical world. By way of example, data and information that is made available via the Internet is often inaccurate. Such information can relate to the individual, can represent current subject matter, history, and the like. Once incorrect data and information are placed on the Internet, it is often extremely difficult to have them removed. We can regard the presence of incorrect and erroneous data/information as representing a form of digital pollution, and its existence can make it difficult for us to discern fact from fiction, and fiction from nonsense.

12.5 The pace of change

As we have mentioned in previous chapters, IT and IT-related disciplines are advancing at a tremendous pace – not only in terms of the performance of the underlying digital systems and associated software, but also in terms of the deployment of digital technologies. In the first part of this section, we use the topical issue of digital fingerprint technologies to highlight the pace at which one rapidly growing area has developed. In the second part of the section, we discuss issues that are in a continual state of flux and which can impact upon larger scale IT projects.

Biometric fingerprint technologies

In late 2006, Mark Ballard (Ballard, 2006) described a pilot scheme concerning the deployment of fingerprint scanning technology in pubs in Yeovil. He writes:

> The extent of interest among local authorities to install fingerprinting security in pubs and clubs around the country has been revealed by the police brains behind the pilot scheme in Yeovil.

> Yet there are still doubts about how well it discourages drunken violence after the latest statistics from Yeovil showed this week that alcohol-related crime was not falling as fast in venues that fingerprinted their punters as elsewhere in the town.

It is interesting to note his description of the operation of this pilot scheme, which reads as follows:

> The scheme involves pub and bar licensees making notes about the behaviour of their patrons against their pub photo and fingerprint records. The information is shared around those pubs signed up to the scheme, so other bar staff can see what their customers have been up to. If they were abusive to bar staff it would be noted and another venue would be able to see and decide perhaps to say, 'we'll let you in, but we'll keep an eye on you.'

> "There's just one or two people who spoil it for everyone and this system is designed to stop them." [said the police officer responsible for the scheme.]

> She added that the scheme should also be hooked up to pub CCTV systems. She hoped that within the year every pub and club in Yeovil centre would be using the fingerprinting system.

> South Somerset District Council released new crime statistics this week that showed how alcohol-related crime had dropped 23.5 per cent in the six venues involved in Yeovil's fingerprint security pilot.

> Yet, the council revealed last Friday that alcohol-related crime in the rest of the town down had dropped by 48 per cent. Statistics had also shown that there had been a rise in domestic violence.

The Register: **www.theregister.co.uk/2006/10/26/pub_fingerprint_plan**

From the perspective of our current discussions there are two key points of interest. Firstly, that the information concerning patrons is shared between pubs, which clearly indicates that this information is not held in a secure manner.

This has potential ramifications – particularly when we consider the accidental or deliberate insertion of erroneous data by workers in pubs who are often casual employees. It is also interesting to note that the local district council seemingly released questionable statistics indicating the value of the scheme. This provides one simple demonstration of the enthusiasm with which finger printing technologies are currently being deployed within the UK.

In terms of security it is important to note that in principle it is not the image of the fingerprint that is stored, but data derived from the fingerprint. This is a primary reason why it has been possible to deploy similar fingerprinting technologies within schools without the law dictating that parental consent has to be obtained prior to the use of such technologies in connection with children. At the time of writing there is an indication that approximately 3,500 schools in the UK are currently employing fingerprinting technologies. These are used, for example, to log children who borrow books from libraries and play a part in many aspects of day-to-day school activity.

As mentioned above, there are many who embrace the use of emerging technologies. Others question the ramifications, and here it must be said that there is a somewhat emotive perspective. When considered from a historical point of view, fingerprinting is commonly associated with criminals, so if one were to be fingerprinted, there may be a feeling that this implies wrong-doing. Furthermore, when we consider the use of fingerprinting and other biometric techniques, coupled with their potential use, it is natural to wonder what impact this will ultimately have on that all-important legal concept of 'presumption of innocence'.

From a wholly rational point of view, many believe that the very idea of gathering fingerprints from children as young as three years old and using this information as a means of monitoring and managing the child's everyday life in school, is preposterous. Furthermore, there is concern as to where this sort of undertaking will eventually lead. The issue of fingerprinting children is contentious and the use of fingerprints in connection with ID cards also raises issues in relation to personal liberty. As we have already mentioned, at the time of writing there is the intention to crosscheck fingerprints collected for use with ID cards against some 900,000 unsolved crimes in the UK. Again, this has ethical and legal ramifications as far as the presumption of innocence is concerned. One of the organisations working against the fingerprinting of children is the LTKA (**www.leavethemkidsalone.com**) and in an article appearing on their website written by Brian Drury (an IT security consultant), he comments:

> If a child has never touched a fingerprint scanner, there is zero probability of being incorrectly investigated for a crime. Once a child has touched a scanner, he or she will be at the mercy of the matching algorithm for the rest of their lives.

Figure 12.2: Other ethical uses of computers?

While this may be an overstatement, it clearly highlights the issue of security – security can never be guaranteed, and in the case of the pilot scheme in Yeovil there seems to have been little attempt to ensure security. Unfortunately, as far as younger children are concerned, there are reported cases of children being encouraged to use the scanning technology as though it were some form of game, and of parents only being notified in retrospect (or finding out accidentally) that their children have been fingerprinted. It is this type of cavalier attitude, and the lack of regulation, which is likely to give this sort of project a bad name – however well intentioned those working upon it may actually be.

Impact on IT projects

The rapid pace of change within IT can have a negative impact upon bringing IT projects to a successful conclusion. In Figure 12.3 we note four different aspects of change that can have important ramifications as far as IT projects are concerned.

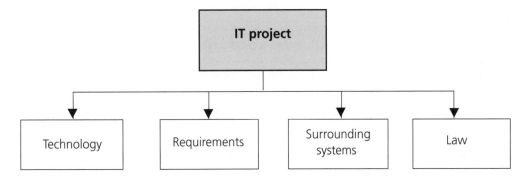

Figure 12.3: During the design, implementation and testing of an IT project, many changes will occur. This greatly increases the difficulty of successfully executing such projects.

Technology

Technology is rapidly advancing. In many IT projects there is a desire to embrace the latest technologies, and this can cause problems. Furthermore, in the case of larger projects where the development work occupies a longer period, by the time the project is concluded the state-of-the-art technologies which were adopted at its outset can already be dated. This can lead to a natural desire on the part of a client to incorporate newer technologies as the project unfolds. This can introduce unanticipated problems and will generally lead to project delays. In addition, following the initial completion of the project there will often be a desire to undertake further upgrade work so as to accommodate new technologies, ever-changing requirements and the like. Unless software systems are properly designed (particularly in the context of anticipating future changes in technology) problems can again occur and the cost of upgrade development can escalate.

Requirements

One of the most difficult aspects of any software development project is accurately determining current and future client requirements. This is an area that requires close collaboration between the client and the developer, and any ambiguities are likely to undermine the development process. We have already mentioned the pace at which technologies are progressing. The client will often be unaware of not only the latest currently available technologies, but also of technologies that are to be released in the near future.

In addition, the developer has to take into account how the proposed system will impact upon working practices, and new opportunities that it can accommodate. For these and other reasons, the accurate specification of requirements is an extremely difficult undertaking and here it is important to note that any uncertainties in this specification may not only impact upon technical aspects of the project, but also upon the delivery and cost estimates. There can be no doubt that if the field of IT was not advancing at such a rapid pace, the development of an accurate requirements specification would be made somewhat simpler.

Surrounding systems

As indicated in Chapter 10, IT systems do not operate in isolation but must interface with (and sometimes encapsulate) other systems. However, these systems are seldom static and are often continually being developed. This again adds complication to any IT project and increases the amount of communication that must take place between the many parties who are often involved – not only with the system that is being developed, but also with the relevant peripheral systems.

Law

Given the rate at which computing and IT-related technologies are advancing and being deployed, there is a continual need to provide an up-to-date and relevant legal framework which addresses the ramifications of the technologies. Thus, the law relevant to IT is continually being updated. Those involved in any longer-term IT projects must therefore look ahead in order to appreciate not only current law, but also law that is in the process of being formulated or enacted. In Chapter Two, we referred to the Computer Misuse Act (1990). From the point of view of IT, this act is most important. However, additions and amendments have since been made. These appear in the extensive Police and Justice Act (2006). The Fraud Act (2006) provides us with another example of recently introduced and relevant legislation.

12.6 Summary

In this chapter we have highlighted and raised questions relating to the ethical and social consequences of various current issues. We began by considering the ramifications of moving towards the so-called 'database society' and the introduction of ID cards coupled with the National Identity Register. In addition we briefly discussed some of the issues arising from the establishment of databases specifically designed to store information concerning children. Here, we referred to the use of such databases for the identification of children who may ultimately exhibit delinquent behaviour. Subsequently, we demonstrated that the use of digital technologies can not only offer users greater freedoms but may also be used to restrict choice and impose constraints. Within this context we considered digital rights management – within the context of the Content Protection and Copy Management scheme.

We have considered three of the real-world ethical dilemmas introduced in previous chapters and, in the final section of this chapter, we discussed issues relating to the pace at which computing and IT in general is advancing. Within this context we have highlighted several social and ethical issues relating to the deployment and use of fingerprint technologies.

12.7 Feedback on activities

Feedback on activity 12.1

Medical: This can be directly determined (in detail) from the recently introduced NHS database.

Race: This can often be inferred from marriage records, selection of school for children, immigration data, religion, shopping habits, medical records, among others.

Feedback on activity 12.2

There is no feedback for this activity.

References

- Ballard, M (26th Oct 2006), Home Office Thumbs Up for Yeovil Pub Fingerprint Plan. *The Register*. Available at: **www.theregister.co.uk/2006/10/26/pub_fingerprint_plan/**.
- Electronic Frontier Foundation (EFF) article, (13th March 2007), *Who Controls Your Television*? Available at: **www.eff.org/IP/DVB/dvb_briefing_paper.php**

Further reading

- BBC Action Network, **www.bbc.co.uk/dna/actionnetwork/A12660301**
- Foundation for Information Policy Research (2006), Children's Databases: Safety and Privacy. Available at: **www.cl.cam.ac.uk/~rja14/Papers/kids.pdf**
- Leave Them Kids Alone website, **www.leavethemkidsalone.com/**
- No2ID website, **www.no2id.net/index.php**
- Slade, G (2006), *Made to Break: Technology and Obsolescence in America*, Harvard University Press.

Answers to review questions

Chapter 1

Review question 1.1

The first is *invisible abuse*, that is 'the intentional use of the invisible operations of a computer to engage in unethical conduct'. For example, a programmer in a bank instructing the computer to deposit fractions of interest to his own bank account. Another example could be employee monitoring, and even, as will be discussed in a later chapter, 'spyware'.

The second type of invisibility is the presence of *invisible programming values*. That is, values that are embedded into a computer program.

The third aspect of invisibility is the *invisible complex calculation*.

Review question 1.2

In favour of Kant's theory is that it assumes equality. It is based on logic and rationality (on the premise that human beings are rational agents). Therefore, if something is good enough for one person, logically it must be good enough for another person. Arguments against this theory are that it does not take into account conflicting priorities, or special circumstances, such as those given in the example regarding stealing food. To claim that stealing food from someone who has more than enough is wrong seems to go against our intuitions.

Review question 1.3

Utilitarian theory says that a good outcome is that which brings 'the greatest benefit to the greatest number of people'. Therefore stealing, for example, is a morally permissible act if it brings greater benefit to the greatest number. Consider, for instance, that a dictator has a warehouse full of food when most of the people in the country are starving. In this instance, stealing the food to distribute it to the starving people would be the right thing to do.

Review question 1.4

- The law

- Codes of conduct

- Ethical theory

- Social norms and other arguments.

Chapter 2

Review question 2.1

In the 1960s and 1970s the term 'hacker' was used to describe an individual working with computers who was technically gifted. The traditional view of a hacker was that of an expert, skilled programmer. In the early days of computing there was no implication that someone known as a computer hacker would act illegally.

The social and computing environment, however, has changed greatly since the 1960s. The currently accepted view of a hacker is someone who uses specialised knowledge of computer systems to obtain 'unauthorised access'. The connotations of the term 'hacker' have clearly shifted away from the earlier definition towards a legal definition, used by the state authorities. Hacking has been criminalised. The term suggests something more malicious or subversive. Typical actions that now fall under hacking include breaking into public and private databases, defrauding banks, stealing credit card details, finding out private information, and spreading viruses.

Review question 2.2

Some of the different potential motives for hacking are as follows:

- The satisfaction gained from the intellectual challenge involved, breaking into systems simply to see if it is possible. The guessing of passwords and bypassing of file protections pose intriguing problems like that of solving a crossword puzzle

- Exposure of loopholes and vulnerabilities in computer systems. Hackers can expose bugs in software and alert software developers so that fixes can be made

- Hacking as a practical joke or prank, where no harm is intended

- Malicious hacking, involving the creation and distribution of viruses

- Hacking as vengeance by disgruntled employees against former employers, or by individuals with grudges

- Hacking as a form of political activism, to make a protest, to get a particular message across, or to correct a perceived injustice.

- Hacking by, or on behalf of, government security agencies or the military for the purposes of espionage, sabotage or cyber war

- Hacking on behalf of law enforcement agencies for the purposes of crime prevention and detection or, increasingly, counter-terrorism

- Hacking as a tool to commit crimes of theft, fraud, extortion or forgery.

Review question 2.3

A virus is a self-replicating piece of programming code inserted into other programming to cause some unexpected, and usually, undesirable event. Viruses can be transmitted by downloading a program from another computer, or can be present on a disk.

The virus lies dormant until circumstances cause its code to be executed by the computer. Some viruses are playful in intent and effect, while others can be harmful, erasing data or causing your hard disk to require reformatting.

A Trojan horse is a programme in which malicious or harmful code is disguised inside apparently harmless programming or data such as an image or sound file, or an e-mail attachment. The victim is tricked into executing the program code by opening the file or attachment, initiating a malicious sequence of events. This may include damage to files, programs or the hard disk. It may enable access to be gained to a computer, through a back door, in such a way as to gain control of a computer.

A worm, like a virus, is self-replicating code, that situates itself in a computer system. Worms tend to be standalone programmes that do not require a specific host computer, but run independently, travelling across networks. Worms tend to exist in memory and are non-permanent. Worm programs entail the deletion of portions of a computer's memory, thus creating a hole of missing information. Crucially, they use up system resources, slowing down a network, or shutting it down completely.

Time bombs or logic bombs are programs that are triggered to act when they detect a certain sequence of events, or after a particular period of time has elapsed. They involve the insertion of routines that can be triggered later by the computer's clock or a combination of events. When the bomb goes off, the entire system will crash. A popular form of logic bomb monitors employment files and initiates systems damage (such as erasure of hard disks or corruption of key programs) once the programmer's employment has been terminated.

Review question 2.4

The Hacker Ethic is comprised of five principal values:

1. Access to computers, and anything which might teach you something about the way the world works, should be unlimited and total. Always yield to the hands-on imperative.

2. All information should be free.

3. Mistrust authority – promote decentralisation.

4. Hackers should be judged by their hacking, not bogus criteria such as academic excellence, age, race or position.

5. You can create art and beauty on a computer.

Comments: Points 1 and 2, advocating open access to information and technology, for self-education, and emphasising hands-on experience and practical skills, are laudable values. But 'unlimited', 'total' and 'free'? This might be a little too idealistic and unrealistic.

Decentralisation (of power and information?) is another worthy principle, and some mistrust of authority is healthy in a democratic society. But could this be used as an excuse for no-holds barred, irresponsible hacking? Point 4 is another important value which corresponds to statements about equality of opportunity in the codes of conduct of many professional bodies. Point 5 also has some rhetorical value – surely there is something artistic and aesthetically pleasing about a skilful piece of programming, or a good 'hack'?

The focus of the Hacker Ethic is, perhaps understandably, on the hacker. Among the areas left out are the rights of owners and users of computer systems, and consideration of a computer professional's responsibilities to them.

Review question 2.5

The primary legal constraint for computer hacking in the UK is the Computer Misuse Act, 1990. The US federal equivalent is the Computer Fraud and Abuse Act, though individual states also each have their own anti-hacking legislation.

Review question 2.6

The three main categories of offences under the Computer Misuse Act are as follows:

1. Unauthorised access to computer material or 'simple hacking' – for example, using a computer without permission.

2. Unauthorised access to computer material with the intent to commit or facilitate commission of further offences. For example, attempting to use the contents of an e-mail message for blackmail, or stealing credit card numbers.

3. Unauthorised modification of computer material. For example, distributing a computer virus, malicious deletion of files, or direct actions such as altering an account to obtain fraudulent credit.

Chapter 3

Review question 3.1

Computer crime can be defined broadly as a criminal act that has been committed using a computer as the principal tool; in other words, where a computer has been the object, subject or instrument of a crime. A further distinction can be made between crimes where the role of the computer is purely incidental, and those where the computer is an essential part of the crime. In the first category are computer-assisted crimes, many of which were committed long before the advent of computers. These include electronic versions of 'traditional' crimes, like fraud, forgery, extortion or theft. In the latter category are crimes that could not have been committed without a computer and which require some degree of computer knowledge and expertise. This latter definition of computer crime is a narrower one, and includes 'new' cyber crimes which are specific to computers, such as hacking, virus attacks, and identity theft.

Review question 3.2

- Piggybacking refers to tapping into communication lines, and riding into a system, behind a legitimate user with a password

- Data diddling is swapping one piece of data for another so it is almost impossible to tell that funds have been stolen

- A Salami involves theft of tiny sums of money from many thousands of accounts. The haul is thus spread over a large number of transactions, to eventually accumulate a large sum

- Corporate espionage involves the theft of corporate assets or trade secrets from competitors, such as product development plans, customer contact lists, product specifications, manufacturing process knowledge, and strategic plans.

Review question 3.3

Theft of computer time involves the use of an employer's computer resources for personal work. This is a grey area because, while some unauthorised use of computer resources is technically theft of processing and storage power, most employers turn a blind eye to employees using the company's computers in moderation for such purposes. Using company computers for financial gain, however, such as private consulting work, is unethical, unless permitted by the employee's employment contract.

Review question 3.4

A number of factors have contributed to the general increase in the amount of computer crime. These include the availability of point and click interfaces, that are much easier to use by the technically less competent, and the availability of software which can be easily downloaded from the Internet and used for criminal purposes. In addition, there has been a general increase in computer literacy in the wider population, and greater access to computer technology. Other reasons include the fact that computer crimes often involve very little physical risk, compared to crimes like bank robberies. Many computer crimes can be committed anonymously, without having to confront the victims. Moreover, computer crimes can often appear not to be 'criminal' acts. This partly explains why many perpetrators do not consider their crimes to be 'dishonest'. Computer crimes are increasingly carried out from remote locations, like Internet cafes, and from mobile sites, with the greater availability and power of laptop computers, PDAs and mobile phones. Finally, computer crimes can be committed alone, without talkative associates, thus further reducing the risk of detection.

Review question 3.5

There are two main reasons why the amount of computer crime is much greater than is estimated.

- Firstly, many crimes go completely undetected and are often only discovered by accident. This is because computer crimes, by their very nature, are very hard to detect – it is not always easy to know when someone has gained unauthorised access to a computer system. This is compounded by the problems of tracing and tracking down computer criminals because of the anonymous, remote and increasingly transnational nature of the crimes concerned

- Secondly, many crimes go unreported. This is partly because there is often very little perceived benefit for the victim. The law is unlikely to be able to undo the damage caused, and the criminal is unlikely to be convicted. More importantly, perhaps, wider knowledge of the crime is likely to harm the future prospects of the organisation that has been the victim of the crime. Very few computer frauds, for example, are made public because companies, especially banks and other financial institutions are loath to admit that their security systems are fallible and vulnerable. Publicity of this nature could lead to a major loss of customer confidence.

Review question 3.6

The main elements of a password policy are as follows:

- Passwords allowing access to a network must not be obvious

- Passwords should include at least 8 characters, with a mixture of numbers and lower- and upper-case letters, and should not be words found in any conventional dictionary

- Passwords should be issued only to the minimum number of people requiring access

- Passwords must be kept confidential at all times and should not be disclosed to anyone else

- Passwords should be changed on a regular basis (every two to four weeks)

- Logins need to be monitored to see the date and time of recent activity, and all unsuccessful login attempts since the previous successful login

- The password database needs to be protected.

Review question 3.7

There are three main drawbacks to encryption:

1. Ensuring the security of the keys, themselves, which can be stolen or hacked.

2. Ensuring an adequate level of encryption. The strength of encryption is measured by the number of bits used in the key to encode the message or data. It is generally recognised within the computer security field that the default 40-bit encryption used by web browsers is inadequate. The Secure Socket Layer used by browsers when purchasing goods online, for example, can easily be hacked into.

3. As the level of encryption is increased, there is a corresponding increase in the amount of time needed to encrypt and decrypt data. This can lead to delays (latencies) in the data transfer process.

Chapter 4

Review question 4.1

Intellectual property includes original musical compositions, poems, novels, inventions, and product formulas. Intellectual objects are non-exclusive because many people can use them simultaneously and their use by some does not preclude their use by others. Furthermore, the cost of reproducing intellectual objects, once developed, is usually marginal.

Review question 4.2

- Standard digitised formats for storing information (such as text, sound and graphics)

- High-volume, inexpensive digital storage media, such as hard disks, CD-ROMs, and DVDs

- Character scanners and image scanners, which convert printed text, photos, and artwork to digitised electronic form

- Compression formats, such as MP3, that make music and movie files small enough to download, copy, and store

- Computer networks which make it easier to distribute digitised material

- The World Wide Web, which makes it easy to find and download material

- Peer-to-peer technology, which permits easy transfer of files over the Internet without any centralised system or service.

Review question 4.3

Copyrights protect literary, musical, dramatic, artistic, architectural, audio or audio-visual works. An example would be software.

Patents protect original, useful and non-obvious inventions, such as machines and processes or compositions of matter. Examples include computer hardware, such as circuits, microprocessors, and some computer software, such as online shopping systems.

Trademarks offer protection to a word, phrase, or symbol, which uniquely identifies a product or a service. An example is the bitten 'apple' logo of Apple Computers.

Review question 4.4

Librarians, universities and other organisations and individuals oppose the DMCA's ban on circumvention methods because it criminalises tools that make possible fair use of copyrighted material for research and education, and ordinary consumer uses for information and entertainment. Researchers oppose the ban because it hinders open discussion of the relevant technologies, such as encryption.

Review question 4.5

The fair use provision of the Copyright Act allows reproduction and other uses of copyrighted works under certain conditions for purposes such as:

- Criticism

- Comment

- News reporting

- Teaching (including multiple copies for classroom use)

- Scholarship or research.

The purpose of the fair use provision is to serve the public interest by promoting the dissemination of knowledge, and allowing public access to copyrighted materials.

Review question 4.6

KaZaA has proven more difficult to shut down than Napster because of the way it is designed, with a different implementation of peer-to-peer file sharing. Whereas Napster relied upon a central computer to maintain a global index of all files available for sharing, KaZaA distributed the index of available files among a large number of 'supernode' computers. Any computer with a high-speed Internet connection running KaZaA Media Desktop had the potential to become a supernode. The use of multiple supernodes made it much more difficult for legal authorities to shut down the file sharing network, because the creators of KaZaA could argue that they could not control, and hence should not be held responsible for, the actions of the people who were using KaZaA.

Review question 4.7

An idea cannot be 'owned' by solely one individual. Probably any idea that we have is not ours alone. Most of our ideas come from someone or somewhere else. 'Originality' means expressing an idea in a new way, perhaps seeing new associations between ideas that were not noticed before. Anything creative that is achieved is the adding of something to pre-existing ideas, which have been obtained from others.

It could be argued that if all ideas were in the public domain, and if anyone could work on and develop anything, regardless of where the idea originated, we would all be better off because more would be developed.

Artists, academics and scientists frequently create without reward. They do so for other reasons: acknowledgement, recognition, gratitude, fame, improving the lives of others. Perhaps, in some circumstances, creation is its own reward.

No one has the right to own concepts, knowledge, or information, partly because this would mean the right to exclude others from using and building upon those ideas. By placing a monetary value on intellectual property are we not controlling who can use and enjoy it?

Assigning property rights to intellectual objects is antithetical to many of the goals and traditions of a free society. Ownership might restrict progress and free exchange of ideas, for example in the scientific or artistic fields, by withholding new knowledge and preventing the free dissemination of ideas to the public.

Review question 4.8

Open source software:

- Allows users access to the source code

- Enables programmers to fix bugs

- Encourages incremental enhancements in software development

- Uses the collective wisdom of many thousands of programmers, creating better software than any individual, or group of individuals, could create.

Chapter 5

Review question 5.1

Censorship is the suppression or regulation of speech that is considered immoral, heretical, subversive, libellous, damaging to state security, or otherwise offensive. It is the control and regulation both of what people can and cannot say or express, and what they are permitted to see, read and view.

Review question 5.2

Plato, in *The Republic,* emphasised the influence of the environment on growing minds and called for rigid control of music and poetry in education. For Plato, carefully selecting the sorts of stories which young people ought, or ought not, to hear from their earliest childhood, would produce citizens who honoured the gods, their parents and would know how important it was to love one another. Plato's arguments still have a remarkable contemporary resonance if we transpose his ideas to the 21st-century world of the Internet and the mass media. Pro-censorship advocates identify forms of expression in music, art, film and computer games that are deemed unfit for consumption by minors.

Review question 5.3

The First Amendment to the US Constitution which guarantees freedom of speech, and of the press, as follows: 'Congress shall make no law respecting an establishment of religion, or prohibiting the free exercise thereof; or abridging the freedom of speech, or of the press; or the right of the people peaceably to assemble, and to petition the Government for a redress of grievances.'

The UK Human Rights Act, 1998. Article 10, states that: 'Everyone has the right of freedom of expression. This right shall include freedom to hold opinions and to receive and impart information and ideas without interference by public authority and regardless of frontiers.'

Review question 5.4

The Official Secrets Act, 1989, prohibits the disclosure of confidential material from government sources by employees. It is an offence for a member, or former member, of the security and intelligence services, or those working closely with them, to disclose information about their work. Journalists who repeat such disclosures may also be prosecuted.

Review question 5.5

- The Internet supports many-to-many communications. Whereas it is relatively easy for a government to shut down a newspaper or a radio station, it is very difficult for a government to prevent an idea from being published on the Internet, where millions of people have the ability to post web pages

- The Internet is dynamic. Millions of new computers are being connected to the Internet each year

- The Internet is huge. There is no way for a team of human censors to keep track of everything that is posted on the Web

- The Internet is global. National governments have limited authority to restrict activities happening outside their borders

- It is hard to distinguish between children and adults on the Internet.

Review question 5.6

Being anonymous can encourage people to speak out in circumstances that may be intimidating, repressive or dangerous, such as the following:

- Social intolerance may require some individuals to rely on anonymity to communicate openly about an embarrassing medical condition or an awkward disability

- Whistle-blowers may be reluctant to come forward with information unless they can remain anonymous. Such information might include exposures of corruption, wrongdoing or abuses of power within an organisation

- Anonymity, to express political dissent, is crucial in the struggle against repression in situations or countries where the expression of dissent could be dangerous.

Review question 5.7

- **Direct state intervention:** the existing laws of each nation can govern the Internet; thus, the state can amend or extend its current laws so that they apply to pertinent activities in cyberspace.

- **Coordinated international intervention:** a new intergovernmental organisation composed of representatives from countries that use the Internet can establish new rules and regulations for cyberspace that will have international jurisdiction

- **Self-governance:** the Internet will develop its own semi-official political structure; it will be governed by charters established by non-profit organisations that represent the Internet's stakeholders.

Chapter 6

Review question 6.1

- **Confidentiality** (the right to limit the spread of knowledge about oneself)

- **Anonymity** (the right to be free from unwanted attention)

- **Solitude** (the right to one's own space, or lack of physical proximity to others).

Review question 6.2

- **Secondary use of personal information:** personal information that is gathered from sources such as product guarantee cards, cookies, and customer details recorded during online and offline transactions. This information is then used for purposes other than those for which the data was supplied, for example direct marketing and advertising

- **Profiling:** using data in computer files to determine characteristics of people most likely to engage in certain behaviour. Businesses use profiling to find people who are likely customers for particular products and services

- **Data matching:** combining information about a person from different databases. Personal information that is supplied or collected for one purpose is cross-referenced to information in other databases, where personal data may have been gathered for an entirely different purpose. An individual's details can thus be searched across a number of different databases, enabling a fairly detailed picture to be built up about that person.

Review question 6.3

Cookies are small files placed on a person's computer when they visit a website – for example, with a reference to a password, so the user does not have to log in each time they visit the site. They may contain personal data, and can be collected by sites you have not even visited. The privacy implications of cookies are that they can be used to surreptitiously collect information about the user for third parties without the user's knowledge or consent.

Review question 6.4

Spam is unsolicited bulk e-mail consisting of marketing and advertising e-mails, junk mail (such as get-rich-quick scams and pornography), chain letters, and occupational spam (inter-office memos and global e-mails within an organisation). The fact that most spam is unsolicited (that is unwanted or not asked for), and that it clogs up the inbox of a user's e-mail program, has led to it being seen as an intrusive invasion of privacy.

Review question 6.5

Under an opt-out policy, one must check a box on a contract, membership form, or agreement, or call or write to the organisation to request removal from distribution lists. If the consumer does not take action, the presumption is that his or her information may be used. Under an opt-in policy, personal information is not distributed to other businesses or organisations unless the consumer has explicitly checked a box or signed a form permitting disclosure.

Review question 6.6

- US: Fourth Amendment to the US Constitution

- UK: Human Rights Act, 1998, Article 8.

Review question 6.7

Some of the concerns include the following:

- RIPA allows the government to access a person's electronic communications in a very unrestricted manner, thus infringing the privacy of their correspondence in a manner many would not tolerate regarding their postal communications

- The terms under which 'warranted interception' is justified are sufficiently vague to permit electronic surveillance of anyone, under any circumstance

- Government's powers to require ISPs to fit surveillance equipment could mean ISPs have to install 'back doors' into their systems for the purposes of monitoring. Such back doors are serious vulnerabilities

- Legal requirements to hand over decryption keys undermine the use of public key systems, such as PGP, to protect information that is communicated between people. It puts people who use PGP at risk of having to disclose their private keys (thus compromising the security of all the information sent to them) or going to prison for destroying, forgetting or losing a key.

Review question 6.8

Racial or ethnic origin; political opinions; religious beliefs; membership of a trade union; physical or mental health condition; sexual life; commission or alleged commission of any offence; proceedings regarding any offence or alleged offence; the sentence of a court in such proceedings.

Chapter 7

Review question 7.1

The argument put forward is that in this 'information age' anyone that does not have access is disadvantaged in a number of ways. Jeremy Moss [2002] states that people without access are disadvantaged because:

- Their access to knowledge is significantly limited

- Their ability to participate fully in the political process and to receive important information is greatly diminished

- Their economic prospects are severely hindered.

Review question 7.2

- The medical model is the traditional and most common view of disability, and as we have pointed out, places the emphasis on the person. This has resulted in a general conception of the disabled person as a victim – someone who has some condition which we sympathise with (and are relieved that we do not have). To remove the problem these people face, we would need to remove the medical condition

- The social model places the emphasis on the way society is physically constructed. So, disabled people are 'people with impairments who are disabled by society' (Busby [2001]). A solution to this problem is to try to 'design' society in a different way.

The difference between these two outlooks is that in the first case the problem is the condition which needs to be resolved, and in the second it is the way our society is constructed that needs to be resolved. The medical model removes any responsibility from society to make any changes; the social model puts a responsibility on society to make changes.

Review question 7.3

A computer professional should be aware of the difficulties people with disabilities have, and consider in all aspects of their work whether they are making provisions for disabled people. This means paying attention to the design of the artefact (the keyboard, monitor etc). We should not forget also that information and communication devices are getting smaller – mobile phones and PDAs for example. These may pose accessibility problems. Other considerations, for the programmer, would be the display of instructions (background/foreground colour, font size, typeface), and using alternatives such as sound. For the systems manager, the areas of consideration might be knowledge of assistive devices, and possibly some attention to password systems (length and configuration of passwords for example, the display of passwords, methods of input).

Chapter 8

Review question 8.1

The three main reasons were:

- The introduction of computers into the workplace was much slower than expected because of a host of financial, technical, human and organisational problems, including oversell by the computer industry

- Unemployment did not increase at such a high rate as predicted, and indeed fell steadily in many developed countries

- Particularly in the US and Europe, the 'baby boom' generation's entry into the workforce was largely complete and the arrival of the 'baby bust' generation in the 1990s actually resulted in some shortages of labour developing.

Review question 8.2

- Skilled workers are an ever-present threat to management, because they are in a position to set their own pace of work and thus effectively control the work process. Managers do not like skilled workers because they are semi-autonomous; they therefore seek to remove skills from workers and transfer them to machines

- In manufacturing plants, this transfer of skills to machines creates more jobs for less-skilled machine minders but fewer jobs for skilled workers. Despite the promise that new technology can improve the quality of working life, many of the new jobs being created in futuristic factories are every bit as tedious, fast paced and stressful as the old-style assembly line jobs.

Review question 8.3

- Stress and stress-related illness, leading to loss of job satisfaction, low morale, absenteeism and poor management labour relations

- Increased sense of depersonalisation, resulting in a sense of anonymity, a lack of respect for the system and its resources, and a diminished sense of ethics, values and morals

- Depersonalisation can also increase the temptation to commit misdeeds, diminish human initiative and cause the abdication of decision-making responsibility.

Review question 8.4

- Prolonged use of computer displays has been linked to eyestrain, tension, headaches, backache and perhaps even miscarriages and birth defects

- Repetitive strain injury (RSI). Typists and word-processor operators making up to 45,000 keystrokes per hour are particularly vulnerable to RSI. This can irritate or inflame tendons, leading to unpredictable and excruciating pain. Poor ergonomic design of equipment is associated with RSI, and work practices such as speed-ups, heavier workloads, greater monotony, fewer rest breaks and non-standard hours are also related to the incidence of RSI.

Review question 8.5

- Companies need to protect themselves, legally, against the possibly illegal activities of their employees (including downloading unauthorised software, copyright infringement, libel, and distributing obscene material)

- Monitoring is used to provide incentives for employees and effectively rewards individuals for true merit and efficient work

- Performance measurements are factual, and promotion is more objectively based. Diligent workers can legitimately argue a case for better pay and conditions that does not rely upon personal opinions and personalities

- Monitoring can help eliminate rampant waste: for example, personal use of employers' resources – phone calls, online shopping, Internet browsing etc

- Monitoring on a computer network can assist in troubleshooting and fine-tuning of a system, as well as streamlining job design and fairly apportioning workloads

- Computerised monitoring is constant, cheap and reliable

- Supervisors are no longer limited by what they can observe with their own eyes

- Managers are under ever-increasing pressure to improve productivity and competitive performance.

Review question 8.6

Health benefits include:

- Reduced spread of communicable illnesses though the office environment

- Reduction in stress-related illnesses

- Relief from stressful commuting

- Reduced production of pollutants (carbon emissions) that lead to increased health problems. Improved access to individual health needs for persons with existing health problems or disabilities.

Additional social benefits include:

- Flexibility of working hours

- Potential for increased care of children in their own homes.

Chapter 9

Review question 9.1

- To respond to situations very flexibly. In lectures we present lecture notes usually either via slides on an overhead projector (OHP), or using PowerPoint slides and a data projector. Either method may fail due to technical difficulties, and we have to adjust our teaching method to overcome the changed circumstances

- To take advantage of fortuitous circumstances. A good way of 'getting the message across' in teaching is to use real-world examples – if there is some current news reporting related to our teaching, we will use it

- To make sense out of ambiguous or contradictory messages This is something we are constantly engaged in during our teaching – we often ask for a verbal response from students to gain feedback on understanding, and sometimes the students' ideas are not clear. We need to search for the essence of what is being said

- To recognise the relative importance of different elements of a situation. An example of this could be where seminar or lecture times are reduced for some reason, and the lecturer needs to assess what material must be included in a lecture, and what can be left out

- To find similarities between situations despite differences which may separate them

- To draw distinctions between situations despite similarities which may link them. As lecturers, we need to understand that although our 'audience' is comprised of students generally, different students have different approaches to learning – these differences could be described as active and passive learning

- To synthesise new concepts by taking old concepts and putting them together in new ways. This idea is at the heart of learning and teaching – if students do not understand a concept delivered in one way, we need to put the concept in a new way that may make more sense

- To come up with ideas in new ways. Again, this is at the heart of our profession – as lecturers we generate ideas, and new ideas are stimulated by our discussions with students.

Review question 9.2

To give an example of how you might approach this exercise, we list the benefits and the disadvantages of the first example: the in-car Intelligent Speed Adaptation system.

The MIRA-designed ISA system uses a GPS receiver to continuously identify the position of the vehicle and match its location with a digital map of permitted speeds. The speed limit is displayed inside the car and also sent to the throttle. When the driver reaches the speed limit, the ISA system will intervene so that, however hard the driver presses on the accelerator pedal, the engine produces no further power. (*IEE Review*, February 2004)

Benefits

The user (the driver)

- Does not have to be continuously on the alert for changing speed limit signs

- Is unlikely to exceed the speed limit in error

- Has a considerably reduced risk of a fine (particularly in areas where speed cameras are in operation)

- Has the responsibility of speed removed from them and assigned to the technical capabilities of the car.

The community

- The incidents of speeding within built-up areas will be reduced

- The number of accidents (particularly involving pedestrians) will be reduced

- The incidence of 'joy riding' (that is, stealing cars purely for the purpose of speeding) will be reduced

- Criminals will not be able to outrun police and are more likely to be caught.

Disadvantages

The user (the driver)

- Loss of personal control in driving

- System may put the user at risk if it fails

- If the system fails and the user exceeds the speed limit, resulting in a fine, it is not clear whether the responsibility is with the user or the car manufacturer

- Occasionally, accidents may be avoided by accelerating – the system may prevent this possibility.

The community

- In a broad sense the community may feel a loss of personal autonomy in favour of a coercion to obey the law.

Review question 9.3

Some basic assumptions, pointed out in the extract, are taken from existing social norms. They are listed in the table below, along with some alternatives. The aim of this exercise is to show that the designer of the program has an image of what happens in a dance context, and that the image is culturally biased.

Assumption	Alternative choice
Males will want to dance with females	a. Males with males b. Females with females c. Any free dancer of either sex
Males will approach the female with a request to dance	a. Females may approach a male to request a dance b. Females may approach a female to request a dance c. Males may approach a male to request a dance d. Any dancer may approach any other dancer
If not dancing, then go to bar	a. Go to a seating area and rest b. Join friends elsewhere c. Take a comfort break d. Leave the room for fresh air

Review question 9.4

For the purposes of this question, we have chosen the 'smart home' example.

The list of issues for consideration by computer professionals is given below as a reminder:

- Reliability

- Trustworthiness – both in the functioning, and the limits of decision making

- Privacy issues – where data is stored, such as user preferences, this information should meet privacy requirements

- Security issues – information should be secure; ownership of the device should be secure

- Burden on the user – is there a burden on the user in respect of managing the device?

- Identity verification – can anyone else impersonate the user?

- Decision-making procedures – can they, or should they, be controlled by the user?

Chapter 10

Review question 10.1

Three forms of misrepresentation are:

- Fraudulent

- Negligent

- Innocent.

Review question 10.2

1. Customers are often unfamiliar with the latest IT developments, so unable to judge whether suppliers are overselling a particular technology and the ease with which it can be delivered.

2. Technological advances can make projects obsolete before they have been completed.

3. There is a tendency to desire 'cutting edge' solutions, which carry a greater risk, rather than use tested, commercial, 'off the shelf' products as far as possible.

Review question 10.3

IT projects generally have interfaces with other systems, which may also be changing. Ensuring these systems interact successfully is often a major challenge, and, without an overall plan, new systems can reinforce differences between services rather than helping to join them together.

Review question 10.4

Correspondence failure is the failure to deliver in accordance with the specification.

Review question 10.5

Key technical issues that should be taken into consideration are:

- Requirements capture

- Systems architecture

- Integration

- Reuse

- Verification

- Validation.

Review question 10.6

The BCS defines what it means to be chartered professionals as follows:

- They will take personal responsibility for their actions, which will be bound by the Code of Conduct

- They are normally educated to a four-year degree (or equivalent level), where the course of study should be accredited by a professional body

- They will then be required to demonstrate their technical and managerial competences over four to five years, which must be peer-approved

- They are also required to maintain their professional competence throughout their active professional careers, for example via the CPD programme.

Review question 10.7

The professional responsibilities, listed in the BCS Code of Conduct, are grouped around the following four sections:

1. The public interest.

2. Duty to relevant authority (the person or organisation which has authority over the IT practitioner, i.e. an employer or client. In the case of a student this will an academic institution.).

3. Duty to the profession.

4. Professional competence and integrity.

Review question 10.8

Computer hardware, if it is sold, will be subject to the Sale of Goods Act, 1979.

Review question 10.9

An agreement for bespoke software will be within the scope of the Supply of Goods and Services Act, 1982.

Chapter 11

Review question 11.1

Given that much software that is not bespoke is global in its application, then there is an argument for a single, global professional body that could set international standards. This might work for a code of conduct but far less so for a professional body.

The problem with setting up a global professional body is that different countries have different laws and cultures. The likelihood would be that one country would dominate such a single professional body (almost certainly the US at the moment). A better solution would be for a forum of national professional bodies similar to the United Nations.

Review question 11.2

Clearly, there is such a need, for example when an organisation suffers some form of new IT project failure and those responsible for the new IT system are not BCS members.

The BCS's website could be improved to make it obvious to such organisations who and how they should contact the BCS about IT project problems. There is probably a need for the BCS to target a very large number of organisations and perhaps offer a mediation service between IT supplier and purchaser organisations.

Review question 11.3

Yes, the number could be reduced and this would be desirable. One way to achieve this is to abandon the four sections as many of the items in each section overlap with items in other sections. For example, item 6 refers to 'due care and diligence' which might be more appropriate in the final section on 'Professional competence and integrity', where the phrase does not occur.

Review question 11.4

The cynical, but probably correct answer, is that most BCS members are no more than vaguely aware of the Code's existence (see the 'ethical dilemma' given earlier in this chapter). The Code probably needs a shortened version, perhaps presented as slogans with the current Code underneath the slogans to support their explanation. Perhaps one could have a simple checklist that members should apply to every IT project they work on, or even to each phase of each project they undertake.